# PATTERNS
# OF CULTURE

*Cover design by William Barss*

# PATTERNS
# OF CULTURE

## By Ruth Benedict

<small>WITH A NEW PREFACE<br/>BY MARGARET MEAD</small>

<small>SENTRY EDITION</small>

HOUGHTON MIFFLIN COMPANY BOSTON
The Riverside Press Cambridge

FIFTH PRINTING SENTRY EDITION C



The Riverside Press

CAMBRIDGE • MASSACHUSETTS

PRINTED IN THE U.S.A.

In the beginning God gave to every people a cup of clay, and from this cup they drank their life.

*Proverb of Digger Indians*

# A NEW PREFACE
# BY MARGARET MEAD

For a quarter of a century, Ruth Benedict's *Patterns of Culture* has provided a felicitous and provocative introduction to the understanding of anthropology. Translated into fourteen languages, with more than 800,000 copies printed in the Mentor edition alone at this writing, *Patterns of Culture* has helped to knit the sciences and the humanities together during a period when they had drawn very far apart.

When Ruth Benedict began her work in anthropology in 1921, the term "culture," as we use it today for the systematic body of learned behavior which is transmitted from parents to children, was part of the vocabulary of a small and technical group of professional anthropologists. That today the modern world is on such easy terms with the concept of culture, that the words "in our culture" slip from the lips of educated men and women almost as effortlessly as do the phrases that refer to period and to place, is in very great part due to this book.

For the book was and is important in several ways. First, it is the best introduction we have to the widening of horizons by a comparative study of different cultures, through which we can see our own socially transmitted customary behavior set beside that of other and strangely different peoples. In her use of this comparative method Ruth Benedict spoke for the whole developing science of anthropology in the United States, England and France. Her distinction is that she spoke with such clarity and style.

On this basis she developed her own special contribution, her view of human cultures as "personality writ large," her view that it was possible to see each culture, no matter how small and primitive or how large and complex, as having selected from the great arc of human potentialities certain characteristics and then having elaborated them with greater strength and intensity than any single individual could ever do in one lifetime. She named the emphases in the cultures she described, Apollonian, Dionysian and Paranoid, drawing on descriptions of individual personality to give point to her argument. But she was building no typology; she held no belief that Nietzschian or psychiatric labels were suitable for all societies. Nor did she believe that any closed system could be constructed into which all human societies, past, present and future, would fit. Rather, she was committed to a picture of developing human cultures for which no limit could be set because the possible combinations were so many and so varied as to be inexhaustible. But, as her knowledge of different cultures grew, so her initial sense that the individual was the creature of culture and so was in no way responsible for the discomfort of his position if he was born or accidentally bred to deviance, changed to a detailed consideration of where and in what ways men could shape their culture closer to their highest vision. The belief that this was possible was to grow.

Originally a student of literature, she hoped "to find a really important undiscovered country," but at first she thought of this adventure as learning Russian or French well enough "to be really at home in the verse." Later she came to feel that each primitive culture represented something comparable to a great work of art or literature, and that this is how the comparison between modern individual works of art and primitive culture should be made, rather than by comparing the scratched designs on the edge of a pot with the ceiling of the Sistine Chapel or berrypicking songs with Shakespeare. When only single arts were compared, primitive cultures had little to offer; but if one took these cultures whole — the religion, the mythology, the everyday ways of men and women — then the internal consistency and the intricacy was as aesthetically satisfying to the would-be explorer as was any single work of art.

On another level, *Patterns of Culture* is concerned with a problem that was central to Ruth Benedict's own life — the relationship between each human being, with a specific hereditary endowment and particular life history, and the culture in which he or she lived. In her own search for identity, she had persistently wondered whether she would have fitted better into another period or another culture than she fitted into contemporary America. She was particularly concerned with the extent to which one culture could find a place for extremes of behavior — in the mystic, the seer, the artist — which another culture branded as abnormal or worthless. Here again, she was not concerned with the question of normal and abnormal behavior as these problems concern the student of mental health. Because she asked the question about the relationship between cultures and abnormality, she opened the way for inquiries by students who were interested in the way in which mental disease differed from one culture to another. But she herself was rather concerned with the question of how narrow definitions of normal behavior penalize or give preference to certain innate capacities, and of how the widening of cultural definitions might enrich our culture and lighten the load of rejection under which the cultural deviant now labors. In her relationships with her colleagues and her students it was the unusual talent or personal destiny, the rare combination, the precious uniqueness which aroused her active solicitude and her quick compassion.

Finally, I believe *Patterns of Culture* has lived because of her robust conviction that a knowledge of how culture works gives to human beings a greater control over their own future than they have ever known before. It comes as a surprise to the reader, first caught in a recognition of the strength of the cultural web, to have this very strength in the end turned back into the context of a mankind, grown wise through knowledge of the very cultural web in which he first appeared to be caught. This belief was to grow stronger through the years as Ruth Benedict assumed greater and greater responsibility for attitudes toward race, toward education, toward winning the war and winning the peace.

In 1939, when Nazi racism threatened freedom everywhere, she devoted her one free semester to writing *Race: Science and Politics*. During the war she brought her talents for cultural analysis through working with living informants to a study of cultures made inaccessible by wartime conditions — Romania, Germany, the Netherlands, Thailand and, finally, Japan. At the end of the war she wrote *The Chrysanthemum and the Sword* in the hope that an understanding of Japanese ability to try new paths would make Americans wiser in their post-war relationships with Japan. Here was a sturdy belief, nourished on years of combining research and policy decisions. But in *Patterns of Culture* the hope of how anthropology might be used by men for their chosen ends was fresh and young, and this freshness lies like dew upon her words, to entrance each reader who meets this view of the world for the first time.

NEW YORK, OCTOBER 1958

# ACKNOWLEDGMENTS

THE three primitive peoples described in this volume have been chosen because knowledge of these tribes is comparatively full and satisfactory and because I was able to supplement published descriptions with many discussions with the field ethnologists who have lived intimately with these peoples and who have written the authoritative descriptions of the tribes in question. I have myself lived several summers in the pueblo of Zuñi, and among some of the neighbouring tribes which I have used to contrast with pueblo culture. I owe a great debt to Dr. Ruth L. Bunzel, who learned the Zuñi language and whose accounts of Zuñi and collections of texts are the best of all the available pueblo studies. For the description of Dobu I am indebted to Dr. Reo F. Fortune's invaluable monograph, *The Sorcerers of Dobu*, and to many delightful conversations. For the Northwest Coast of America I have used not only Professor Franz Boas's text publications and detailed compilations of Kwakiutl life, but his still unpublished material and his penetrating comment upon his experience on the Northwest Coast extending over forty years.

For the presentations here I am alone responsible and it may be that I have carried some interpretations further than one or another of the field-workers would have done. But the chapters have been read and verified as to facts by these authorities upon these tribes, and references to their detailed studies are given for those who wish to consult the full accounts.

# ACKNOWLEDGMENTS

I wish to make grateful acknowledgment to the original publishers for permission to reprint certain paragraphs from the following articles: 'The Science of Custom,' in *The Century Magazine*; 'Configurations of Culture in North America,' in *The American Anthropologist*; and 'Anthropology and the Abnormal,' in *The Journal of General Psychology*.

Thanks are due also to E. P. Dutton and Company, publishers of *Sorcerers of Dobu*.

RUTH BENEDICT

# CONTENTS

# CONTENTS

# INTRODUCTION

DURING the present century many new approaches to the problems of social anthropology have developed. The old method of constructing a history of human culture based on bits of evidence, torn out of their natural contacts, and collected from all times and all parts of the world, has lost much of its hold. It was followed by a period of painstaking attempts at reconstruction of historical connections based on studies of distribution of special features and supplemented by archæological evidence. Wider and wider areas were looked upon from this viewpoint. Attempts were made to establish firm connections between various cultural features and these were used to establish wider historical connections. The possibility of independent development of analogous cultural features which is a postulate of a general history of culture has been denied or at least consigned to an inconsequential rôle. Both the evolutionary method and the analysis of independent local cultures were devoted to unravelling the sequences of cultural forms. While by means of the former it was hoped to build up a unified picture of the history of culture and civilization, the adherents of the latter methods, at least among its more conservative adherents, saw each culture as a single unit and as an individual historical problem.

Under the influence of the intensive analysis of cultures the indispensable collection of facts relating to cultural forms has received a strong stimulus. The material so collected gave us information on social life, as though it consisted of strictly separated categories, such as economic life, technology, art, social organization, religion, and the unifying bond was difficult to find. The position of the anthropologist seemed like that satirized by Gœthe:

Wer will was Lebendig's erkennen und beschreiben,
Sucht erst den Geist heraus zu treiben,
Dann hat er die Teile in seiner Hand,
Fehlt leider nur das geistige Band.

The occupation with living cultures has created a stronger interest in the totality of each culture. It is felt more and more that hardly any trait of culture can be understood when taken out of its general setting. The attempt to conceive a whole culture as controlled by a single set of conditions did not solve the problem. The purely anthropo-geographical, economic, or in other ways formalistic approach seemed to give distorted pictures.

The desire to grasp the meaning of a culture as a whole compels us to consider descriptions of standardized behaviour merely as a stepping-stone leading to other problems. We must understand the individual as living in his culture; and the culture as lived by individuals. The interest in these socio-psychological problems is not in any way opposed to the historical approach. On the contrary, it reveals dynamic processes that have been active in cultural changes and enables us to evaluate evidence obtained from the detailed comparison of related cultures.

On account of the character of the material the problem of cultural life presents itself often as that of the interrelation between various aspects of culture. In some cases this study leads to a better appreciation of the intensity or lack of integration of a culture. It brings out clearly the forms of integration in various types of culture which prove that the relations between different aspects of cul-

# INTRODUCTION

ture follow the most diverse patterns and do not lend themselves profitably to generalizations. However, it leads rarely, and only indirectly, to an understanding of the relation between individual and culture.

This requires a deep penetration into the genius of the culture, a knowledge of the attitudes controlling individual and group behaviour. Dr. Benedict calls the genius of culture its configuration. In the present volume the author has set before us this problem and has illustrated it by the example of three cultures that are permeated each by one dominating idea. This treatment is distinct from the so-called functional approach to social phenomena in so far as it is concerned rather with the discovery of fundamental attitudes than with the functional relations of every cultural item. It is not historical except in so far as the general configuration, as long as it lasts, limits the directions of change that remain subject to it. In comparison to changes of content of culture the configuration has often remarkable permanency.

As the author points out, not every culture is characterized by a dominant character, but it seems probable that the more intimate our knowledge of the cultural drives that actuate the behaviour of the individual, the more we shall find that certain controls of emotion, certain ideals of conduct, prevail that account for what seem to us as abnormal attitudes when viewed from the standpoint of our civilization. The relativity of what is considered social or asocial, normal or abnormal, is seen in a new light.

The extreme cases selected by the author make clear the importance of the problem.

FRANZ BOAS

# PATTERNS
# OF CULTURE

# I

## The Science of Custom

ANTHROPOLOGY is the study of human beings as creatures of society. It fastens its attention upon those physical characteristics and industrial techniques, those conventions and values, which distinguish one community from all others that belong to a different tradition.

The distinguishing mark of anthropology among the social sciences is that it includes for serious study other societies than our own. For its purposes any social regulation of mating and reproduction is as significant as our own, though it may be that of the Sea Dyaks, and have no possible historical relation to that of our civilization. To the anthropologist, our customs and those of a New Guinea tribe are two possible social schemes for dealing with a common problem, and in so far as he remains an anthropologist he is bound to avoid any weighting of one in favour of the other. He is interested in human behaviour, not as it is shaped by one tradition, our own, but as it has been shaped by any tradition whatsoever. He is interested in the great gamut of custom that is found in various cultures, and his object is to understand the way in which these cultures change and differentiate, the different forms through which they express themselves, and the manner in which the customs of any peoples function in the lives of the individuals who compose them.

Now custom has not been commonly regarded as a subject of any great moment. The inner workings of our own brains we feel to be uniquely worthy of investigation, but custom, we have a way of thinking, is behaviour at its most commonplace. As a matter of fact, it is the other way around. Traditional custom, taken the world over, is a mass of detailed behavior more astonishing than what any one person can ever evolve in individual actions no matter how aberrant. Yet that is a rather trivial aspect of the matter. The fact of first-rate importance is the predominant rôle that custom plays in experience and in belief, and the very great varieties it may manifest.

No man ever looks at the world with pristine eyes. He sees it edited by a definite set of customs and institutions and ways of thinking. Even in his philosophical probings he cannot go behind these stereotypes; his very concepts of the true and the false will still have reference to his particular traditional customs. John Dewey has said in all seriousness that the part played by custom in shaping the behaviour of the individual as over against any way in which he can affect traditional custom, is as the proportion of the total vocabulary of his mother tongue over against those words of his own baby talk that are taken up into the vernacular of his family. When one seriously studies social orders that have had the opportunity to develop autonomously, the figure becomes no more than an exact and matter-of-fact observation. The life-history of the individual is first and foremost an accommodation to the patterns and standards traditionally handed down in his community. From the moment of his birth the customs into which he is born shape his experience and behaviour. By the time he can talk, he is the little creature of his culture, and by the time he is grown and able to take part in its activities, its habits are his habits, its beliefs his beliefs, its impossibilities his impossibilities. Every child that is born into his group will share them with him, and no child born into one on the opposite side of the globe can ever achieve the thousandth part. There is no social problem it is more incumbent upon us to understand than this of the rôle of custom. Until we are intelligent as to its laws and varieties, the main complicating facts of human life must remain unintelligible.

The study of custom can be profitable only after certain preliminary propositions have been accepted, and some of these propositions have been violently opposed. In the first place any scientific study requires that there be no preferential weighting of one or another of the items in the series it selects for its consideration. In all the less controversial fields like the study of cacti or termites or the nature of nebulæ, the necessary method of study is to group the relevant material and to take note of all possible variant forms and conditions. In this way we have learned all that we know of the laws of astronomy, or of the habits of the social insects, let us say. It is only in the study of man himself that the major social sciences have substituted the study of one local variation, that of Western civilization.

Anthropology was by definition impossible as long as these distinctions between ourselves and the primitive, ourselves and the barbarian, ourselves and the pagan, held sway over people's minds. It was necessary first to arrive at that degree of sophistication where we no longer set our own belief over against our neighbour's superstition. It was necessary to recognize that those institutions which are based on the same premises, let us say the supernatural, must be considered together, our own among the rest.

In the first half of the nineteenth century this elementary postulate of anthropology could not occur to the most enlightened person of Western civilization. Man, all down his history, has defended his uniqueness like a point of honour. In Copernicus' time this claim to supremacy was so inclusive that it took in even the earth on which we live, and the fourteenth century refused with passion to have this planet subordinated to a place in the solar scheme. By Darwin's time, having granted the solar system to the enemy, man fought with all the weapons at his command for the uniqueness of the soul, an unknowable attribute given by God to man in such a manner that it disproved man's ancestry in the animal kingdom. No lack of continuity in the argument, no doubts of the nature of this 'soul,' not even the fact that the nineteenth century did not care in the least to defend its brotherhood with any group of aliens — none of these facts counted against the first-rate excitement that raged on account of the indignity evolution proposed against the notion of man's uniqueness.

Both these battles we may fairly count as won — if not yet, then soon; but the fighting has only massed itself upon another front. We are quite willing to admit now that the revolution of the earth about the sun, or the animal ancestry of man, has next to nothing to do with the uniqueness of our human achievements. If we inhabit one chance planet out of a myriad solar systems, so much the greater glory, and if all the ill-assorted human races are linked by evolution with the animal, the provable differences between ourselves and them are the more extreme

4

and the uniqueness of our institutions the more remarkable. But *our* achievements, *our* institutions are unique; they are of a different order from those of lesser races and must be protected at all costs. So that today, whether it is a question of imperialism, or of race prejudice, or of a comparison between Christianity and paganism, we are still preoccupied with the uniqueness, not of the human institutions of the world at large, which no one has ever cared about anyway, but of our own institutions and achievements, our own civilization.

Western civilization, because of fortuitous historical circumstances, has spread itself more widely than any other local group that has so far been known. It has standardized itself over most of the globe, and we have been led, therefore, to accept a belief in the uniformity of human behaviour that under other circumstances would not have arisen. Even very primitive peoples are sometimes far more conscious of the rôle of cultural traits than we are, and for good reason. They have had intimate experience of different cultures. They have seen their religion, their economic system, their marriage prohibitions, go down before the white man's. They have laid down the one and accepted the other, often uncomprehendingly enough, but they are quite clear that there are variant arrangements of human life. They will sometimes attribute dominant characteristics of the white man to his commercial competition, or to his institution of warfare, very much in the fashion of the anthropologist.

The white man has had a different experience. He has never seen an outsider, perhaps, unless the outsider has been already Europeanized. If he has travelled, he has very likely been around the world without ever staying outside a cosmopolitan hotel. He knows little of any ways

5

of life but his own. The uniformity of custom, of outlook, that he sees spread about him seems convincing enough, and conceals from him the fact that it is after all an historical accident. He accepts without more ado the equivalence of human nature and his own cultural standards.

Yet the great spread of white civilization is not an isolated historical circumstance. The Polynesian group, in comparatively recent times, has spread itself from Ontong, Java, to Easter Island, from Hawaii to New Zealand, and the Bantu-speaking tribes spread from the Sahara to southern Africa. But in neither case do we regard these peoples as more than an overgrown local variation of the human species. Western civilization has had all its inventions in transportation and all its far-flung commercial arrangements to back up its great dispersion, and it is easy to understand historically how this came about.

The psychological consequences of this spread of white culture have been out of all proportion to the materialistic. This world-wide cultural diffusion has protected us as man had never been protected before from having to take seriously the civilizations of other peoples; it has given to our culture a massive universality that we have long ceased to account for historically, and which we read off rather as necessary and inevitable. We interpret our dependence, in our civilization, upon economic competition, as proof that this is the prime motivation that human nature can rely upon, or we read off the behaviour of small children as it is moulded in our civilization and recorded in child clinics, as child psychology or the way in which the young human animal is bound to behave. It is the same whether it is a question of our ethics or of our family organization. It is the inevitability of each familiar motivation that we defend, attempting always to identify our own local ways of behaving with Behaviour, or our own socialized habits with Human Nature.

Now modern man has made this thesis one of the living issues in his thought and in his practical behaviour, but the sources of it go far back into what appears to be, from its universal distribution among primitive peoples, one of the earliest of human distinctions, the difference in kind between 'my own' closed group and the outsider. All primitive tribes agree in recognizing this category of the outsiders, those who are not only outside the provisions of the moral code which holds within the limits of one's own people, but who are summarily denied a place anywhere in the human scheme. A great number of the tribal names in common use, Zuñi, Déné, Kiowa, and the rest, are names by which primitive peoples know themselves, and are only their native terms for 'the human beings,' that is, themselves. Outside of the closed group there are no human beings. And this is in spite of the fact that from an objective point of view each tribe is surrounded by peoples sharing in its arts and material inventions, in elaborate practices that have grown up by a mutual give-and-take of behaviour from one people to another.

Primitive man never looked out over the world and saw 'mankind' as a group and felt his common cause with his species. From the beginning he was a provincial who raised the barriers high. Whether it was a question of choosing a wife or of taking a head, the first and important distinction was between his own human group and those beyond the pale. His own group, and all its ways of behaving, was unique.

So modern man, differentiating into Chosen People and

dangerous aliens, groups within his own civilization genetically and culturally related to one another as any
tribes in the Australian bush are among themselves, has
the justification of a vast historical continuity behind his
attitude. The Pygmies have made the same claims. We
are not likely to clear ourselves easily of so fundamental
a human trait, but we can at least learn to recognize its
history and its hydra manifestations.

One of these manifestations, and one which is often
spoken of as primary and motivated rather by religious
emotions than by this more generalized provincialism, is
the attitude that has universally held in Western civilizations so long as religion remained a living issue among
them. The distinction between any closed group and
outside peoples, becomes in terms of religion that between the true believers and the heathen. Between these
two categories for thousands of years there were no common meeting-points. No ideas or institutions that held in
the one were valid in the other. Rather all institutions
were seen in opposing terms according as they belonged
to one or the other of the very often slightly differentiated
religions: on the one side it was a question of Divine
Truth and the true believer, of revelation and of God; on
the other it was a matter of mortal error, of fables, of the
damned and of devils. There could be no question of
equating the attitudes of the opposed groups and hence
no question of understanding from objectively studied
data the nature of this important human trait, religion.

We feel a justified superiority when we read a description such as this of the standard religious attitude. At
least we have thrown off that particular absurdity, and
we have accepted the study of comparative religion. But
considering the scope a similar attitude has had in our

8

civilization in the form of race prejudices, for example, we are justified in a little scepticism as to whether our sophistication in the matter of religion is due to the fact that we have outgrown naïve childishness, or simply to the fact that religion is no longer the area of life in which the important modern battles are staged. In the really live issues of our civilization we seem to be far from having gained the detachment that we have so largely achieved in the field of religion.

There is another circumstance that has made the serious study of custom a late and often a half-heartedly pursued discipline, and it is a difficulty harder to surmount than those of which we have just spoken. Custom did not challenge the attention of social theorists because it was the very stuff of their own thinking: it was the lens without which they could not see at all. Precisely in proportion as it was fundamental, it had its existence outside the field of conscious attention. There is nothing mystical about this blindness. When a student has assembled the vast data for a study of international credits, or of the process of learning, or of narcissism as a factor in psychoneuroses, it is through and in this body of data that the economist or the psychologist or the psychiatrist operates. He does not reckon with the fact of other social arrangements where all the factors, it may be, are differently arranged. He does not reckon, that is, with cultural conditioning. He sees the trait he is studying as having known and inevitable manifestations, and he projects these as absolute because they are all the materials he has to think with. He identifies local attitudes of the 1930's with Human Nature, the description of them with Economics or Psychology.

Practically, it often does not matter. Our children must

be educated in our pedagogical tradition, and the study of the process of learning in our schools is of paramount importance. There is the same kind of justification for the shrug of the shoulders with which we often greet a discussion of other economic systems. After all, we must live within the framework of mine and thine that our own culture institutionalizes.

That is true, and the fact that the varieties of culture can best be discussed as they exist in space gives colour to our nonchalance. But it is only limitation of historical material that prevents examples from being drawn rather from the succession of cultures in time. That succession we cannot escape if we would, and when we look back even a generation we realize the extent to which revision has taken place, sometimes in our most intimate behaviour. So far these revisions have been blind, the result of circumstances we can chart only in retrospect. Except for our unwillingness to face cultural change in intimate matters until it is forced upon us, it would not be impossible to take a more intelligent and directive attitude. The resistance is in large measure a result of our misunderstanding of cultural conventions, and especially an exaltation of those that happen to belong to our nation and decade. A very little acquaintance with other conventions, and a knowledge of how various these may be, would do much to promote a rational social order.

The study of different cultures has another important bearing upon present-day thought and behaviour. Modern existence has thrown many civilizations into close contact, and at the moment the overwhelming response to this situation is nationalism and racial snobbery. There has never been a time when civilization stood more in need of individuals who are genuinely culture-conscious, who can see objectively the socially conditioned behaviour of other peoples without fear and recrimination.

Contempt for the alien is not the only possible solution of our present contact of races and nationalities. It is not even a scientifically founded solution. Traditional Anglo-Saxon intolerance is a local and temporal culture-trait like any other. Even people as nearly of the same blood and culture as the Spanish have not had it, and race prejudice in the Spanish-settled countries is a thoroughly different thing from that in countries dominated by England and the United States. In this country it is obviously not an intolerance directed against the mixture of blood of biologically far-separated races, for upon occasion excitement mounts as high against the Irish Catholic in Boston, or the Italian in New England mill towns, as against the Oriental in California. It is the old distinction of the in-group and the out-group, and if we carry on the primitive tradition in this matter, we have far less excuse than savage tribes. We have travelled, we pride ourselves on our sophistication. But we have failed to understand the relativity of cultural habits, and we remain debarred from much profit and enjoyment in our human relations with peoples of different standards, and untrustworthy in our dealings with them.

The recognition of the cultural basis of race prejudice is a desperate need in present Western civilization. We have come to the point where we entertain race prejudice against our blood brothers the Irish, and where Norway and Sweden speak of their enmity as if they too represented different blood. The so-called race line, during a war in which France and Germany fight on opposite sides, is held to divide the people of Baden from those of Alsace, though in bodily form they alike belong to the Alpine sub-race.

11

In a day of footloose movements of people and of mixed marriages in the ancestry of the most desirable elements of the community, we preach unabashed the gospel of the pure race.

To this anthropology makes two answers. The first is as to the nature of culture and the second is as to the nature of inheritance. The answer as to the nature of culture takes us back to prehuman societies. There are societies where Nature perpetuates the slightest mode of behaviour by biological mechanisms, but these are societies not of men but of the social insects. The queen ant, removed to a solitary nest, will reproduce each trait of sex behaviour, each detail of the nest. The social insects represent Nature in a mood when she was taking no chances. The pattern of the entire social structure she committed to the ant's instinctive behaviour. There is no greater chance that the social classes of an ant society, or its patterns of agriculture, will be lost by an ant's isolation from its group than that the ant will fail to reproduce the shape of its antennæ or the structure of its abdomen.

For better or for worse, man's solution lies at the opposite pole. Not one item of his tribal social organization, of his language, of his local religion, is carried in his germcell. In Europe, in other centuries, when children were occasionally found who had been abandoned and had maintained themselves in forests apart from other human beings, they were all so much alike that Linnæus classified them as a distinct species, *Homo ferus,* and supposed that they were a kind of gnome that man seldom ran across. He could not conceive that these half-witted brutes were born human, these creatures with no interest in what went on about them, rocking themselves rhythmically back and forth like some wild animal in a zoo, with organs of speech and hearing that could hardly be trained to do service, who withstood freezing weather in rags and plucked potatoes out of boiling water without discomfort. There is no doubt, of course, that they were children abandoned in infancy, and what they had all of them lacked was association with their kind, through which alone man's faculties are sharpened and given form.

We do not come across wild children in our more humane civilization. But the point is made as clearly in any case of adoption of an infant into another race and culture. An Oriental child adopted by an Occidental family learns English, shows toward its foster parents the attitudes current among the children he plays with, and grows up to the same professions that they elect. He learns the entire set of the cultural traits of the adopted society, and the set of his real parents' group plays no part. The same process happens on a grand scale when entire peoples in a couple of generations shake off their traditional culture and put on the customs of an alien group. The culture of the American Negro in northern cities has come to approximate in detail that of the whites in the same cities. A few years ago, when a cultural survey was made of Harlem, one of the traits peculiar to the Negroes was their fashion of gambling on the last three unit figures of the next day's stock turnover. At least it cost less than the whites' corresponding predilection for gambling in the stocks themselves and was no less uncertain and exciting. It was a variation on the white pattern, though hardly a great departure. And most Harlem traits keep still closer to the forms that are current in white groups.

All over the world, since the beginning of human history, it can be shown that peoples have been able to adopt the culture of peoples of another blood. There is nothing in

the biological structure of man that makes it even difficult. Man is not committed in detail by his biological
constitution to any particular variety of behaviour. The
great diversity of social solutions that man has worked
out in different cultures in regard to mating, for example,
or trade, are all equally possible on the basis of his original
endowment. Culture is not a biologically transmitted
complex.

What is lost in Nature's guaranty of safety is made up
in the advantage of greater plasticity. The human animal
does not, like the bear, grow himself a polar coat in order
to adapt himself, after many generations, to the Arctic.
He learns to sew himself a coat and put up a snow house.
From all we can learn of the history of intelligence in prehuman as well as human societies, this plasticity has been
the soil in which human progress began and in which it
has maintained itself. In the ages of the mammoths, species after species without plasticity arose, overreached
itself, and died out, undone by the development of the
very traits it had biologically produced in order to cope
with its environment. The beasts of prey and finally
the higher apes came slowly to rely upon other than biological adaptations, and upon the consequent increased
plasticity the foundations were laid, bit by bit, for the development of intelligence. Perhaps, as is often suggested,
man will destroy himself by this very development of intelligence. But no one has suggested any means by which
we can return to the biological mechanisms of the social
insect, and we are left no alternative. The human cultural
heritage, for better or for worse, is not biologically transmitted.

The corollary in modern politics is that there is no basis
for the argument that we can trust our spiritual and cul-

tural achievements to any selected hereditary germ-plasms. In our Western civilization, leadership has passed successively in different periods to the Semitic-speaking peoples, to the Hamitic, to the Mediterranean sub-group of the white race, and lately to the Nordic. There is no doubt about the cultural continuity of the civilization, no matter who its carriers were at the moment. We must accept all the implications of our human inheritance, one of the most important of which is the small scope of biologically transmitted behaviour, and the enormous rôle of the cultural process of the transmission of tradition.

The second answer anthropology makes to the argument of the racial purist concerns the nature of heredity. The racial purist is the victim of a mythology. For what is 'racial inheritance'? We know roughly what heredity is from father to son. Within a family line the importance of heredity is tremendous. But heredity is an affair of family lines. Beyond that it is mythology. In small and static communities like an isolated Eskimo village, 'racial' heredity and the heredity of child and parent are practically equivalent, and racial heredity therefore has meaning. But as a concept applied to groups distributed over a wide area, let us say, to Nordics, it has no basis in reality. In the first place, in all Nordic nations there are family lines which are represented also in Alpine or Mediterranean communities. Any analysis of the physical make-up of a European population shows overlapping: the dark-eyed, dark-haired Swede represents family lines that are more concentrated farther south, but he is to be understood in relation to what we know of these latter groups. His heredity, so far as it has any physical reality, is a matter of his family line, which is not confined to

Sweden. We do not know how far physical types may vary without intermixture. We know that inbreeding brings about a local type. But this is a situation that in our cosmopolitan white civilization hardly exists, and when 'racial heredity' is invoked, as it usually is, to rally a group of persons of about the same economic status, graduating from much the same schools, and reading the same weeklies, such a category is merely another version of the in- and the out-group and does not refer to the actual biological homogeneity of the group.

What really binds men together is their culture, — the ideas and the standards they have in common. If instead of selecting a symbol like common blood heredity and making a slogan of it, the nation turned its attention rather to the culture that unites its people, emphasizing its major merits and recognizing the different values which may develop in a different culture, it would substitute realistic thinking for a kind of symbolism which is dangerous because it is misleading.

A knowledge of cultural forms is necessary in social thinking, and the present volume is concerned with this problem of culture. As we have just seen, bodily form, or race, is separable from culture, and can for our purposes be laid to one side except at certain points where for some special reason it becomes relevant. The chief requirement for a discussion of culture is that it should be based on a wide selection of possible cultural forms. It is only by means of such facts that we can possibly differentiate between those human adjustments that are culturally conditioned and those that are common and, so far as we can see, inevitable in mankind. We cannot discover by introspection or by observation of any one society what behaviour is 'instinctive,' that is, organically determined.

# THE SCIENCE OF CUSTOM

In order to class any behaviour as instinctive, much more is necessary than that it should be proved to be automatic. The conditioned response is as automatic as the organically determined, and culturally conditioned responses make up the greater part of our huge equipment of automatic behaviour.

Therefore the most illuminating material for a discussion of cultural forms and processes is that of societies historically as little related as possible to our own and to one another. With the vast network of historical contact which has spread the great civilizations over tremendous areas, primitive cultures are now the one source to which we can turn. They are a laboratory in which we may study the diversity of human institutions. With their comparative isolation, many primitive regions have had centuries in which to elaborate the cultural themes they have made their own. They provide ready to our hand the necessary information concerning the possible great variations in human adjustments, and a critical examination of them is essential for any understanding of cultural processes. It is the only laboratory of social forms that we have or shall have.

This laboratory has another advantage. The problems are set in simpler terms than in the great Western civilizations. With the inventions that make for ease of transportation, international cables and telephones and radio transmission, those that ensure permanence and widespread distribution to the printed page, the development of competing professional groups and cults and classes and their standardization over the world, modern civilization has grown too complex for adequate analysis except as it is broken up for the purpose into small artificial sections. And these partial analyses are inadequate because so

17

many outside factors cannot be controlled. A survey of any one group involves individuals out of opposed heterogeneous groups, with different standards, social aims, home relations, and morality. The interrelation of these groups is too complicated to evaluate in the necessary detail. In primitive society, the cultural tradition is simple enough to be contained within the knowledge of individual adults, and the manners and morals of the group are moulded to one well-defined general pattern. It is possible to estimate the interrelation of traits in this simple environment in a way which is impossible in the cross-currents of our complex civilization.

Neither of these reasons for stressing the facts of primitive culture has anything to do with the use that has been classically made of this material. This use had to do with a reconstruction of origins. Early anthropologists tried to arrange all traits of different cultures in an evolutionary sequence from the earliest forms to their final development in Western civilization. But there is no reason to suppose that by discussing Australian religion rather than our own we are uncovering primordial religion, or that by discussing Iroquoian social organization we are returning to the mating habits of man's early ancestors.

Since we are forced to believe that the race of man is one species, it follows that man everywhere has an equally long history behind him. Some primitive tribes may have held relatively closer to primordial forms of behaviour than civilized man, but this can only be relative and our guesses are as likely to be wrong as right. There is no justification for identifying some one contemporary primitive custom with the original type of human behaviour. Methodologically there is only one means by which we may gain an approximate knowledge of these early beginnings. That is by a study of the distribution of those few traits that are universal or near-universal in human society. There are several that are well known. Of these everyone agrees upon animism, and the exogamous restrictions upon marriage. The conceptions, diverse as they prove to be, of the human soul, and of an after-life, raise more question. Beliefs as nearly universal as these we may justifiably regard as exceedingly old human inventions. This is not equivalent to regarding them as biologically determined, for they may have been very early inventions of the human race, 'cradle' traits which have become fundamental in all human thinking. In the last analysis they may be as socially conditioned as any local custom. But they have long since become automatic in human behaviour. They are old, and they are universal. All this, however, does not make the forms that can be observed today the original forms that arose in primordial times. Nor is there any way of reconstructing these origins from the study of their varieties. One may isolate the universal core of the belief and differentiate from this its local forms, but it is still possible that the trait took its rise in a pronounced local form and not in some original least common denominator of all observed traits.

For this reason the use of primitive customs to establish origins is speculative. It is possible to build up an argument for any origin that can be desired, origins that are mutually exclusive as well as those that are complementary. Of all the uses of anthropological material, this is the one in which speculation has followed speculation most rapidly, and where in the nature of the case no proof can be given.

Nor does the reason for using primitive societies for the discussion of social forms have necessary connection with a romantic return to the primitive. It is put forward in no spirit of poeticizing the simpler peoples. There are many ways in which the culture of one or another people appeals to us strongly in this era of heterogeneous standards and confused mechanical bustle. But it is not in a return to ideals preserved for us by primitive peoples that our society will heal itself of its maladies. The romantic Utopianism that reaches out toward the simpler primitive, attractive as it sometimes may be, is as often, in ethnological study, a hindrance as a help.

The careful study of primitive societies is important today rather, as we have said, because they provide case material for the study of cultural forms and processes. They help us to differentiate between those responses that are specific to local cultural types and those that are general to mankind. Beyond this, they help us to gauge and understand the immensely important rôle of culturally conditioned behaviour. Culture, with its processes and functions, is a subject upon which we need all the enlightenment we can achieve, and there is no direction in which we can seek with greater reward than in the facts of preliterate societies.

# II

## The Diversity of Cultures

A CHIEF of the Digger Indians, as the Californians call
them, talked to me a great deal about the ways of his
people in the old days. He was a Christian and a leader
among his people in the planting of peaches and apricots
on irrigated land, but when he talked of the shamans who
had transformed themselves into bears before his eyes in
the bear dance, his hands trembled and his voice broke
with excitement. It was an incomparable thing, the
power his people had had in the old days. He liked best
to talk of the desert foods they had eaten. He brought
each uprooted plant lovingly and with an unfailing sense
of its importance. In those days his people had eaten 'the
health of the desert,' he said, and knew nothing of the in-
sides of tin cans and the things for sale at butcher shops.
It was such innovations that had degraded them in these
latter days.

One day, without transition, Ramon broke in upon his
descriptions of grinding mesquite and preparing acorn
soup. 'In the beginning,' he said, 'God gave to every
people a cup, a cup of clay, and from this cup they drank
their life.' I do not know whether the figure occurred in
some traditional ritual of his people that I never found, or
whether it was his own imagery. It is hard to imagine
that he had heard it from the whites he had known at

Banning; they were not given to discussing the ethos of different peoples. At any rate, in the mind of this humble Indian the figure of speech was clear and full of meaning. 'They all dipped in the water,' he continued, 'but their cups were different. Our cup is broken now. It has passed away.'

*Our cup is broken.* Those things that had given significance to the life of his people, the domestic rituals of eating, the obligations of the economic system, the succession of ceremonials in the villages, possession in the bear dance, their standards of right and wrong — these were gone, and with them the shape and meaning of their life. The old man was still vigorous and a leader in relationships with the whites. He did not mean that there was any question of the extinction of his people. But he had in mind the loss of something that had value equal to that of life itself, the whole fabric of his people's standards and beliefs. There were other cups of living left, and they held perhaps the same water, but the loss was irreparable. It was no matter of tinkering with an addition here, lopping off something there. The modelling had been fundamental, it was somehow all of a piece. It had been their own.

Ramon had had personal experience of the matter of which he spoke. He straddled two cultures whose values and ways of thought were incommensurable. It is a hard fate. In Western civilization our experiences have been different. We are bred to one cosmopolitan culture, and our social sciences, our psychology, and our theology persistently ignore the truth expressed in Ramon's figure.

The course of life and the pressure of environment, not to speak of the fertility of human imagination, provide an incredible number of possible leads, all of which, it appears, may serve a society to live by. There are the schemes of ownership, with the social hierarchy that may be associated with possessions; there are material things and their elaborate technology; there are all the facets of sex life, parenthood and post-parenthood; there are the guilds or cults which may give structure to the society; there is economic exchange; there are the gods and supernatural sanctions. Each one of these and many more may be followed out with a cultural and ceremonial elaboration which monopolizes the cultural energy and leaves small surplus for the building of other traits. Aspects of life that seem to us most important have been passed over with small regard by peoples whose culture, oriented in another direction, has been far from poor. Or the same trait may be so greatly elaborated that we reckon it as fantastic.

It is in cultural life as it is in speech; selection is the prime necessity. The numbers of sounds that can be produced by our vocal cords and our oral and nasal cavities are practically unlimited. The three or four dozen of the English language are a selection which coincides not even with those of such closely related dialects as German and French. The total that are used in different languages of the world no one has even dared to estimate. But each language must make its selection and abide by it on pain of not being intelligible at all. A language that used even a few hundreds of the possible — and actually recorded — phonetic elements could not be used for communication. On the other hand a great deal of our misunderstanding of languages unrelated to our own has arisen from our attempts to refer alien phonetic systems back to ours as a point of reference. We recognize only one *k*. If other people have five *k* sounds placed in different positions in the throat and mouth, distinctions of vocabulary and of syntax that depend on these differences are impossible to us until we master them. We have a *d* and an *n*. They may have an intermediate sound which, if we fail to identify it, we write now *d* and now *n*, introducing distinctions which do not exist. The elementary prerequisite of linguistic analysis is a consciousness of these incredibly numerous available sounds from which each language makes its own selections.

In culture too we must imagine a great arc on which are ranged the possible interests provided either by the human age-cycle or by the environment or by man's various activities. A culture that capitalized even a considerable proportion of these would be as unintelligible as a language that used all the clicks, all the glottal stops, all the labials, dentals, sibilants, and gutturals from voiceless to voiced and from oral to nasal. Its identity as a culture depends upon the selection of some segments of this arc. Every human society everywhere has made such selection in its cultural institutions. Each from the point of view of another ignores fundamentals and exploits irrelevancies. One culture hardly recognizes monetary values; another has made them fundamental in every field of behaviour. In one society technology is unbelievably slighted even in those aspects of life which seem necessary to ensure survival; in another, equally simple, technological achievements are complex and fitted with admirable nicety to the situation. One builds an enormous cultural superstructure upon adolescence, one upon death, one upon after-life.

The case of adolescence is particularly interesting, because it is in the limelight in our own civilization and because we have plentiful information from other cultures. In our own civilization a whole library of psychological studies has emphasized the inevitable unrest of the period of puberty. It is in our tradition a physiological state as definitely characterized by domestic explosions and rebellion as typhoid is marked by fever. There is no question of the facts. They are common in America. The question is rather of their inevitability.

The most casual survey of the ways in which different societies have handled adolescence makes one fact inescapable: even in those cultures which have made most of the trait, the age upon which they focus their attention varies over a great range of years. At the outset, therefore, it is clear that the so-called puberty institutions are a misnomer if we continue to think of biological puberty. The puberty they recognize is social, and the ceremonies are a recognition in some fashion or other of the child's new status of adulthood. This investiture with new occupations and obligations is in consequence as various and as culturally conditioned as the occupations and obligations themselves. If the sole honourable duty of manhood is conceived to be deeds of war, the investiture of the warrior is later and of a different sort from that in a society where adulthood gives chiefly the privilege of dancing in a representation of masked gods. In order to understand puberty institutions, we do not most need analyses of the necessary nature of *rites de passage*; we need rather to know what is identified in different cultures with the beginning of adulthood and their methods of admitting to the new status. Not biological puberty, but what adulthood means in that culture conditions the puberty ceremony.

Adulthood in central North America means warfare. Honour in it is the great goal of all men. The constantly recurring theme of the youth's coming-of-age, as also of preparation for the warpath at any age, is a magic ritual for success in war. They torture not one another, but themselves: they cut strips of skin from their arms and legs, they strike off their fingers, they drag heavy weights pinned to their chest or leg muscles. Their reward is enhanced prowess in deeds of warfare.

In Australia, on the other hand, adulthood means participation in an exclusively male cult whose fundamental trait is the exclusion of women. Any woman is put to death if she so much as hears the sound of the bull-roarer at the ceremonies, and she must never know of the rites. Puberty ceremonies are elaborate and symbolic repudiations of the bonds with the female sex; the men are symbolically made self-sufficient and the wholly responsible element of the community. To attain this end they use drastic sexual rites and bestow supernatural guaranties.

The clear physiological facts of adolescence, therefore, are first socially interpreted even where they are stressed. But a survey of puberty institutions makes clear a further fact: puberty is physiologically a different matter in the life-cycle of the male and the female. If cultural emphasis followed the physiological emphasis, girls' ceremonies would be more marked than boys'; but it is not so. The ceremonies emphasize a social fact: the adult prerogatives of men are more far-reaching in every culture than women's, and consequently, as in the above instances, it is more common for societies to take note of this period in boys than in girls.

Girls' and boys' puberty, however, may be socially celebrated in the same tribe in identical ways. Where, as in the interior of British Columbia, adolescent rites are a magical training for all occupations, girls are included on the same terms as boys. Boys roll stones down mountains and beat them to the bottom to be swift of foot, or throw gambling-sticks to be lucky in gambling; girls carry water from distant springs, or drop stones down inside their dresses that their children may be born as easily as the pebble drops to the ground.

In such a tribe as the Nandi of the lake region of East Africa, also, girls and boys share an even-handed puberty rite, though, because of the man's dominant rôle in the culture, his boyhood training period is more stressed than the woman's. Here adolescent rites are an ordeal inflicted by those already admitted to adult status upon those they are now forced to admit. They require of them the most complete stoicism in the face of ingenious tortures associated with circumcision. The rites for the two sexes are separate, but they follow the same pattern. In both the novices wear for the ceremony the clothing of their sweethearts. During the operation their faces are watched for any twinge of pain, and the reward of bravery is given with great rejoicing by the lover, who runs forward to receive back some of his adornments. For both the girl and the boy the rites mark their *entrée* into a new sex status: the boy is now a warrior and may take a sweetheart, the girl is marriageable. The adolescent tests are for both a pre-marital ordeal in which the palm is awarded by their lovers.

Puberty rites may also be built upon the facts of girls' puberty and admit of no extension to boys. One of the most naïve of these is the institution of the fatting-house for girls in central Africa. In the region where feminine beauty is all but identified with obesity, the girl at puberty is segregated, sometimes for years, fed with sweet and fatty foods, allowed no activity, and her body rubbed as-

27

siduously with oils. She is taught during this time her future duties, and her seclusion ends with a parade of her corpulence that is followed by her marriage to her proud bridegroom. It is not regarded as necessary for the man to achieve pulchritude before marriage in a similar fashion.

The usual ideas around which girls' puberty institutions are centred, and which are not readily extended to boys', are those concerned with menstruation. The uncleanness of the menstruating woman is a very widespread idea, and in a few regions first menstruation has been made the focus of all the associated attitudes. Puberty rites in these cases are of a thoroughly different character from any of which we have spoken. Among the Carrier Indians of British Columbia, the fear and horror of a girl's puberty was at its height. Her three or four years of seclusion was called 'the burying alive,' and she lived for all that time alone in the wilderness, in a hut of branches far from all beaten trails. She was a threat to any person who might so much as catch a glimpse of her, and her mere footstep defiled a path or a river. She was covered with a great headdress of tanned skin that shrouded her face and breasts and fell to the ground behind. Her arms and legs were loaded with sinew bands to protect her from the evil spirit with which she was filled. She was herself in danger and she was a source of danger to everybody else.

Girls' puberty ceremonies built upon ideas associated with the menses are readily convertible into what is, from the point of view of the individual concerned, exactly opposite behaviour. There are always two possible aspects to the sacred: it may be a source of peril or it may be a source of blessing. In some tribes the first menses of girls are a potent supernatural blessing. Among the Apaches I have seen the priests themselves pass on their knees before the row of solemn little girls to receive from them the blessing of their touch. All the babies and the old people come also of necessity to have illness removed from them. The adolescent girls are not segregated as sources of danger, but court is paid to them as to direct sources of supernatural blessing. Since the ideas that underlie puberty rites for girls, both among the Carrier and among the Apache, are founded on beliefs concerning menstruation, they are not extended to boys, and boys' puberty is marked instead, and lightly, with simple tests and proofs of manhood.

The adolescent behaviour, therefore, even of girls was not dictated by some physiological characteristic of the period itself, but rather by marital or magic requirements socially connected with it. These beliefs made adolescence in one tribe serenely religious and beneficent, and in another so dangerously unclean that the child had to cry out in warning that others might avoid her in the woods. The adolescence of girls may equally, as we have seen, be a theme which a culture does not institutionalize. Even where, as in most of Australia, boys' adolescence is given elaborate treatment, it may be that the rites are an induction into the status of manhood and male participation in tribal matters, and female adolescence passes without any kind of formal recognition.

These facts, however, still leave the fundamental question unanswered. Do not all cultures have to cope with the natural turbulence of this period, even though it may not be given institutional expression? Dr. Mead has studied this question in Samoa. There the girl's life passes through well-marked periods. Her first years out of babyhood are passed in small neighbourhood gangs of age mates from which the little boys are strictly excluded. The corner of the village to which she belongs is all-important, and the little boys are traditional enemies. She has one duty, that of baby-tending, but she takes the baby with her rather than stays home to mind it, and her play is not seriously hampered. A couple of years before puberty, when she grows strong enough to have more difficult tasks required of her and old enough to learn more skilled techniques, the little girls' play group in which she grew up ceases to exist. She assumes woman's dress and must contribute to the work of the household. It is an uninteresting period of life to her and quite without turmoil. Puberty brings no change at all.

A few years after she has come of age, she will begin the pleasant years of casual and irresponsible love affairs that she will prolong as far as possible into the period when marriage is already considered fitting. Puberty itself is marked by no social recognition, no change of attitude or of expectancy. Her pre-adolescent shyness is supposed to remain unchanged for a couple of years. The girl's life in Samoa is blocked out by other considerations than those of physiological sex maturity, and puberty falls in a particularly unstressed and peaceful period during which no adolescent conflicts manifest themselves. Adolescence, therefore, may not only be culturally passed over without ceremonial; it may also be without importance in the emotional life of the child and in the attitude of the village toward her.

Warfare is another social theme that may or may not be used in any culture. Where war is made much of, it may be with contrasting objectives, with contrasting organization in relation to the state, and with contrasting sanctions. War may be, as it was among the Aztecs, a way of getting captives for the religious sacrifices. Since the Spaniards fought to kill, according to Aztec standards they broke the rules of the game. The Aztecs fell back in dismay and Cortez walked as victor into the capital.

There are even quainter notions, from our standpoint, associated with warfare in different parts of the world. For our purposes it is sufficient to notice those regions where organized resort to mutual slaughter never occurs between social groups. Only our familiarity with war makes it intelligible that a state of warfare should alternate with a state of peace in one tribe's dealings with another. The idea is quite common over the world, of course. But on the one hand it is impossible for certain peoples to conceive the possibility of a state of peace, which in their notion would be equivalent to admitting enemy tribes to the category of human beings, which by definition they are not even though the excluded tribe may be of their own race and culture.

On the other hand, it may be just as impossible for a people to conceive of the possibility of a state of war. Rasmussen tells of the blankness with which the Eskimo met his exposition of our custom. Eskimos very well understand the act of killing a man. If he is in your way, you cast up your estimate of your own strength, and if you are ready to take it upon yourself, you kill him. If you are strong, there is no social retribution. But the idea of an Eskimo village going out against another Eskimo village in battle array or a tribe against a tribe, or even of another village being fair game in ambush warfare, is alien to them. All killing comes under one head, and is not separated, as ours is, into categories, the one meritorious, the other a capital offence.

I myself tried to talk of warfare to the Mission Indian of California, but it was impossible. Their misunderstanding of warfare was abysmal. They did not have the basis in their own culture upon which the idea could exist, and their attempts to reason it out reduced the great wars to which we are able to dedicate ourselves with moral fervour to the level of alley brawls. They did not happen to have a cultural pattern that distinguished between them.

War is, we have been forced to admit even in the face of its huge place in our own civilization, an asocial trait. In the chaos following the World War all the wartime arguments that expounded its fostering of courage, of altruism, of spiritual values, give out a false and offensive ring. War in our own civilization is as good an illustration as one can take of the destructive lengths to which the development of a culturally selected trait may go. If we justify war, it is because all peoples always justify the traits of which they find themselves possessed, not because war will bear an objective examination of its merits.

Warfare is not an isolated case. From every part of the world and from all levels of cultural complexity it is possible to illustrate the overweening and finally often the asocial elaboration of a cultural trait. Those cases are clearest where, as in dietary or mating regulations, for example, traditional usage runs counter to biological drives. Social organization, in anthropology, has a quite specialized meaning owing to the unanimity of all human societies in stressing relationship groups within which marriage is forbidden. No known people regard all women as possible mates. This is not in an effort, as is so often supposed, to prevent inbreeding in our sense, for over great parts of the world it is an own cousin, often the daughter of one's mother's brother, who is the predestined spouse. The relatives to whom the prohibition refers differ utterly among different peoples, but all human societies are alike in placing a restriction. No human idea has received more constant and complex elaboration in culture than this of incest. The incest groups are often the most important functioning units of the tribe, and the duties of every individual in relation to any other are defined by their relative positions in these groups. These groups function as units in religious ceremonials and in cycles of economic exchange, and it is impossible to exaggerate the importance of the rôle they have played in social history.

Some areas handle the incest tabu with moderation. In spite of the restrictions there may be a considerable number of women available for a man to marry. In others the group that is tabu has been extended by a social fiction to include vast numbers of individuals who have no traceable ancestors in common, and choice of a mate is in consequence excessively limited. This social fiction receives unequivocal expression in the terms of relationship which are used. Instead of distinguishing lineal from collateral kin as we do in the distinction between father and uncle, brother and cousin, one term means literally 'man of my father's group (relationship, locality, etc.) of his generation,' not distinguishing between direct and collateral lines, but making other distinctions that are foreign to us. Certain tribes of eastern Australia use an extreme form of this so-called classificatory kinship system. Those whom they call brothers and sisters are all those of their generation with whom they recognize any relationship. There is no cousin category or anything that corresponds to it; all relatives of one's own generation are one's brothers and sisters.

This manner of reckoning relationship is not uncommon in the world, but Australia has in addition an unparalleled horror of sister marriage and an unparalleled development of exogamous restrictions. So the Kurnai, with their extreme classificatory relationship system, feel the Australian horror of sex relationship with all their 'sisters,' that is, women of their own generation who are in any way related to them. Besides this, the Kurnai have strict locality rules in the choice of a mate. Sometimes two localities, out of the fifteen or sixteen of which the tribe is composed, must exchange women, and can have no mates in any other group. Sometimes there is a group of two or three localities that may exchange with two or three others. Still further, as in all Australia, the old men are a privileged group, and their prerogatives extend to marrying the young and attractive girls. The consequence of these rules is, of course, that in all the local group which must by absolute prescription furnish a young man with his wife, there is no girl who is not touched by one of these tabus. Either she is one of those who through relationship with his mother is his 'sister,' or she is already bargained for by an old man, or for some lesser reason she is forbidden to him.

That does not bring the Kurnai to reformulate their exogamous rules. They insist upon them with every show of violence. Therefore, the only way they are usually able to marry is by flying violently in the face of the regulations. They elope. As soon as the village knows that an elopement has occurred, it sets out in pursuit, and if the couple are caught the two are killed. It does not matter that possibly all of the pursuers were married by elopement in the same fashion. Moral indignation runs high. There is, however, an island traditionally recognized as a safe haven, and if the couple can reach it and remain away till the birth of a child, they are received again with blows, it is true, but they may defend themselves. After they have run the gauntlet and been given their drubbing, they take up the status of married people in the tribe.

The Kurnai meet their cultural dilemma typically enough. They have extended and complicated a particular aspect of behaviour until it is a social liability. They must either modify it, or get by with a subterfuge. And they use the subterfuge. They avoid extinction, and they maintain their ethics without acknowledged revision. This manner of dealing with the *mores* has lost nothing in the progress of civilization. The older generation of our own civilization similarly maintained monogamy and supported prostitution, and the panegyrics of monogamy were never so fervent as in the great days of the red-light districts. Societies have always justified favourite traditional forms. When these traits get out of hand and some form of supplementary behaviour is called in, lip service is given as readily to the traditional form as if the supplementary behaviour did not exist.

Such a bird's-eye survey of human cultural forms makes clear several common misconceptions. In the first place, the institutions that human cultures build up upon the hints presented by the environment or by man's physical necessities do not keep as close to the original impulse as we easily imagine. These hints are, in reality, mere rough sketches, a list of bare facts. They are pin-point potentialities, and the elaboration that takes place around them is dictated by many alien considerations. Warfare is not the expression of the instinct of pugnacity. Man's pugnacity is so small a hint in the human equipment that it may not be given any expression in inter-tribal relations. When it is institutionalized, the form it takes follows other grooves of thought than those implied in the original impulse. Pugnacity is no more than the touch to the ball of custom, a touch also that may be withheld.

Such a view of cultural processes calls for a recasting of many of our current arguments upholding our traditional institutions. These arguments are usually based on the impossibility of man's functioning without these particular traditional forms. Even very special traits come in for this kind of validation, such as the particular form of economic drive that arises under our particular system of property ownership. This is a remarkably special motivation and there are evidences that even in our generation it is being strongly modified. At any rate, we do not have to confuse the issue by discussing it as if it were a matter of biological survival values. Self-support is a motive our civilization has capitalized. If our economic structure changes so that this motive is no longer so potent a drive as it was in the era of the great frontier and expanding industrialism, there are many other motives that would be appropriate to a changed economic organization. Every culture, every era, exploits some few out of a great number of possibilities. Changes may be very disquieting, and involve great losses, but this is due to the difficulty of change itself, not to the fact that our age and country has hit upon the one possible motivation under which human life can be conducted. Change, we must remember, with all its difficulties, is inescapable. Our fears over even very minor shifts in custom are usually quite beside the point. Civilizations might change far more radically than any human authority has ever had the will or the imagination to change them, and still be completely workable. The minor changes that occasion so much denunciation today, such as the increase of divorce, the growing secularization in our cities, the prevalence of the petting party, and many more, could be taken up quite readily into a slightly different pattern of culture. Becoming traditional, they would be given the same richness of content, the same importance and value, that the older patterns had in other generations.

The truth of the matter is rather that the possible human institutions and motives are legion, on every plane of cultural simplicity or complexity, and that wisdom consists in a greatly increased tolerance toward their divergencies. No man can thoroughly participate in any culture unless he has been brought up and has lived according to its forms, but he can grant to other cultures the same significance to their participants which he recognizes in his own.

## II

The diversity of culture results not only from the ease with which societies elaborate or reject possible aspects of existence. It is due even more to a complex interweaving of cultural traits. The final form of any traditional institution, as we have just said, goes far beyond the original human impulse. In great measure this final form depends upon the way in which the trait has merged with other traits from different fields of experience.

A widespread trait may be saturated with religious beliefs among one people and function as an important aspect of their religion. In another area it may be wholly a matter of economic transfer and be therefore an aspect of their monetary arrangements. The possibilities are endless and the adjustments are often bizarre. The nature of the trait will be quite different in the different areas according to the elements with which it has combined.

It is important to make this process clear to ourselves

37

because otherwise we fall easily into the temptation to generalize into a sociological law the results of a local merging of traits, or we assume their union to be a universal phenomenon. The great period of European plastic art was religiously motivated. Art pictured and made common property the religious scenes and dogmas which were fundamental in the outlook of that period. Modern European æsthetics would have been quite different if mediæval art had been purely decorative and had not made common cause with religion.

As a matter of history great developments in art have often been remarkably separate from religious motivation and use. Art may be kept definitely apart from religion even where both are highly developed. In the pueblos of the Southwest of the United States, art-forms in pottery and textiles command the respect of the artist in any culture, but their sacred bowls carried by the priests or set out on the altars are shoddy and the decorations crude and unstylized. Museums have been known to throw out Southwest religious objects because they were so far below the traditional standard of workmanship. 'We have to put a frog there,' the Zuñi Indians say, meaning that the religious exigencies eliminate any need of artistry. This separation between art and religion is not a unique trait of the Pueblos. Tribes of South America and of Siberia make the same distinction, though they motivate it in various ways. They do not use their artistic skill in the service of religion. Instead, therefore, of finding the sources of art in a locally important subject matter, religion, as older critics of art have sometimes done, we need rather to explore the extent to which these two can mutually interpenetrate, and the consequences of such merging for both art and religion.

38

# THE DIVERSITY OF CULTURES

The interpenetration of different fields of experience, and the consequent modification of both of them, can be shown from all phases of existence: economics, sex relations, folklore, material culture, and religion. The process can be illustrated in one of the widespread religious traits of the North American Indians. Up and down the continent, in every culture area except that of the pueblos of the Southwest, supernatural power was obtained in a dream or vision. Success in life, according to their beliefs, was due to personal contact with the supernatural. Each man's vision gave him power for his lifetime, and in some tribes he was constantly renewing his personal relationship with the spirits by seeking further visions. Whatever he saw, an animal or a star, a plant or a supernatural being, adopted him as a personal protégé, and he could call upon him in need. He had duties to perform for his visionary patron, gifts to give him and obligations of all kinds. In return the spirit gave him the specific powers he promised him in his vision.

In every great region of North America this guardian spirit complex took different form according to the other traits of the culture with which it was most closely associated. In the plateaus of British Columbia it merged with the adolescent ceremonies we have just spoken of. Both boys and girls, among these tribes, went out into the mountains at adolescence for a magic training. Puberty ceremonies have a wide distribution up and down the Pacific Coast, and over most of this region they are quite distinct from the guardian spirit practices. But in British Columbia they were merged. The climax of the magic adolescent training for boys was the acquisition of a guardian spirit who by its gifts dictated the lifetime profession of the young man. He became a warrior, a shaman,

39

a hunter, or a gambler according to the supernatural visitant. Girls also received guardian spirits representing their domestic duties. So strongly is the guardian spirit experience among these peoples moulded by its association with the ceremonial of adolescence that anthropologists who know this region have argued that the entire vision complex of the American Indians had its origin in puberty rites. But the two are not genetically connected. They are locally merged, and in the merging both traits have taken special and characteristic forms.

In other parts of the continent, the guardian spirit is not sought at puberty, nor by all the youths of the tribe. Consequently the complex has in these cultures no kind of relationship with puberty rites even when any such exist. On the southern plains it is adult men who must acquire mystic sanctions. The vision complex merged with a trait very different from puberty rites. The Osage are organized in kinship groups in which descent is traced through the father and disregards the mother's line. These clan groups have a common inheritance of supernatural blessing. The legend of each clan tells how its ancestor sought a vision, and was blessed by the animal whose name the clan has inherited. The ancestor of the mussel clan sought seven times, with the tears running down his face, a supernatural blessing. At last he met the mussel and spoke to it, saying:

O grandfather,
The little ones have nothing of which to make their bodies.

Thereupon the mussel answered him:

You say the little ones have nothing of which to make their
    bodies.
Let the little ones make of me their bodies.

# THE DIVERSITY OF CULTURES

When the little ones make of me their bodies,
They shall always live to see old age.
Behold the wrinkles upon my skin [shell]
Which I have made to be the means of reaching old age.
When the little ones make of me their bodies
They shall always live to see the signs of old age upon their skins.
The seven bends of the river [of life]
I pass successfully.
And in my travels the gods themselves have not the power to see
    the trail that I make.
When the little ones make of me their bodies
No one, not even the gods, shall be able to see the trail they
    make.

Among these people all the familiar elements of the vision quest are present, but it was attained by a first ancestor of the clan, and its blessings are inherited by a
blood-relationship group.

This situation among the Osage presents one of the fullest pictures in the world of totemism, that close mingling
of social organization and of religious veneration for the
ancestor. Totemism is described from all parts of the
world, and anthropologists have argued that the clan
totem originated in the 'personal totem,' or guardian
spirit. But the situation is exactly analogous to that of
the plateaus of British Columbia where the vision quest
merged with the adolescent rites, only that here it has
merged with hereditary privileges of the clan. So strong
has this new association become that a vision is no longer
thought to give a man power automatically. The blessings
of the vision are attained only by inheritance, and among
the Osage long chants have grown up describing the ancestor's encounters, and detailing the blessings which his
descendants may claim in consequence.

In both these cases it is not only the vision complex

which receives a different character in different regions as it merges with puberty rites or clan organization. The adolescence ceremonies and the social organization are equally coloured by the interweaving of the vision quest. The interaction is mutual. The vision complex, the puberty rites, the clan organization, and many other traits that enter also into close relationship with the vision, are strands which are braided in many combinations. The consequences of the different combinations that result from this intermingling of traits cannot be exaggerated. In both the regions of which we have just spoken, both where the religious experience was merged with puberty rites and where it was merged with clan organization, as a natural corollary of the associated practices all individuals of the tribe could receive power from the vision for success in any undertaking. Achievement in any occupation was credited to the individual's claim upon a vision experience. A successful gambler or a successful hunter drew his power from it just as a successful shaman did. According to their dogma all avenues of advancement were closed to those who had failed to obtain a supernatural patron.

In California, however, the vision was the professional warrant of the shaman. It marked him as a person apart. It was just in this region, therefore, that the most aberrant aspects of this experience were developed. The vision was no longer a slight hallucination for which the stage could be set by fasting and torture and isolation. It was a trance experience which overtook the exceptionally unstable members of the community and especially the women. Among the Shasta it was the convention that only women were so blessed. The required experience was definitely cataleptic and came upon the novice after a preliminary dreaming had prepared the way. She fell senseless and rigid to the ground. When she came to herself, blood oozed from her mouth. All the ceremonies by which for years after she validated her call to be a shaman were further demonstrations of her liability to cataleptic seizures and were regarded as the cure by which her life was saved. In tribes like the Shasta not only the vision experience had changed its character to a violent seizure which differentiated religious practitioners from all others, but the character of the shamans was equally modified by the nature of the trance experience. They were definitely the unstable members of the community. In this region contests between shamans took the form of dancing each other down, that is, of seeing which one could withstand longest in a dance the cataleptic seizure which would inevitably overtake them. Both the vision experience and shamanism had been profoundly affected by the close relationship into which they had entered. The merging of the two traits, no less than the merging of the vision experience and puberty rites or clan organization, had drastically modified both fields of behaviour.

In the same way in our own civilization the separateness of the church and of the marriage sanction is historically clear, yet the religious sacrament of wedlock for centuries dictated developments both in sex behaviour and in the church. The peculiar character of marriage during those centuries was due to the merging of two essentially unrelated cultural traits. On the other hand, marriage has often been the means by which wealth was traditionally transferred. In cultures where this is true, the close association of marriage with economic transfer may quite obliterate the fact that marriage is fundamentally a matter of sexual and child-rearing adjustments. Marriage in each case must be understood in relation to other traits to which it has become assimilated, and we should not run into the mistake of thinking that 'marriage' can be understood in the two cases by the same set of ideas. We must allow for the different components which have been built up into the resulting trait.

We greatly need the ability to analyze traits of our own cultural heritage into their several parts. Our discussions of the social order would gain in clarity if we learned to understand in this way the complexity of even our simplest behaviour. Racial differences and prestige prerogatives have so merged among Anglo-Saxon peoples that we fail to separate biological racial matters from our most socially conditioned prejudices. Even among nations as nearly related to the Anglo-Saxons as the Latin peoples, such prejudices take different forms, so that, in Spanish-colonized countries and in British colonies racial differences have not the same social significance. Christianity and the position of women, similarly, are historically interrelated traits, and they have at different times interacted very differently. The present high position of women in Christian countries is no more a 'result' of Christianity than was Origen's coupling of woman with the deadly temptations. These interpenetrations of traits occur and disappear, and the history of culture is in considerable degree a history of their nature and fates and associations. But the genetic connection we so easily see in a complex trait and our horror at any disturbance of its interrelationships is largely illusory. The diversity of the possible combinations is endless, and adequate social orders can be built indiscriminately upon a great variety of these foundations.

# III

---

*The Integration of Culture*

---

THE diversity of cultures can be endlessly documented. A field of human behaviour may be ignored in some societies until it barely exists; it may even be in some cases unimagined. Or it may almost monopolize the whole organized behaviour of the society, and the most alien situations be manipulated only in its terms. Traits having no intrinsic relation one with the other, and historically independent, merge and become inextricable, providing the occasion for behaviour that has no counterpart in regions that do not make these identifications. It is a corollary of this that standards, no matter in what aspect of behaviour, range in different cultures from the positive to the negative pole. We might suppose that in the matter of taking life all peoples would agree in condemnation. On the contrary, in a matter of homicide, it may be held that one is blameless if diplomatic relations have been severed between neighbouring countries, or that one kills by custom his first two children, or that a husband has right of life and death over his wife, or that it is the duty of the child to kill his parents before they are old. It may be that those are killed who steal a fowl, or who cut their upper teeth first, or who are born on a Wednesday. Among some peoples a person suffers torments at having caused an accidental death; among others it is a matter of no consequence. Suicide also may be a light matter, the recourse of anyone who has suffered some slight rebuff, an act that occurs constantly in a tribe. It may be the highest and noblest act a wise man can perform. The very tale of it, on the other hand, may be a matter for incredulous mirth, and the act itself impossible to conceive as a human possibility. Or it may be a crime punishable by law, or regarded as a sin against the gods.

The diversity of custom in the world is not, however, a matter which we can only helplessly chronicle. Self-torture here, head-hunting there, prenuptial chastity in one tribe and adolescent licence in another, are not a list of unrelated facts, each of them to be greeted with surprise wherever it is found or wherever it is absent. The tabus on killing oneself or another, similarly, though they relate to no absolute standard, are not therefore fortuitous. The significance of cultural behaviour is not exhausted when we have clearly understood that it is local and man-made and hugely variable. It tends also to be integrated. A culture, like an individual, is a more or less consistent pattern of thought and action. Within each culture there come into being characteristic purposes not necessarily shared by other types of society. In obedience to these purposes, each people further and further consolidates its experience, and in proportion to the urgency of these drives the heterogeneous items of behaviour take more and more congruous shape. Taken up by a well-integrated culture, the most ill-assorted acts become characteristic of its peculiar goals, often by the most unlikely metamorphoses. The form that these acts take we can understand only by understanding first the emotional and intellectual mainsprings of that society.

Such patterning of culture cannot be ignored as if it

were an unimportant detail. The whole, as modern science is insisting in many fields, is not merely the sum of all its parts, but the result of a unique arrangement and interrelation of the parts that has brought about a new entity. Gunpowder is not merely the sum of sulphur and charcoal and saltpeter, and no amount of knowledge even of all three of its elements in all the forms they take in the natural world will demonstrate the nature of gunpowder. New potentialities have come into being in the resulting compound that were not present in its elements, and its mode of behaviour is indefinitely changed from that of any of its elements in other combinations.

Cultures, likewise, are more than the sum of their traits. We may know all about the distribution of a tribe's form of marriage, ritual dances, and puberty initiations, and yet understand nothing of the culture as a whole which has used these elements to its own purpose. This purpose selects from among the possible traits in the surrounding regions those which it can use, and discards those which it cannot. Other traits it recasts into conformity with its demands. The process of course need never be conscious during its whole course, but to overlook it in the study of the patternings of human behaviour is to renounce the possibility of intelligent interpretation.

This integration of cultures is not in the least mystical. It is the same process by which a style in art comes into being and persists. Gothic architecture, beginning in what was hardly more than a preference for altitude and light, became, by the operation of some canon of taste that developed within its technique, the unique and homogeneous art of the thirteenth century. It discarded elements that were incongruous, modified others to its purposes, and invented others that accorded with its taste.

When we describe the process historically, we inevitably use animistic forms of expression as if there were choice and purpose in the growth of this great art-form. But this is due to the difficulty in our language-forms. There was no conscious choice, and no purpose. What was at first no more than a slight bias in local forms and techniques expressed itself more and more forcibly, integrated itself in more and more definite standards, and eventuated in Gothic art.

What has happened in the great art-styles happens also in cultures as a whole. All the miscellaneous behaviour directed toward getting a living, mating, warring, and worshipping the gods, is made over into consistent patterns in accordance with unconscious canons of choice that develop within the culture. Some cultures, like some periods of art, fail of such integration, and about many others we know too little to understand the motives that actuate them. But cultures at every level of complexity, even the simplest, have achieved it. Such cultures are more or less successful attainments of integrated behaviour, and the marvel is that there can be so many of these possible configurations.

Anthropological work has been overwhelmingly devoted to the analysis of culture traits, however, rather than to the study of cultures as articulated wholes. This has been due in great measure to the nature of earlier ethnological descriptions. The classical anthropologists did not write out of first-hand knowledge of primitive people. They were armchair students who had at their disposal the anecdotes of travellers and missionaries and the formal and schematic accounts of the early ethnologists. It was possible to trace from these details the distribution of the custom of knocking out teeth, or of divination by entrails, but it was not possible to see how these traits were embedded in different tribes in characteristic configurations that gave form and meaning to the procedures.

Studies of culture like *The Golden Bough* and the usual comparative ethnological volumes are analytical discussions of traits and ignore all the aspects of cultural integration. Mating or death practices are illustrated by bits of behaviour selected indiscriminately from the most different cultures, and the discussion builds up a kind of mechanical Frankenstein's monster with a right eye from Fiji, a left from Europe, one leg from Tierra del Fuego, and one from Tahiti, and all the fingers and toes from still different regions. Such a figure corresponds to no reality in the past or present, and the fundamental difficulty is the same as if, let us say, psychiatry ended with a catalogue of the symbols of which psychopathic individuals make use, and ignored the study of patterns of symptomatic behaviour — schizophrenia, hysteria, and manic-depressive disorders — into which they are built. The rôle of the trait in the behaviour of the psychotic, the degree to which it is dynamic in the total personality, and its relation to all other items of experience, differ completely. If we are interested in mental processes, we can satisfy ourselves only by relating the particular symbol to the total configuration of the individual.

There is as great an unreality in similar studies of culture. If we are interested in cultural processes, the only way in which we can know the significance of the selected detail of behaviour is against the background of the motives and emotions and values that are institutionalized in that culture. The first essential, so it seems today, is to study the living culture, to know its habits of thought and the functions of its institutions, and such knowledge

49

cannot come out of post-mortem dissections and reconstructions.

The necessity for functional studies of culture has been stressed over and over again by Malinowski. He criticizes the usual diffusion studies as post-mortem dissections of organisms we might rather study in their living and functioning vitality. One of the best and earliest of the full-length pictures of a primitive people which have made modern ethnology possible is Malinowski's extended account of the Trobriand Islanders of Melanesia. Malinowski, however, in his ethnological generalizations is content to emphasize that traits have a living context in the culture of which they are a part, that they function. He then generalizes the Trobriand traits — the importance of reciprocal obligations, the local character of magic, the Trobriand domestic family — as valid for the primitive world instead of recognizing the Trobriand configuration as one of many observed types, each with its characteristic arrangements in the economic, the religious, and the domestic sphere.

The study of cultural behaviour, however, can no longer be handled by equating particular local arrangements with the generic primitive. Anthropologists are turning from the study of primitive culture to that of primitive cultures, and the implications of this change from the singular to the plural are only just beginning to be evident.

The importance of the study of the whole configuration as over against the continued analysis of its parts is stressed in field after field of modern science. Wilhelm Stern has made it basic in his work in philosophy and psychology. He insists that the undivided totality of the person must be the point of departure. He criticizes the atomistic studies that have been almost universal both in introspective and experimental psychology, and he substitutes investigation into the configuration of personality. The whole *Struktur* school has devoted itself to work of this kind in various fields. Worringer has shown how fundamental a difference this approach makes in the field of æsthetics. He contrasts the highly developed art of two periods, the Greek and the Byzantine. The older criticism, he insists, which defined art in absolute terms and identified it with the classical standards, could not possibly understand the processes of art as they are represented in Byzantine painting or mosaic. Achievement in one cannot be judged in terms of the other, because each was attempting to achieve quite different ends. The Greeks in their art attempted to give expression to their own pleasure in activity; they sought to embody their identification of their vitality with the objective world. Byzantine art, on the other hand, objectified abstraction, a profound feeling of separation in the face of outside nature. Any understanding of the two must take account, not only of comparisons of artistic ability, but far more of differences of artistic intention. The two forms were contrasting, integrated configurations, each of which could make use of forms and standards that were incredible in the other.

The *Gestalt* (configuration) psychology has done some of the most striking work in justifying the importance of this point of departure from the whole rather than from its parts. *Gestalt* psychologists have shown that in the simplest sense-perception no analysis of the separate percepts can account for the total experience. It is not enough to divide perceptions up into objective fragments. The subjective framework, the forms provided by past experience, are crucial and cannot be omitted. The 'wholeness-

51

properties' and the 'wholeness-tendencies' must be studied in addition to the simple association mechanisms with which psychology has been satisfied since the time of Locke. The whole determines its parts, not only their relation but their very nature. Between two wholes there is a discontinuity in kind, and any understanding must take account of their different natures, over and above a recognition of the similar elements that have entered into the two. The work in *Gestalt* psychology has been chiefly in those fields where evidence can be experimentally arrived at in the laboratory, but its implications reach far beyond the simple demonstrations which are associated with its work.

In the social sciences the importance of integration and configuration was stressed in the last generation by Wilhelm Dilthey. His primary interest was in the great philosophies and interpretations of life. Especially in *Die Typen der Weltanschauung* he analyzes part of the history of thought to show the relativity of philosophical systems. He sees them as great expressions of the variety of life, moods, *Lebensstimmungen*, integrated attitudes the fundamental categories of which cannot be resolved one into another. He argues vigorously against the assumption that any one of them can be final. He does not formulate as cultural the different attitudes he discusses, but because he takes for discussion great philosophical configurations, and historical periods like that of Frederick the Great, his work has led naturally to more and more conscious recognition of the rôle of culture.

This recognition has been given its most elaborate expression by Oswald Spengler. His *Decline of the West* takes its title not from its theme of destiny ideas, as he calls the dominant patterning of a civilization, but from a thesis which has no bearing upon our present discussion, namely, that these cultural configurations have, like any organism, a span of life they cannot overpass. This thesis of the doom of civilizations is argued on the basis of the shift of cultural centres in Western civilization and the periodicity of high cultural achievement. He buttresses this description with the analogy, which can never be more than an analogy, with the birth- and death-cycle of living organisms. Every civilization, he believes, has its lusty youth, its strong manhood, and its disintegrating senescence.

It is this latter interpretation of history which is generally identified with *The Decline of the West*, but Spengler's far more valuable and original analysis is that of contrasting configurations in Western civilization. He distinguishes two great destiny ideas: the Apollonian of the classical world and the Faustian of the modern world. Apollonian man conceived of his soul 'as a cosmos ordered in a group of excellent parts.' There was no place in his universe for will, and conflict was an evil which his philosophy decried. The idea of an inward development of the personality was alien to him, and he saw life as under the shadow of catastrophe always brutally threatening from the outside. His tragic climaxes were wanton destructions of the pleasant landscape of normal existence. The same event might have befallen another individual in the same way and with the same results.

On the other hand, the Faustian's picture of himself is as a force endlessly combating obstacles. His version of the course of individual life is that of an inner development, and the catastrophes of existence come as the inevitable culmination of his past choices and experiences. Conflict is the essence of existence. Without it personal life has no meaning, and only the more superficial values of existence can be attained. Faustian man longs for the infinite, and his art attempts to reach out toward it. Faustian and Apollonian are opposed interpretations of existence, and the values that arise in the one are alien and trivial to the other.

The civilization of the classical world was built upon the Apollonian view of life, and the modern world has been working out in all its institutions the implications of the Faustian view. Spengler glances aside also at the Egyptian, 'which saw itself as moving down a narrow and inexorably prescribed life-path to come at last before the judges of the dead,' and at the Magian with its strict dualism of body and soul. But his great subjects are the Apollonian and the Faustian, and he considers mathematics, architecture, music, and painting as expressing these two great opposed philosophies of different periods of Western civilization.

The confused impression which is given by Spengler's volumes is due only partially to the manner of presentation. To an even greater degree it is the consequence of the unresolved complexities of the civilizations with which he deals. Western civilizations, with their historical diversity, their stratification into occupations and classes, their incomparable richness of detail, are not yet well enough understood to be summarized under a couple of catchwords. Outside of certain very restricted intellectual and artistic circles, Faustian man, if he occurs, does not have his own way with our civilization. There are the strong men of action and the Babbitts as well as the Faustians, and no ethnologically satisfactory picture of modern civilization can ignore such constantly recurring types. It is quite as convincing to characterize our cultural type as thoroughly extrovert, running about in endless mundane activity, inventing, governing, and as Edward Carpenter says, 'endlessly catching its trains,' as it is to characterize it as Faustian, with a longing for the infinite.

Anthropologically speaking, Spengler's picture of world civilizations suffers from the necessity under which he labours of treating modern stratified society as if it had the essential homogeneity of a folk culture. In our present state of knowledge, the historical data of western European culture are too complex and the social differentiation too thorough-going to yield to the necessary analysis. However suggestive Spengler's discussion of Faustian man is for a study of European literature and philosophy, and however just his emphasis upon the relativity of values, his analysis cannot be final because other equally valid pictures can be drawn. In the retrospect it may be possible to characterize adequately a great and complex whole like Western civilization, but in spite of the importance and the truth of Spengler's postulate of incommensurable destiny ideas, at the present time the attempt to interpret the Western world in terms of any one selected trait results in confusion.

It is one of the philosophical justifications for the study of primitive peoples that the facts of simpler cultures may make clear social facts that are otherwise baffling and not open to demonstration. This is nowhere more true than in the matter of the fundamental and distinctive cultural configurations that pattern existence and condition the thoughts and emotions of the individuals who participate in those cultures. The whole problem of the formation of the individual's habit-patterns under the influence of traditional custom can best be understood at the present time through the study of simpler peoples. This does not mean that the facts and processes we can discover in this way are limited in their application to primitive civilizations. Cultural configurations are as compelling and as significant in the highest and most complex societies of which we have knowledge. But the material is too intricate and too close to our eyes for us to cope with it successfully.

The understanding we need of our own cultural processes can most economically be arrived at by a détour. When the historical relations of human beings and their immediate forbears in the animal kingdom were too involved to use in establishing the fact of biological evolution, Darwin made use instead of the structure of beetles, and the process, which in the complex physical organization of the human is confused, in the simpler material was transparent in its cogency. It is the same in the study of cultural mechanisms. We need all the enlightenment we can obtain from the study of thought and behaviour as it is organized in the less complicated groups.

I have chosen three primitive civilizations to picture in some detail. A few cultures understood as coherent organizations of behaviour are more enlightening than many touched upon only at their high spots. The relation of motivations and purposes to the separate items of cultural behaviour at birth, at death, at puberty, and at marriage can never be made clear by a comprehensive survey of the world. We must hold ourselves to the less ambitious task, the many-sided understanding of a few cultures.

# IV

## The Pueblos of New Mexico

THE Pueblo Indians of the Southwest are one of the most widely known primitive peoples in Western civilization. They live in the midst of America, within easy reach of any transcontinental traveller. And they are living after the old native fashion. Their culture has not disintegrated like that of all the Indian communities outside of Arizona and New Mexico. Month by month and year by year, the old dances of the gods are danced in their stone villages, life follows essentially the old routines, and what they have taken from our civilization they have remodelled and subordinated to their own attitudes.

They have a romantic history. All through that part of America which they still inhabit are found the homes of their cultural ancestors, the cliff-dwellings and great planned valley cities of the golden age of the Pueblos. Their unbelievably numerous cities were built in the twelfth and thirteenth centuries, but we can follow their history much further back to its simple beginnings in one-room stone houses to each of which an underground ceremonial chamber was attached. These early Pueblo people, however, were not the first who had taken this Southwest desert for their home. An earlier people, the Basketmakers, had lived there so long before that we cannot calculate the period of their occupancy, and they were

57

supplanted, and perhaps largely exterminated, by the early Pueblo people.

The Pueblo culture flourished greatly after it had settled upon its arid plateau. It had brought with it the bow and arrow, a knowledge of stone architecture, and a diversified agriculture. Why it chose for the site of its greatest development the inhospitable, almost waterless valley of the San Juan, which flows into the Colorado River from the north, no one ventures to explain. It seems one of the most forbidding regions in the whole of what is now the United States, yet it was here that there grew up the greatest Indian cities north of Mexico. These were of two kinds, and they seem to have been built by the same civilization at the same period: the cliff-dwellings, and the semicircular valley citadels. The cliff-dwellings dug into the sheer face of the precipice, or built on a ledge hundreds of feet from the valley floor, are some of the most romantic habitations of mankind. We cannot guess what the circumstances were that led to the construction of these homes, far from the cornfields and far from any water-supply, which must have been serious if they were planned as fortifications, but some of the ruins enduringly challenge our admiration of ingenuity and beauty. One thing is never omitted in them, no matter how solid the rock ledge upon which the pueblo is built: the underground ceremonial chamber, the kiva, is hewed out to accommodate a man upright, and is large enough to serve as a gathering-room. It is entered by a ladder through a hatchway.

The other type of dwelling was a prototype of the modern planned city: a semicircular sweep of wall that rose three stories at the fortified exterior and was terraced inward as it approached the underground kivas that clustered in the embrace of the great masonry arms. Some of these great valley cities of this type have not only the small kivas, but one great additional temple similarly sunk into the earth and of the most finished and perfect masonry.

The peak of Pueblo civilization had been reached and passed before the Spanish adventurers came searching for cities of gold. It seems likely that the Navajo-Apache tribes from the north cut off the supplies of water from the cities of these ancient peoples and overcame them. When the Spanish came, they had already abandoned their cliff-dwellings and great semicircular cities and had settled along the Rio Grande in villages they still occupy. Toward the west there were also Acoma, Zuñi, and Hopi, the great western Pueblos.

Pueblo culture, therefore, has a long homogeneous history behind it, and we have special need of this knowledge of it because the cultural life of these peoples is so at variance with that of the rest of North America. Unfortunately archæology cannot go further and tell us how it came about that here in this small region of America a culture gradually differentiated itself from all those that surrounded it and came always more and more drastically to express a consistent and particular attitude toward existence.

We cannot understand the Pueblo configuration of culture without a certain acquaintance with their customs and modes of living. Before we discuss their cultural goals, we must set before ourselves briefly the framework of their society.

The Zuñi are a ceremonious people, a people who value sobriety and inoffensiveness above all other virtues. Their interest is centred upon their rich and complex ceremonial life. Their cults of the masked gods, of healing, of the sun, of the sacred fetishes, of war, of the dead, are formal and established bodies of ritual with priestly officials and calendric observances. No field of activity competes with ritual for foremost place in their attention. Probably most grown men among the western Pueblos give to it the greater part of their waking life. It requires the memorizing of an amount of word-perfect ritual that our less trained minds find staggering, and the performance of neatly dovetailed ceremonies that are charted by the calendar and complexly interlock all the different cults and the governing body in endless formal procedure.

The ceremonial life not only demands their time; it preoccupies their attention. Not only those who are responsible for the ritual and those who take part in it, but all the people of the pueblo, women and families who 'have nothing,' that is, that have no ritual possessions, centre their daily conversation about it. While it is in progress, they stand all day as spectators. If a priest is ill, or if no rain comes during his retreat, village gossip runs over and over his ceremonial missteps and the implications of his failure. Did the priest of the masked gods give offence to some supernatural being? Did he break his retreat by going home to his wife before the days were up? These are the subjects of talk in the village for a fortnight. If an impersonator wears a new feather on his mask, it eclipses all talk of sheep or gardens or marriage or divorce.

This preoccupation with detail is logical enough. Zuñi religious practices are believed to be supernaturally powerful in their own right. At every step of the way, if the procedure is correct, the costume of the masked god traditional to the last detail, the offerings unimpeachable, the words of the hours-long prayers letter-perfect, the effect will follow according to man's desires. One has only, in the phrase they have always on their tongues, to 'know how.' According to all the tenets of their religion, it is a major matter if one of the eagle feathers of a mask has been taken from the shoulder of the bird instead of from the breast. Every detail has magical efficacy.

Zuñi places great reliance upon imitative magic. In the priests' retreats for rain they roll round stones across the floor to produce thunder, water is sprinkled to cause the rain, a bowl of water is placed upon the altar that the springs may be full, suds are beaten up from a native plant that clouds may pile in the heavens, tobacco smoke is blown out that the gods 'may not withhold their misty breath.' In the masked-god dances mortals clothe themselves with the 'flesh' of the supernaturals, that is, their paint and their masks, and by this means the gods are constrained to grant their blessings. Even the observances that are less obviously in the realm of magic partake in Zuñi thought of the same mechanistic efficacy. One of the obligations that rest upon every priest or official during the time when he is actively participating in religious observances is that of feeling no anger. But anger is not tabu in order to facilitate communication with a righteous god who can only be approached by those with a clean heart. It is rather a sign of concentration upon supernatural affairs, a state of mind that constrains the supernaturals and makes it impossible for them to withhold their share of the bargain. It has magical efficacy.

Their prayers also are formulas, the effectiveness of which comes from their faithful rendition. The amount of traditional prayer forms of this sort in Zuñi can hardly be exaggerated. Typically they describe in ritualistic language the whole course of the reciter's ceremonial obligations leading up to the present culmination of the ceremony. They itemize the appointment of the impersonator, the gathering of willow shoots for prayer-sticks, the binding of the bird feathers to them with cotton string, the painting of the sticks, the offering to the gods of the finished plume wands, the visits to sacred springs, the periods of retreat. No less than the original religious act, the recital must be meticulously correct.

Seeking yonder along the river courses
The ones who are our fathers,
Male willow,
Female willow,
Four times cutting the straight young shoots,
To my house
I brought my road.
This day
With my warm human hands
I took hold of them.
I gave my prayer-sticks human form.
With the striped cloud tail
Of the one who is my grandfather,
The male turkey,
With eagle's thin cloud tail,
With the striped cloud wings
And massed cloud tails
Of all the birds of summer,
With these four times I gave my prayer-sticks human form.
With the flesh of the one who is my mother,
Cotton woman,
Even a poorly made cotton thread,
Four times encircling them and tying it about their bodies,
I gave my prayer-sticks human form.
With the flesh of the one who is our mother,
Black paint woman,
Four times covering them with flesh,
I gave my prayer-sticks human form.

Prayer in Zuñi is never an outpouring of the human heart. There are some ordinary prayers that can be slightly varied, but this means little more than that they can be made longer or shorter. And the prayers are never remarkable for their intensity. They are always mild and ceremonious in form, asking for orderly life, pleasant days, shelter from violence. Even war priests conclude their prayer:

I have sent forth my prayers.
Our children,
Even those who have erected their shelters
At the edge of the wilderness,
May their roads come in safely,
May the forests
And the brush
Stretch out their water-filled arms
To shield their hearts;
May their roads come in safely;
May their roads all be fulfilled,
May it not somehow become difficult for them
When they have gone but a little way.
May all the little boys,
All the little girls,
And those whose roads are ahead,
May they have powerful hearts,
Strong spirits;
On roads reaching to Dawn Lake
May you grow old;
May your roads be fulfilled;
May you be blessed with life.
Where the life-giving road of your sun father comes out,
May your roads reach;
May your roads be fulfilled.

If they are asked the purpose of any religious observance, they have a ready answer. It is for rain. This is of course a more or less conventional answer. But it reflects a deep-seated Zuñi attitude. Fertility is above all else the

63

blessing within the bestowal of the gods, and in the desert country of the Zuñi plateau, rain is the prime requisite for the growth of crops. The retreats of the priests, the dances of the masked gods, even many of the activities of the medicine societies are judged by whether or not there has been rain. To 'bless with water' is the synonym of all blessing. Thus, in the prayers, the fixed epithet the gods apply in blessing to the rooms in Zuñi to which they come, is 'water-filled,' their ladders are 'water-ladders,' and the scalp taken in warfare is 'the water-filled covering.' The dead, too, come back in the rain clouds, bringing the universal blessing. People say to the children when the summer afternoon rain clouds come up the sky, 'Your grandfathers are coming,' and the reference is not to individual dead relatives, but applies impersonally to all forbears. The masked gods also are the rain and when they dance they constrain their own being — rain — to descend upon the people. The priests, again, in their retreat before their altars sit motionless and withdrawn for eight days, summoning the rain.

> From wherever you abide permanently
> You will make your roads come forth.
> Your little wind blown clouds,
> Your thin wisp of clouds
> Replete with living waters,
> You will send forth to stay with us.
> Your fine rain caressing the earth,
> Here at Itiwana,[1]
> The abiding place of our fathers,
> Our mothers,
> The ones who first had being,
> With your great pile of waters
> You will come together.

[1] 'The Middle,' the ceremonial name of Zuñi, the centre of the world.

Rain, however, is only one of the aspects of fertility for which prayers are constantly made in Zuñi. Increase in the gardens and increase in the tribe are thought of together. They desire to be blessed with happy women:

> Even those who are with child,
> Carrying one child on the back,
> Holding another on a cradle board,
> Leading one by the hand,
> With yet another going before.

Their means of promoting human fertility are strangely symbolic and impersonal, as we shall see, but fertility is one of the recognized objects of religious observances.

This ceremonial life that preoccupies Zuñi attention is organized like a series of interlocking wheels. The priesthoods have their sacred objects, their retreats, their dances, their prayers, and their year-long programme is annually initiated by the great winter solstice ceremony that makes use of all the different groups and sacred things and focuses all their functions. The tribal masked-god society has similar possessions and calendric observances, and these culminate in the great winter tribal masked-god ceremony, the Shalako. In like fashion the medicine societies, with their special relation to curing, function throughout the year, and have their annual culminating ceremony for tribal health. These three major cults of Zuñi ceremonial life are not mutually exclusive. A man may be, and often is, for the greater part of his life, a member of all three. They each give him sacred possessions 'to live by' and demand of him exacting ceremonial knowledge.

The priesthoods stand on the highest level of sanctity. There are four major and eight minor priesthoods. They

65

'hold their children [1] fast.' They are holy men. Their sacred medicine bundles, in which their power resides, are, as Dr. Bunzel says, of 'indescribable sanctity.' They are kept in great covered jars, in bare, inner rooms of the priests' houses, and they consist of pairs of stoppered reeds, one filled with water, in which there are miniature frogs, and the other with corn. The two are wrapped together with yards and yards of unspun native cotton. No one ever enters the holy room of the priests' medicine bundle except the priests when they go in for their rituals, and an elder woman of the household or the youngest girl child, who go in before every meal to feed the bundle. Anyone entering, for either purpose, removes his moccasins.

The priests, as such, do not hold public ceremonies, though in great numbers of the rites their presence is necessary or they initiate essential first steps in the undertaking. Their retreats before their sacred bundle are secret and sacrosanct. In June, when rain is needed for the corn, at that time about a foot above the ground, the series of retreats begins. In order, each new priesthood going 'in' as the preceding one comes out, they 'make their days.' The heads of the sun cult and of the war cult are included also in this series of the priests' retreats. They must sit motionless, with their thoughts fixed upon ceremonial things, eight days for the major priesthoods, four for the lesser. All Zuñi awaits the granting of rain during these days, and priests blessed with rain are greeted and thanked by everyone upon the street after their retreat is ended. They have blessed their people with more than rain. They have upheld them in all their ways of life. Their position as guardians of their people has been vindicated. The prayers

[1] That is, the people of Zuñi.

66

they have prayed during their retreat have been answered:

> All my ladder-descending children,
> All of them I hold in my hands,
> May no one fall from my grasp
> After going but a little way.
> Even every little beetle,
> Even every dirty little beetle
> Let me hold them all fast in my hands,
> Let none of them fall from my grasp.
> May my children's roads all be fulfilled;
> May they grow old;
> May their roads reach all the way to Dawn Lake;
> May their roads be fulfilled;
> In order that your thoughts may bend to this
> Your days are made.

The heads of the major priesthoods, with the chief priest
of the sun cult and the two chief priests of the war cult,
constitute the ruling body, the council, of Zuñi. Zuñi is a
theocracy to the last implication. Since priests are holy
men and must never during the prosecution of their duties
feel anger, nothing is brought before them about which
there will not be unanimous agreement. They initiate the
great ceremonial events of the Zuñi calendar, they make
ritual appointments, and they give judgment in cases of
witchcraft. To our sense of what a governing body should
be, they are without jurisdiction and without authority.

If the priesthoods stand on the level of greatest sanctity,
the cult of the masked gods is most popular. It has first
claim in Zuñi affection, and it flourishes today like the
green bay tree.

There are two kinds of masked gods: the masked gods
proper, the kachinas; and the kachina priests. These
kachina priests are the chiefs of the supernatural world

and are themselves impersonated with masks by Zuñi dancers. Their sanctity in Zuñi eyes makes it necessary that their cult should be quite separate from that of the dancing gods proper. The dancing gods are happy and comradely supernaturals who live at the bottom of a lake far off in the empty desert south of Zuñi. There they are always dancing. But they like best to return to Zuñi to dance. To impersonate them, therefore, is to give them the pleasure they most desire. A man, when he puts on the mask of the god, becomes for the time being the supernatural himself. He has no longer human speech, but only the cry which is peculiar to that god. He is tabu, and must assume all the obligations of anyone who is for the time being sacred. He not only dances, but he observes an esoteric retreat before the dance, and plants prayer-sticks and observes continence.

There are more than a hundred different masked gods of the Zuñi pantheon, and many of these are dance groups that come in sets, thirty or forty of a kind. Others come in sets of six, coloured for the six directions — for Zuñi counts up and down as cardinal points. Each of these gods has individual details of costuming, an individual mask, an individual place in the hierarchy of the gods, myths that recount his doings, and ceremonies during which he is expected.

The dances of the masked gods are administered and carried out by a tribal society of all adult males. Women too may be initiated 'to save their lives,' but it is not customary. They are not excluded because of any tabu, but membership for a woman is not customary, and there are today only three women members. As far back as tradition reaches there seem not to have been many more at any one time. The men's tribal society is organized in six groups, each with its kiva or ceremonial chamber. Each kiva has its officials, its dances that belong to it, and its own roll of members.

Membership in one or the other of these kivas follows from the choice of a boy's ceremonial father at birth, but there is no initiation till the child is between five and nine years old. It is his first attainment of ceremonial status. This initiation, as Dr. Bunzel points out, does not teach him esoteric mysteries; it establishes a bond with supernatural forces. It makes him strong, and, as they say, valuable. The 'scare kachinas,' the punitive masked gods, come for the initiation, and they whip the children with their yucca whips. It is a rite of exorcism, 'to take off the bad happenings,' and to make future events propitious. In Zuñi whipping is never used as a corrective of children. The fact that white parents use it in punishment is a matter for unending amazement. In the initiation children are supposed to be very frightened, and they are not shamed if they cry aloud. It makes the rite the more valuable.

Later, traditionally when the boy is about fourteen and old enough to be responsible, he is whipped again by even stronger masked gods. It is at this initiation that the kachina mask is put upon his head, and it is revealed to him that the dancers, instead of being the supernaturals from the Sacred Lake, are in reality his neighbours and his relatives. After the final whipping, the four tallest boys are made to stand face to face with the scare kachinas who have whipped them. The priests lift the masks from their heads and place them upon the heads of the boys. It is the great revelation. The boys are terrified. The yucca whips are taken from the hands of the scare kachinas and put in the hands of the boys who face them, now with the masks upon their heads. They are commanded to whip the kachinas. It is their first object lesson in the truth that they, as mortals, must exercise all the functions which the uninitiated ascribe to the supernaturals themselves. The boys whip them, four times on the right arm, four on the left, four times on the right leg, four on the left. Afterward the kachinas are whipped in turn in the same way by all the boys, and the priests tell them the long myth of the boy who let fall the secret that the kachinas were merely impersonations and was killed by the masked gods. They cut his head from his body and kicked it all the way to the Sacred Lake. His body they left lying in the plaza. The boys must never, never tell. They are now members of the cult and may impersonate the masked gods.

They do not yet possess masks. They will not have masks made until they are married men of some substance. Then a man plants lavishly for the year and makes known to the head of his kiva that he wishes the initiation of the mask. He is whipped again by the kachinas who whipped him as a boy, and feasts his kiva and those who have danced. His mask is his, for he keeps it in his house and it makes his house valuable. At his death it will be buried with him to ensure his joining the troop of kachina dancers in the Sacred Lake. Any man, however, who has not a mask borrows from those who have, at any time, freely and without a return gift. He has it painted to represent any kachina he chooses, for according as it is painted and furnished with accessories, it may be used in the impersonation of a large number of kachinas.

The cult of the kachina priests is quite different. The masks of kachina priests are not made up at request and refurbished for different impersonators at each dance. They are permanent masks which are surrounded by cult

THE PUEBLOS OF NEW MEXICO

observances, and are second in sanctity only to the medicine bundles of the major priesthoods. They are owned
and cared for, as those are, by family lines in the same
houses that have cared for them, they say, since the beginning of the world. Each has its own cult group. These
cults are responsible for the impersonations of these masks
whenever they are required in the round of Zuñi ceremonials. These permanent masks of the kachina priests
are associated with the long rituals that their impersonators memorize and deliver on their appearance. Unlike
the dancing kachinas, they do not come to dance, but to
perform definite ceremonial functions in the calendric
ritual. It is they who come to whip the children at initiation, who come at the great annual ceremony of Shalako,
who 'make the New Year.' They are the counterpart,
upon the supernatural plane, of their 'daylight children,'
the chief priests of Zuñi. They are the chief priests of the
kachinas.

The third great division of the Zuñi ceremonial structure
is that of the medicine societies. The supernatural patrons
of the medicine societies are the beast gods, chief of whom
is the bear. Just as the dancers impersonate the kachinas,
the medicine societies impersonate the bear. In place of
a mask they pull over their arms the skin of the forelegs
of the bear with the claws still in place. Just as the dancers
utter only the cry of the kachina, the impersonators of the
beast gods growl, dangerously, like the bear. It is the bear
who has the supreme powers of healing, and his powers
are constrained, as in the case of the kachinas, by the use
of his bodily substance.

The medicine societies have great stores of esoteric
knowledge, which bit by bit the member learns throughout
his life. Some of these esoteric techniques, like walking

71

on red-hot coals, or swallowing swords, are learned upon further initiation into higher orders of the societies. The doctors are the highest orders of all, those 'whose roads are finished.' Those who aspire to this degree must sit for years at the feet of those who already know.

These medicine men are summoned in case of illness. But the cure is made by virtue of powers belonging to the society and lays upon the patient the obligation of participation in these powers. For this reason he must later take up formal membership in the group of the doctor who has healed him. In other words, initiation into medicine societies is through a cure from serious illness. Men and women alike are members. For those who wish to join and are not ill, other ritual ways are provided, but most persons join after an illness. The initiation is expensive, so that usually years elapse before membership is consummated and the new heart is dramatically given to the initiate.

The medicine societies have altars and sacred objects that command a high place in Zuñi. The doctors have also a personal fetish, a perfect ear of corn entirely covered with the most valuable and beautiful feathers, the butt of the ear covered with a fine basketry base. Throughout its owner's life this is brought out to be set up on every altar of his society, and it is buried, dismantled of its precious feathers, with his body at his death.

The great public ceremony of the medicine societies, the tribal healing, is the culmination of their winter retreat, and the high point of their functioning. On that night all societies are convened in their society rooms, the altars are set up, and the bear and the other beast gods are impersonated by the members. Everyone goes; it insures the removal of illnesses and the achievement of sound bodily health.

72

In Zuñi thought, war and hunting and clowning cults are grouped with the medicine societies. There are naturally points of difference. Only those who have killed someone join the war society. The circumstances of the killing do not matter. Anyone who has spilled blood must join to 'save his life,' that is, to escape the danger of having taken life. The cult members have charge of the scalp-house and are the protectors of the people. On them falls the duty of policing the village. Like the members of the hunters' society, they do not doctor and only men are members. The clowning society, also, has its characteristic differences, but it is thought of, nevertheless, as belonging with the medicine societies.

No other aspect of existence seriously competes in Zuñi interest with the dances and the religious observances. Domestic affairs like marriage and divorce are casually and individually arranged. Zuñi is a strongly socialized culture and not much interested in those things that are matters for the individual to attend to. Marriage is arranged almost without courtship. Traditionally girls had few opportunities for speaking to a boy alone, but in the evening when all the girls carried the water-jars on their heads to the spring for water, a boy might waylay one and ask for a drink. If she liked him she gave it to him. He might ask her also to make him a throwing stick for the rabbit hunt, and give her afterwards the rabbits he had killed. Boys and girls were supposed to have no other meetings, and certainly there are many Zuñi women today who were married with no more preliminary sex experience than this.

When the boy decides to ask her father for the girl, he goes to her house. As in every Zuñi visit, he first tastes the food that is set before him, and the father says to him

73

as he must say to every visitor, 'Perhaps you came for something.' The boy answers, 'Yes, I came thinking of your daughter.' The father calls his daughter, saying, 'I cannot speak for her. Let her say.' If she is willing, the mother goes into the next room and makes up the pallet and they retire together. Next day she washes his hair. After four days she dresses in her best clothes and carries a large basket of fine corn flour to his mother's house as a present. There are no further formalities and little social interest is aroused in the affair.

If they are not happy together, and think of separating, especially if they have no children that have lived, the wife will make a point of going to serve at the ceremonial feasts. When she has a tête-à-tête with some eligible man they will arrange a meeting. In Zuñi it is never thought to be difficult for a woman to acquire a new husband. There are fewer women than men, and it is more dignified for a man to live with a wife than to remain in his mother's house. Men are perennially willing. When the woman is satisfied that she will not be left husbandless, she gathers together her husband's possessions and places them on the doorsill, in olden times on the roof by the hatchway. There are not many: his extra pair of moccasins, his dance skirt and sash, if he has them, his box of precious feathers for prayer-sticks, his paint-pots for prayer-sticks and for refurbishing masks. All his more important ceremonial possessions he has never brought from his mother's house. When he comes home in the evening he sees the little bundle, picks it up and cries, and returns with it to his mother's house. He and his family weep and are regarded as unfortunate. But the rearrangement of living-quarters is the subject of only fleeting gossip. There is rarely an interplay of deep feeling. Husbands and wives abide by the rules, and these rules hardly provide for violent emotions, either of jealousy or of revenge, or of an attachment that refuses to accept dismissal.

In spite of the casual nature of marriage and divorce, a very large proportion of Zuñi marriages endure through the greater part of a lifetime. Bickering is not liked, and most marriages are peaceful. The permanence of Zuñi marriages is the more striking because marriage, instead of being the social form behind which all the forces of tradition are massed, as in our culture, cuts directly across the most strongly institutionalized social bond in Zuñi.

This is the matrilineal family, which is ceremonially united in its ownership and care of the sacred fetishes. To the women of the household, the grandmother and her sisters, her daughters and their daughters, belong the house and the corn that is stored in it. No matter what may happen to marriages, the women of the household remain with the house for life. They present a solid front. They care for and feed the sacred objects that belong to them. They keep their secrets together. Their husbands are outsiders, and it is their brothers, married now into the houses of other clans, who are united with the household in all affairs of moment. It is they who return for all the retreats when the sacred objects of the house are set out before the altar. It is they, not the women, who learn the word-perfect ritual of their sacred bundle and perpetuate it. A man goes always, for all important occasions, to his mother's house, which, when she dies, becomes his sister's house, and if his marriage breaks up, he returns to the same stronghold.

This blood-relationship group, rooted in the ownership of the house, united in the care of sacred objects, is the important group in Zuñi. It has permanence and impor-

75

tant common concerns. But it is not the economically functioning group. Each married son, each married brother, spends his labour upon the corn which will fill his wife's storeroom. Only when his mother's or sister's house lacks male labour does he care for the cornfield of his blood-relationship group. The economic group is the household that lives together, the old grandmother and her husband, her daughters and their husbands. These husbands count in the economic group, though in the ceremonial group they are outsiders.

For women there is no conflict. They have no allegiance of any kind to their husbands' groups. But for all men there is double allegiance. They are husbands in one group and brothers in another. Certainly in the more important families, in those which care for permanent fetishes, a man's allegiance as brother has more social weight than his allegiance as husband. In all families a man's position derives, not, as with us, from his position as breadwinner, but from his rôle in relation to the sacred objects of the household. The husband, with no such relationship to the ceremonial possessions of his wife's house to trade upon, only gradually attains to position in the household as his children grow to maturity. It is as their father, not as provider or as their mother's husband, that he finally attains some authority in the household where he may have lived for twenty years.

Economic affairs are always as comparatively unimportant in Zuñi as they are in determining the family alignments. Like all the Pueblos, and perhaps in greater degree than the rest, Zuñi is rich. It has gardens and peach orchards and sheep and silver and turquoise. These are important to a man when they make it possible for him to have a mask made for himself, or to pay for the learning of ritual, or to entertain the tribal masked gods at the Shalako. For this last he must build a new house for the gods to bless at housewarming. All that year he must feed the cult members who build for him, he must provide the great beams for the rafters, he must entertain the whole tribe at the final ceremony. There are endless responsibilities he must assume. For this purpose he will plant heavily the year before and increase his herd. He will receive help from his clan group, all of which he must return in kind. Riches used in this way are of course indispensable to a man of prestige, but neither he nor anyone else is concerned with the reckoning of possessions, but with the ceremonial rôle which he has taken. A 'valuable' family, in native parlance, is always a family which owns permanent fetishes, and a man of importance is one who has undertaken many ceremonial rôles.

All the traditional arrangements tend to make wealth play as small a part as possible in the performance of ritual prerogatives. Ceremonial objects, even though they are recognized personal property and attained by the expenditure of money and effort, are free to the use of anyone who can employ them. There are many sacred things too dangerous to be handled except by those who have qualified, but the tabus are not property tabus. Hunting fetishes are owned in the hunters' society, but anyone who is going hunting may take them for his use. He will have to assume the usual responsibilities for using holy things; he will have to plant prayer-sticks and be continent and benevolent for four days. But he pays nothing, and those who possess the fetishes as private property have no monopoly of their supernatural powers. Similarly a man who has no mask borrows one freely and is not thought of as a beggar or a suppliant.

Besides this unusual discontinuity between vested interests and the ownership of ceremonial objects in Zuni, other more common arrangements make wealth of comparative unimportance. Membership in a clan with numerous ceremonial prerogatives outweighs wealth, and a poor man may be sought repeatedly for ritual offices because he is of the required lineage. Most ceremonial participation, in addition, is the responsibility of a group of people. An individual acts in assuming ritual posts as he does in all other affairs of life, as a member of a group. He may be a comparatively poor man, but the household or the kiva acting through him provides the ceremonial necessaries. The group gains always from this participation because of the great blessing that accrues to it, and the property owned by a self-respecting individual is not the count on which he is admitted to or denied ceremonial rôles.

The Pueblos are a ceremonious people. But that is not the essential fashion in which they are set off from the other peoples of North America and Mexico. It goes much deeper than any difference in degree in the amount of ritual that is current among them. The Aztec civilization of Mexico was as ritualistic as the Pueblo, and even the Plains Indians with their sun dance and their men's societies, their tobacco orders and their war rituals, had a rich ceremonialism.

The basic contrast between the Pueblos and the other cultures of North America is the contrast that is named and described by Nietzsche in his studies of Greek tragedy. He discusses two diametrically opposed ways of arriving at the values of existence. The Dionysian pursues them through 'the annihilation of the ordinary bounds and limits of existence'; he seeks to attain in his most valued moments escape from the boundaries imposed upon him by his five senses, to break through into another order of experience. The desire of the Dionysian, in personal experience or in ritual, is to press through it toward a certain psychological state, to achieve excess. The closest analogy to the emotions he seeks is drunkenness, and he values the illuminations of frenzy. With Blake, he believes 'the path of excess leads to the palace of wisdom.' The Apollonian distrusts all this, and has often little idea of the nature of such experiences. He finds means to outlaw them from his conscious life. He 'knows but one law, measure in the Hellenic sense.' He keeps the middle of the road, stays within the known map, does not meddle with disruptive psychological states. In Nietzsche's fine phrase, even in the exaltation of the dance he 'remains what he is, and retains his civic name.'

The Southwest Pueblos are Apollonian. Not all of Nietzsche's discussion of the contrast between Apollonian and Dionysian applies to the contrast between the Pueblos and the surrounding peoples. The fragments I have quoted are faithful descriptions, but there were refinements of the types in Greece that do not occur among the Indians of the Southwest, and among these latter, again, there are refinements that did not occur in Greece. It is with nc thought of equating the civilization of Greece with that of aboriginal America that I use, in describing the cultural configurations of the latter, terms borrowed from the culture of Greece. I use them because they are categories that bring clearly to the fore the major qualities that differentiate Pueblo culture from those of other American Indians, not because all the attitudes that are found in Greece are found also in aboriginal America.

Apollonian institutions have been carried much further in the pueblos than in Greece. Greece was by no means as single-minded. In particular, Greece did not carry out as the Pueblos have the distrust of individualism that the Apollonian way of life implies, but which in Greece was scanted because of forces with which it came in conflict. Zuñi ideals and institutions on the other hand are rigorous on this point. The known map, the middle of the road, to any Apollonian is embodied in the common tradition of his people. To stay always within it is to commit himself to precedent, to tradition. Therefore those influences that are powerful against tradition are uncongenial and minimized in their institutions, and the greatest of these is individualism. It is disruptive, according to Apollonian philosophy in the Southwest, even when it refines upon and enlarges the tradition itself. That is not to say that the Pueblos prevent this. No culture can protect itself from additions and changes. But the process by which these come is suspect and cloaked, and institutions that would give individuals a free hand are outlawed.

It is not possible to understand Pueblo attitudes toward life without some knowledge of the culture from which they have detached themselves: that of the rest of North America. It is by the force of the contrast that we can calculate the strength of their opposite drive and the resistances that have kept out of the Pueblos the most characteristic traits of the American aborigines. For the American Indians as a whole, and including those of Mexico, were passionately Dionysian. They valued all violent experience, all means by which human beings may break through the usual sensory routine, and to all such experiences they attributed the highest value.

The Indians of North America outside the Pueblos have,

of course, anything but a uniform culture. They contrast violently at almost every point, and there are eight of them that it is convenient to differentiate as separate culture areas. But throughout them all, in one or another guise, there run certain fundamental Dionysian practices. The most conspicuous of these is probably their practice of obtaining supernatural power in a dream or vision, of which we have already spoken. On the western plains men sought these visions with hideous tortures. They cut strips from the skin of their arms, they struck off fingers, they swung themselves from tall poles by straps inserted under the muscles of their shoulders. They went without food and water for extreme periods. They sought in every way to achieve an order of experience set apart from daily living. It was grown men, on the plains, who went out after visions. Sometimes they stood motionless, their hands tied behind them, or they staked out a tiny spot from which they could not move till they had received their blessing. Sometimes, in other tribes, they wandered over distant regions, far out into dangerous country. Some tribes chose precipices and places especially associated with danger. At all events a man went alone, or, if he was seeking his vision by torture and someone had to go out with him to tie him to the pole from which he was to swing till he had his supernatural experience, his helper did his part and left him alone for his ordeal.

It was necessary to keep one's mind fixed upon the expected visitation. Concentration was the technique above all others upon which they relied. 'Keep thinking it all the time,' the old medicine men said always. Sometimes it was necessary to keep the face wet with tears so that the spirits would pity the sufferer and grant him his request. 'I am a poor man. Pity me,' is a constant prayer.

'Have nothing,' the medicine men taught, 'and the spirits will come to you.'

On the western plains they believed that when the vision came it determined their life and the success they might expect. If no vision came, they were doomed to failure. 'I was going to be poor; that is why I had no vision.' If the experience was of curing, one had curing powers, if of warfare, one had warrior's powers. If one encountered Double Woman, one was a transvestite and took woman's occupations and habits. If one was blessed by the mythical Water Serpent, one had supernatural power for evil and sacrificed the lives of one's wife and children in payment for becoming a sorcerer. Any man who desired general strengthening or success in particular ventures sought visions often. They were necessary for warpaths and for curings and for all kinds of miscellaneous occasions: calling the buffalo, naming children, mourning, revenge, finding lost articles.

When the vision came, it might be visual or auditory hallucination, but it need not be. Most of the accounts tell of the appearance of some animal. When it first appeared it was often in human form, and it talked with the supplicant and gave him a song and a formula for some supernatural practice. As it was leaving, it turned into an animal, and the supplicant knew what animal it was that had blessed him, and what skin or bone or feathers he must get to keep as a memento of the experience and preserve for life as his sacred medicine bundle. On the other hand some experiences were much more casual. There were tribes that valued especially moments of intimacy with nature, occasions when a person alone by the edge of a river or following the trail felt in some otherwise simple event a compelling significance.

It might be from a dream that the supernatural power came to them. Some of the accounts of visions are unmistakable dream experiences, whether they occurred in sleep or under less normal conditions. Some tribes valued the dreams of sleep more highly than any other experiences. Lewis and Clark complained when they crossed the western plains in the early days that no night was fit for sleeping; some old man was always rousing to beat on his drum and ceremonially rehearse the dream he had just had. It was a valuable source of power.

In any case the criterion of whether or not the experience had power was necessarily a matter for the individual to decide. It was recognized as subjective, no matter what other social curbs were imposed upon its subsequent practice. Some experiences had power and some had not, and they distinguished by the flash of significance that singled out those that were valuable. If it did not communicate this thrill, an experience they had sought even with torture was counted valueless, and they dared not claim power from it for fear that the animal claimed as guardian spirit would visit death and disgrace upon them.

This belief in the power of a vision experience on the western plains is a cultural mechanism which gives a theoretically unlimited freedom to the individual. He might go out and get this supremely coveted power, no matter to what family he belonged. Besides this, he might claim his vision as authority for any innovation, any personal advantage which he might imagine, and this authority he invoked was an experience in solitude which in the nature of the case could not be judged by another person. It was, moreover, probably the experience of greatest instability that he could achieve. It gave individual initiative a scope which is not easily equalled.

Practically, of course, the authority of custom remained unchallenged. Even given the freest scope by their institutions, men are never inventive enough to make more than minute changes. From the point of view of an outsider the most radical innovations in any culture amount to no more than a minor revision, and it is a commonplace that prophets have been put to death for the difference between Tweedledum and Tweedledee. In the same way, the cultural licence that the vision gave was used to establish, according to the instructions of the vision, a Strawberry Order of the Tobacco Society where before there had been a Snowbird Order, or the power of the skunk in warfare where the usual reliance was upon the buffalo. Other limitations were also inevitable. The emphasis might be placed upon trying out the vision. Only those could claim supernatural power for war who had put their vision to the test and had led a successful war party. In some tribes even the proposition to put the vision to the test had to go before the elders, and the body of elders was guided by no mystic communications.

In cultures other than those of the western plains these limitations upon Dionysian practices were carried much further. Wherever vested rights and privileges were important in any community the conflict occasioned by such a cultural trait as the vision is obvious enough. It is a frankly disruptive cultural mechanism. In tribes where the conflict was strong a number of things might happen. The supernatural experience, to which they still gave lip service, might become an empty shell. If prestige was vested in cult groups and in families, these could not afford to grant individuals free access to the supernatural and teach them that all power came from such contact. There was no reason why they could not still teach the dogma of the free and open vision, and they did. But it was an hypocrisy. No man could exercise power by any authority except that of succession to his father's place in the cult in which he had membership. Among the Omaha, although all power passed down strictly within the family line and was valued for the sorcery that it was, they did not revise their traditional dogma of absolute and sole dependence upon the solitary vision as a sanction for supernatural power. On the Northwest Coast, and among the Aztecs of Mexico, where prestige was also a guarded privilege, different compromises occurred, but they were compromises which did not outlaw the Dionysian values.

The Dionysian bent in the North American vision quest, however, did not usually have to make compromise with prestige groups and their privileges. The experience was often sought openly by means of drugs and alcohol. Among the Indian tribes of Mexico the fermented juice of the fruit of the giant cactus was used ceremonially to obtain the blessed state which was to them supremely religious. The great ceremony of the year among the related Pima, by means of which all blessings were obtained, was the brewing of this cactus beer. The priests drank first, and then all the people, 'to get religious.' Intoxication, in their practice and in their poetry, is the synonym of religion. It has the same mingling of clouded vision and of insight. It gives the whole tribe, together, the exaltation that it associated with religion.

Drugs were much commoner means of attaining this experience. The peyote or mescal bean is a cactus button from the highlands of Mexico. The plant is eaten fresh by the Indian tribes within pilgrimage distance, but the button is traded as far as the Canadian border. It is always used ceremonially. Its effect is well known. It gives peculiar sensations of levitation and brilliant colour images, and is accompanied by very strong affect, either ultimate despair or release from all inadequacy and insecurity. There is no motor disturbance and no erotic excitation.

The cult of the peyote among the American Indians is still spreading. It is incorporated as the Indian Church in Oklahoma and among many tribes the older tribal rituals have paled before this cult. It is associated everywhere with some attitude toward the whites, either a religious opposition to their influence, or a doctrine of speedy acceptance of white ways, and it has many Christian elements woven into its fabric. The peyote is passed and eaten in the manner of the sacrament, first the peyote, then the water, round and round, with songs and prayers. It is a dignified all-night ceremony, and the effects prolong themselves during the following day. In other cases it is eaten for four nights, with four days given up to the excitation. Peyote, within the cults that espouse it, is identified with god. A large button of it is placed upon the ground altar and worshipped. All good comes from it. 'It is the only holy thing I have known in my life'; 'this medicine alone is holy, and has rid me of all evil.' And it is the Dionysian experience of the peyote trance that constitutes its appeal and its religious authority.

The datura or the jimson weed is a more drastic poison. It is more local, being used in Mexico and among the tribes of Southern California. In this latter region it was given to boys at initiation, and under its influence they received their visions. I have been told of boys who died as a result of the drink. The boys were comatose, and some tribes speak of this condition continuing for one day and some for four. The Mojave, the eastern neighbours

86

of these tribes, used datura to get luck in gambling and were said to be unconscious for four days. During this time the dream came which gave them the luck they sought.

Everywhere among the North American Indians, therefore, except in the Southwest Pueblos, we encounter this Dionysian dogma and practice of the vision-dream from which comes supernatural power. The Southwest is surrounded by peoples who seek the vision by fasting, by torture, by drugs and alcohol. But the Pueblos do not accept disruptive experiences and they do not derive supernatural power from them. If a Zuñi Indian has by chance a visual or auditory hallucination it is regarded as a sign of death. It is an experience to avoid, not one to seek by fasting. Supernatural power among the Pueblos comes from cult membership, a membership which has been bought and paid for and which involves the learning of verbatim ritual. There is no occasion when they are expected to overpass the boundaries of sobriety either in preparation for membership, or in initiation, or in the subsequent rise, by payment, to the higher grades, or in the exercise of religious prerogatives. They do not seek or value excess. Nevertheless the elements out of which the widespread vision quest is built up are present: the seeking of dangerous places, the friendship with a bird or animal, fasting, the belief in special blessings from supernatural encounters. But they are no longer integrated as a Dionysian experience. There is complete reinterpretation. Among the Pueblos men go out at night to feared or sacred places and listen for a voice, not that they may break through to communication with the supernatural, but that they may take the omens of good luck and bad. It is regarded as a minor ordeal during which they are badly frightened, and the great tabu connected with it is that they must not look behind on the way home, no matter what seems to be following. The objective performance is much the same as in the vision quest; in each case, they go out during the preparation for a difficult undertaking — in the Southwest, often a foot-race — and make capital of the darkness, the solitariness, the appearance of animals. But the experience which is elsewhere conceived as Dionysian, among the Pueblos is a mechanical taking of omens.

Fasting, the technique upon which the American Indian most depended in attaining a self-induced vision, has received the same sort of reinterpretation. It is no longer utilized to dredge up experiences that normally lie below the level of consciousness; among the Pueblos it is a requirement for ceremonial cleanness. Nothing could be more unexpected to a Pueblo Indian than any theory of a connection between fasting and any sort of exaltation. Fasting is required during all priestly retreats, before participation in a dance, in a race, and on endless ceremonial occasions, but it is never followed by power-giving experience; it is never Dionysian.

The fate of the jimson-weed poisoning in the Southwest pueblos is much like that of the technique of fasting. The practice is present, but its teeth are drawn. The one-to-four-day jimson-weed trances of the Indians of Southern California are not for them. The drug is used as it was in ancient Mexico in order to discover a thief. In Zuñi the man who is to take the drug has a small quantity put into his mouth by the officiating priest, who then retires to the next room and listens for the incriminating name from the lips of the man who has taken the jimson-weed. He is not supposed to be comatose at any time; he alternately sleeps and walks about the room. In the morning he is said to have no memory of the insight he has received. The chief care is to remove every trace of the drug and two common desacratizing techniques are employed to take away the dangerous sacredness of the plant: first, he is given an emetic, four times, till every vestige of the drug is supposed to be ejected; then his hair is washed in yucca suds. The other Zuñi use of jimson weed is even further from any Dionysian purpose; members of the priestly orders go out at night to plant prayer-sticks on certain occasions 'to ask the birds to sing for rain,' and at such times a minute quantity of the powdered root is put into the eyes, ears, and mouth of each priest. Here all connections with the physical properties of the drug are lost sight of.

Peyote has had an even more drastic fate. The Pueblos are close to the Mexican plateau where the peyote button is obtained, and the Apache and the tribes of the plains with which they came most in contact were peyote-eaters. But the practice gained no foothold in the pueblos. A small anti-government group in Taos, the most atypical and Plains-like of the Pueblos, has recently taken it up. But elsewhere it has never been accepted. In their strict Apollonian *ethos*, the Pueblos distrust and reject those experiences which take the individual in any way out of bounds and forfeit his sobriety.

This repugnance is so strong that it has even been sufficient to keep American alcohol from becoming an administrative problem. Everywhere else on Indian reservations in the United States alcohol is an inescapable issue. There are no government regulations that can cope with the Indian's passion for whiskey. But in the pueblos the problem has never been important. They did not brew any native intoxicant in the old days, nor do they now.

Nor is it a matter of course, as it is for instance with the near-by Apaches, that every trip to town, for old men or young, is a debauch. It is not that the Pueblos have a religious tabu against drinking. It is deeper than that. Drunkenness is repulsive to them. In Zuñi after the early introduction of liquor, the old men voluntarily outlawed it, and the rule was congenial enough to be honoured.

Torture was even more consistently rejected. The Pueblos, especially the eastern Pueblos, were in contact with two very different cultures in which self-torture was of the greatest importance, the Plains Indians and the Mexican Penitentes. Pueblo culture also shares many traits with the now extinct torture-using civilization of ancient Mexico, where on all occasions one drew blood from parts of one's own body, especially from the tongue, as an offering to the gods. On the plains, self-torture was specialized as a technique for obtaining states of self-oblivion during which one obtained a vision. The Penitentes of New Mexico are the last surviving sect, in a far corner of the world, of the Flagellants of mediæval Spain, and they have retained to the present day the Good Friday observances of identification with the crucified Saviour. The climax of the rite is the crucifixion of the Christ, impersonated by one of the members of the cult. The procession emerges from the house of the Penitentes at dawn of Good Friday, the Christ staggering under the weight of the tremendous cross. Behind him are his brethren with bared backs who lash themselves at every slow step with their great whips of bayonet cactus to which are fastened barbs of the cholla. From a distance their backs look as if covered with a rich red cloth. The 'way' is about a mile and a half, and when they reach the end the Christ is bound upon the cross and raised. If he, or one of the whippers, dies, his shoes are placed upon his doorstep, and no mourning is allowed for him.

The Pueblos do not understand self-torture. Every man's hand has its five fingers, and unless they have been tortured to secure a sorcery confession they are unscarred. There are no cicatrices upon their backs, no marks where strips of skin have been taken off. They have no rites in which they sacrifice their own blood, or use it for fertility. They used to hurt themselves to a certain extent in a few initiations at the moments of greatest excitement, but in such cases the whole matter was almost an affair of collegiate exuberance. In the Cactus Society, a warrior cult, they dashed about striking themselves and each other with cactus-blade whips; in the Fire Society they tossed fire about like confetti. Neither psychic danger nor abnormal experience is sought in either case. Certainly in the observed fire tricks of the Pueblos — as also in the fire tricks of the Plains — it is not self-torture that is sought. In the Fire Walk, whatever the means employed, feet are not burned, and when the fire is taken into the mouth the tongue is not blistered.

The Pueblo practice of beating with stripes is likewise without intent to torture. The lash does not draw blood. Far from glorying in any such excesses, as the Plains Indians do, a Zuñi child, whipped at adolescence or earlier, at the tribal initiation, may cry out and even call for his mother when he is struck by the initiating masked gods. The adults repudiate with distress the idea that the whips might raise welts. Whipping is 'to take off the bad happenings'; that is, it is a trusted rite of exorcism. The fact that it is the same act that is used elsewhere for self-torture has no bearing upon the use that is made of it in this culture.

If ecstasy is not sought by fasting, by torture, or by drugs or alcohol, or under the guise of the vision, neither is it induced in the dance. Perhaps no people in North America spend more time in the dance than the Southwest Pueblos. But their object in it never is to attain self-oblivion. It is by the frenzy of the dance that the Greek cult of Dionysus was best known, and it recurs over and over in North America. The Ghost Dance of the Indians that swept the country in the 1870's was a round dance danced monotonously till the dancers, one after the other, fell rigid, prostrate on the ground. During their seizure they had visions of deliverance from the whites, and meanwhile the dance continued and others fell. It was the custom in most of the dozens of tribes to which it penetrated to hold the dance every Sunday. There were other and older dances also that were thoroughly Dionysian. The tribes of northern Mexico danced, frothing at the mouth, upon the altar. The shamans' dances of California required a cataleptic seizure. The Maidu used to hold shamans' contests in which that one was victor who danced down the others; that is, who did not succumb to the hypnotic suggestions of the dance. On the Northwest Coast the whole winter ceremonial was thought of as being designed to tame the man who had returned mad and possessed by the spirits. The initiates played out their rôle with the frenzy that was expected of them. They danced like Siberian shamans, tethered by four ropes strung to the four directions so that they could be controlled if they ran into harm to themselves or others.

Of all this there is no suggestion in all the dance occasions of Zuñi. The dance, like their ritual poetry, is a monotonous compulsion of natural forces by reiteration. The tireless pounding of their feet draws together the mist

in the sky and heaps it into the piled rain clouds. It forces
out the rain upon the earth. They are bent not at all upon
an ecstatic experience, but upon so thorough-going an
identification with nature that the forces of nature will
swing to their purposes. This intent dictates the form and
spirit of Pueblo dances. There is nothing wild about them.
It is the cumulative force of the rhythm, the perfection of
forty men moving as one, that makes them effective.

No one has conveyed this quality of Pueblo dancing
more precisely than D. H. Lawrence. 'All the men sing
in unison, as they move with the soft, yet heavy bird
tread which is the whole of the dance, with bodies bent a
little forward, shoulders and heads loose and heavy, feet
powerful but soft, the men tread the rhythm into the
centre of the earth. The drums keep up the pulsating heart
beat and for hours, hours, it goes on.' Sometimes they are
dancing the sprouting corn up out of the earth, sometimes
they are calling the game animals by the tramp of their
feet, sometimes they are constraining the white cumulus
clouds that are slowly piling up the sky on a desert afternoon. Even the presence of these in the sky, whether or
not they vouchsafe rain, is a blessing from the supernaturals upon the dance, a sign that their rite is accepted.
If rain comes, that is the sign and seal of the power of their
dance. It is the answer. They dance on through the swift
Southwest downpour, their feathers wet and heavy, their
embroidered kilts and mantles drenched. But they have
been favoured by the gods. The clowns make merry in the
deep adobe mud, sliding at full length in the puddles and
paddling in the half-liquid earth. It is their recognition
that their feet in the dance have the compulsion of natural
forces upon the storm clouds and have been powerful to
bring the rain.

93

# PATTERNS OF CULTURE

Even where the Pueblos share with their near neighbours dance patterns the very forms of which are instinct with Dionysian meaning, they are used among the Pueblos with complete sobriety. The Cora of northern Mexico have a whirling dance, like so many other tribes of that part of the country, and the climax of it comes when the dancer, having reached the greatest velocity and obliviousness of which he is capable, whirls back and back and upon the very ground altar itself. At any other moment, on any other occasion, this is sacrilege. But of such things the highest Dionysian values are made. In his madness the altar is destroyed, trampled into the sand again. At the end the dancer falls upon the destroyed altar.

In the sets of dances in the underground kiva chamber in the Hopi Snake Dance they also dance upon the altar. But there is no frenzy. It is prescribed, like a movement of a Virginia Reel. One of the commonest formal dance patterns of the Pueblos is built up of the alternation of two dance groups who in each set vary a similar theme, appearing from alternate sides of the dancing space. Finally for the last set the two come out simultaneously from both directions. In this kiva snake dance, the Antelope Society dancers are opposed to the Snake dancers. In the first set the Antelope priest dances, squatting, the circuit of the altar, and retires. The Snake priest repeats. In the second set Antelope receives a vine in his mouth and dances before the initiates, trailing it over their knees. He retires. Snake follows, receiving a live rattlesnake in his mouth in the same fashion and trailing it over the initiates' knees. In the final set Antelope and Snake come out together, still in the squatting position, and dance not the circuit of the altar but upon it, ending the dance. It is a formal sequence like that of a Morris dance, and it is danced in complete sobriety.

94

Nor is the dancing with snakes a courting of the dangerous and the terrible in Hopi. There is current in our civilization so common a horror of snakes that we misread the Snake Dance. We readily attribute to the dancers the emotions we should feel in like case. But snakes are not often regarded with horror by the American Indians. They are often reverenced, and occasionally their holiness makes them dangerous, as anything may be that is sacred or *manitou*. But our unreasoned repulsion is no part of their reaction. Nor are snakes especially feared for their attack. There are Indian folktales that end, 'and that is why the rattlesnake is not dangerous.' The habits of the rattlesnake make it easy to subdue and Indians readily cope with it. The feeling tone of the dancers toward the snakes in the Snake Dance is not that of unholy dread or repulsion, but that of cult members toward their animal patron. Moreover, it has been repeatedly verified that the poison sacs of the rattlesnakes are removed for the dance. They are bruised or pinched out, and when the snakes are released after the dance, the sacs grow again and fill with poison as before. But for the period of the dance the snakes are harmless. The situation, therefore, in the mind of the Hopi dancer is not Dionysian either in its secular or in its supernatural aspect. It is an excellent example of the fact that the same objective behaviour may be, according to inculcated ideas, either a Dionysian courting of dangerous and repulsive experience, or a sober and formal ceremonial.

Whether by the use of drugs, of alcohol, of fasting, of torture, or of the dance, no experiences are sought or tolerated among the Pueblos that are outside of ordinary sensory routine. The Pueblos will have nothing to do with disruptive individual experiences of this type. The love of moderation to which their civilization is committed has no place for them. Therefore they have no shamans.

Shamanism is one of the most general human institutions. The shaman is the religious practitioner who, by whatever kind of personal experience is recognized as supernatural in his tribe, gets his power directly from the gods. He is often, like Cassandra and others of those who spoke with tongues, a person whose instability has marked him out for his profession. In North America shamans are characteristically those who have the experience of the vision. The priest, on the other hand, is the depository of ritual and the administrator of cult activities. The Pueblos have no shamans; they have only priests.

The Zuñi priest holds his position because of relationship claims, or because he has bought his way up through various orders of a society, or because he has been chosen by the chief priests to serve for the year as impersonator of the kachina priests. In any case he has qualified by learning vast quantity of ritual, both of act and of word. All his authority is derived from the office he holds, from the ritual he administers. It must be word-perfect, and he is responsible for the traditional correctness of each complicated ceremony he performs. The Zuñi phrase for a person with power is 'one who knows how.' There are persons who 'know how' in the most sacred cults, in racing, in gambling, and in healing. In other words, they have learned their power verbatim from traditional sources. There is no point at which they are licenced to claim the power of their religion as the sanction for any act of their own initiative. They may not even approach the supernatural except with group warrant at stated intervals. Every prayer, every cult act, is performed at an authorized and universally known season, and in the traditional fashion. The most individual religious act in Zuñi is the planting of prayer-sticks, those delicately fashioned offerings to the gods which are half-buried in sacred places and carry their specific prayer to the supernaturals. But even prayer-sticks may not be offered on the initiative even of the highest priests. One of the folk-tales tells of the chief priest of Zuñi who made prayer-sticks and went out to bury them. It was not the time of the moon when prayer-sticks are planted by the members of the medicine societies, and the people said, 'Why does the chief priest plant prayer-sticks? He must be conjuring.' As a matter of fact, he was using his power for a private revenge. If the most personal of all religious acts may not be performed on the private initiative even of the chief priest, more formal acts are doubly fenced about with public sanctions. No one must ever wonder why an individual is moved to pray.

The Pueblos in their institution of the priest, and the rest of aboriginal America in its institution of the shaman, select and reward two opposing types of personality. The Plains Indians in all their institutions gave scope to the self-reliant man who could easily assume authority. He was rewarded beyond all others. The innovations the returned Crow Indian brought back from his vision might be infinitesimal. That is not the point. Every Buddhist monk and every mediæval Christian mystic saw in his vision what his brethren had seen before. But they and the aboriginal Crow claimed power — or godliness — on the authority of their private experience. The Indian went back to his people in the strength of his vision, and the tribe carried out as a sacred privilege the instructions he had received. In healing, each man knew his own individual power, and asked nothing of any other votary. This dogma was modified in practice, for man perpetuates tradition even in those institutions that attempt to flaunt it. But the dogmas of their religion gave cultural warrant for an amazing degree of self-reliance and personal authority.

This self-reliance and personal initiative on the plains were expressed not only in shamanism but in their passionate enthusiasm for the guerrilla warfare that occupied them. Their war parties were ordinarily less than a dozen strong, and the individual acted alone in their simple engagements in a way that stands at the other pole from the rigid discipline and subordination of modern warfare. Their war was a game in which each individual amassed counts. These counts were for cutting loose a picketed horse, or touching an enemy, or taking a scalp. The individual, usually by personal dare-deviltry, acquired as many as he could, and used them for joining societies, giving feasts, qualifying as a chief. Without initiative and the ability to act alone, an Indian of the plains was not recognized in his society. The testimony of early explorers, the rise of outstanding individuals in their conflicts with the whites, the contrast with the Pueblos, all go to show how their institutions fostered personality, almost in the Nietzschean sense of the superman. They saw life as the drama of the individual progressing upward through grades of men's societies, through acquisitions of supernatural power, through feasts and victories. The initiative rested always with him. His deeds of prowess were counted for him personally, and it was his prerogative to boast of them on ritual occasions, and to use them in every way to further his personal ambitions.

The ideal man of the Pueblos is another order of being. Personal authority is perhaps the most vigorously disparaged trait in Zuñi. 'A man who thirsts for power or knowledge, who wishes to be as they scornfully phrase it "a leader of his people," receives nothing but censure and will very likely be persecuted for sorcery,' and he often has been. Native authority of manner is a liability in Zuñi, and witchcraft is the ready charge against a person who possesses it. He is hung by the thumbs until he 'confesses.' It is all Zuñi can do with a man of strong personality. The ideal man in Zuñi is a person of dignity and affability who has never tried to lead, and who has never called forth comment from his neighbours. Any conflict, even though all right is on his side, is held against him. Even in contests of skill like their foot-races, if a man wins habitually he is debarred from running. They are interested in a game that a number can play with even chances, and an outstanding runner spoils the game: they will have none of him.

A good man has, in Dr. Bunzel's words, 'a pleasing address, a yielding disposition, and a generous heart.' The highest praise, describing an impeccable townsman, runs: 'He is a nice polite man. No one ever hears anything from him. He never gets into trouble. He's Badger clan and Muhekwe kiva, and he always dances in the summer dances.' He should 'talk lots,' as they say — that is, he should always set people at their ease — and he should without fail co-operate easily with others either in the field or in ritual, never betraying a suspicion of arrogance or a strong emotion.

He avoids office. He may have it thrust upon him, but he does not seek it. When the kiva offices must be filled, the hatchway of the kiva is fastened and all the men are imprisoned until someone's excuses have been battered down. The folktales always relate of good men their unwillingness to take office — though they always take it. A man must avoid the appearance of leadership. When the chosen person has been prevailed upon and has been initiated in the office, he has not been given authority in our sense. His post carries with it no sanction for important action. The council of Zuñi is made up of the highest priests, and priests have no jurisdiction in cases of conflict or violence. They are holy men and must not have a quarrel put before them. Only the war chiefs have some measure of executive authority, not in war so much as in peace-time policing powers. They make proclamation of a coming rabbit hunt, or coming dances, they summon priests and co-operate with the medicine societies. The crime that they traditionally have to deal with is witch-craft. Another crime, that of betraying to the uninitiated boys the secret of the kachinas, is punished by the masked gods themselves, summoned by the head of the kachina cult. There are no other crimes. Theft rarely occurs and is a private matter. Adultery is no crime and the strain that arises from such an act is easily taken care of under their marriage arrangements. Homicide, in the one case that is remembered, was settled quickly by payments between the two families.

The priests of the high council, therefore, are not disturbed. They administer the main features of the ceremonial calendar. The successful prosecution of their plans could be blocked at every turn by an unco-operative minor priest. He would only have to sulk, refusing, for instance, to set up his altar or to furnish his kachina priest mask. The priestly council could only wait and defer the ceremonial. But everyone co-operates, and no show of authority is called for.

This same lack of personal exercise of authority is as

characteristic of domestic situations as it is of religious. The matrilineal and matrilocal household of course makes necessary a different allocation of authority from that with which we are familiar. But matrilineal societies do not usually dispense with a male person of authority in the household even though the father does not qualify. The mother's brother as the male head of the matrilineal household is arbiter and responsible head. But Zuñi does not recognize any authority as vested in the mother's brother, and certainly not in the father. Neither of them disciplines the children of his household. Babies are much fondled by the men folk. They carry them when they are ailing and hold them in their laps evenings. But they do not discipline them. The virtue of co-operation holds domestic life true to form just as it holds religious life, and no situations arise that need to be drastically handled. What would they be? Marriage is in other cultures the almost universal occasion where some authority is exercised. But among the Pueblos it is arranged with little formality. Marriage elsewhere in the world involves property rights and economic exchange, and on all such occasions the elders have prerogatives. But in Zuñi marriage there are no stakes in which the elders are interested. The slight emphasis upon possessions among the Pueblos makes a casual affair not only of the elsewhere difficult situation of marriage but of a dozen others, all those which according to other cultural forms involve investment of group property for the young man. Zuñi simply eliminates the occasions.

Every arrangement militates against the possibility of the child's suffering from an Œdipus complex. Malinowski has pointed out for the Trobriands that the structure of society gives to the uncle authority that is associated in our culture with the father. In Zuñi, not even the uncles exercise authority. Occasions are not tolerated which would demand its exercise. The child grows up without either the resentments or the compensatory day-dreams of ambition that have their roots in this familiar situation. When the child himself becomes an adult, he has not the motivations that lead him to imagine situations in which authority will be relevant.

Therefore the initiation of boys is the strange event that it is in Zuñi, strange, that is, in comparison with the practices that are constantly met with in the world. For the initiation of boys is very often an uninhibited exercise of their prerogatives by those in authority; it is a hazing by those in power of those whom they must now admit to tribal status. These rites occur in much the same forms in Africa, in South America, and in Australia. In South Africa the boys are herded under men with long sticks who use them freely on all occasions. They must run the gauntlet with blows raining upon them, they must expect constant blows from behind accompanied by jeers. They must sleep naked without blankets in the coldest months of the year, their heads, not their feet, turned toward the fire. They may not smear the ground to keep away the white worms that bite them at night. At the first signs of daybreak they must go to the pool and stay submerged in the cold water till the sun appears. They may not drink a drop of water for the three months of the initiation camp, they are fed with disgusting food. In compensation, unintelligible formulas are taught them with a great show of importance, and esoteric words.

In American Indian tribes so much time is not usually given to boys' initiation, but the ideas are often the same. The Apache, with whom the Zuñi have many relations, say that breaking a boy is like breaking a young colt. They force him to make holes in the ice and bathe, run with water in his mouth, humiliate him on his trial war parties, and generally bully him. The Indians of Southern California bury him in hills of stinging ants.

But in Zuñi the boy's initiation is never in any way an ordeal. It is thought to make the rite very valuable if the children cry even under the mild strokes they receive. The child is accompanied at every step by his ceremonial father and takes his strokes either clasped upon the old man's back or kneeling between his knees. He is given security by his accompanying sponsor, rather than pushed violently out of the nest, like the South African boy. And the final initiation ends when the boy himself takes the yucca whip and strikes the kachina as he has himself been struck. The initiation does not unload upon the children the adults' pitiful will to power. It is an exorcising and purifying rite. It makes the children valuable by giving them group status. The whipping is an act which they have seen their elders court all their lives as a blessing and a cure. It is their accolade in the supernatural world.

The lack of opportunities for the exercise of authority, both in religious and in domestic situations, is knit up with another fundamental trait: the insistence upon sinking the individual in the group. In Zuñi, responsibility and power are always distributed and the group is made the functioning unit. The accepted way to approach the supernatural is in group ritual. The accepted way to secure family subsistence is by household partnership. Neither in religion nor in economics is the individual autonomous. In religion a man who is anxious about his harvest does not offer prayer for the rain that will save it; he dances in the summer rain dances. A man does not pray for the recovery of his son who is ill; he brings the doctors' order of Big Fire Society to cure him. Those individual prayers that are allowed, at the personal planting of prayer-sticks, at the head-washings of ceremonial cleanliness, at the calling of the medicine men or a ceremonial father, have validity only because they are necessary parts of a larger whole, the group ritual to which they belong. They could no more be separated from it and still have power than one word could be taken from the long magic formulas and retain by itself the efficacy of the perfect prayer.

Sanction for all acts comes from the formal structure, not from the individual. A chief priest, as we saw, can plant prayer-sticks only as chief priest and at those times when he is known to be officially functioning. A medicine man doctors because he is a member of the cult of medicine men. Membership in that cult does not merely strengthen powers of his own, as is the case on the plains, but it is the sole source of his powers. Even the killing of Navajos is judged in the same way. A folktale tells a story of consummate treachery. A rich Navajo and his wife came to trade in a Zuñi household, and the men murdered him for his turquoise. 'But they had not the power of the scalp'; that is, they did not join the war cult, which would have made it right for them to have perpetrated the deed. According to Zuñi thought there is institutional sanction even for this act, and they condemn merely the deed that does not avail itself of its institutional warrant.

The Zuñi people therefore devote themselves to the constituted forms of their society. They sink individuality in them. They do not think of office, and possession of priestly bundles, as steps in the upward path of ambition. A man when he can afford it gets himself a mask in order to increase the number of things 'to live by' in his household, and the number of masks his kiva commands. He takes his due part in the calendric rituals and at great expense builds a new house to entertain the kachina priest impersonations at Shalako, but he does it with a degree of anonymity and lack of personal reference that is hard to duplicate in other cultures. Their whole orientation of personal activity is unfamiliar to us.

Just as in religion the acts and motivations of the individual are singularly without personal reference, so too in economic life. The economic unit is, as we have seen, a very unstable group of men folk. The core of the household, the permanent group, is a relationship group of women, but the women are not the ones who function importantly in the great economic enterprises such as agriculture or herding, or even work in turquoise. And the men who are necessary in the fundamental occupations are a shifting group loosely held together. The husbands of the daughters of the household will return to their maternal households upon a domestic storm and will henceforth have no responsibility for feeding or housing their children whom they leave behind. There are, besides, in the household the miscellaneous male blood relatives of the female relationship group: the unmarried, the widowed, the divorced, and those who are awaiting the passing of temporary unpleasantness in their wives' households. Yet this miscellaneous group, whatever its momentary composition, pools its work in filling the common corn storeroom, and this corn remains the collective property of the women of the household. Even if some newly cultivated fields belong as private property to any of these men, all the men jointly farm them for the common storeroom just as they do ancestral fields.

The custom is the same in regard to houses. The men build them, and jointly, and they belong to the women. A man, leaving his wife in the fall, may be leaving behind him the house he has spent his year building and a full cornroom, the result of his season's farming. But there is no thought of his having any individual claim upon either; and he is not thought of as defrauded. He pooled his work in his household's, and the results are a group supply; if he is no longer a member of that group, that is his affair. Sheep are today a considerable source of income, and are owned by men individually. But they are co-operatively herded by groups of male kindred, and new economic motivations are very slow in making their appearance.

Just as according to the Zuñi ideal a man sinks his activities in those of the group and claims no personal authority, so also he is never violent. Their Apollonian commitment to the mean in the Greek sense is never clearer than in their cultural handling of the emotions. Whether it is anger or love or jealousy or grief, moderation is the first virtue. The fundamental tabu upon their holy men during their periods of office is against any suspicion of anger. Controversies, whether they are ceremonial or economic or domestic, are carried out with an unparalleled lack of vehemence.

Every day in Zuñi there are fresh instances of their mildness. One summer a family I knew well had given me a house to live in, and because of some complicated circumstances another family claimed the right to dispose of the dwelling. When feeling was at its height, Quatsia, the owner of the house, and her husband were with me in the living-room when a man I did not know began cutting down the flowering weeds that had not yet been hoed out of the yard. Keeping the yard free of growth is a chief prerogative of a house-owner, and therefore the man who claimed the right to dispose of the house was taking this occasion to put his claim publicly upon record. He did not enter the house or challenge Quatsia and Leo, who were inside, but he hacked slowly at the weeds. Inside, Leo sat immobile on his heels against the wall, peaceably chewing a leaf. Quatsia, however, allowed herself to flush. 'It is an insult,' she said to me. 'The man out there knows that Leo is serving as priest this year and he can't be angry. He shames us before the whole village by taking care of our yard.' The interloper finally raked up his wilted weeds, looked proudly at the neat yard, and went home. No words were ever spoken between them. For Zuñi it was an insult of sorts, and by his morning's work on the yard the rival claimant sufficiently expressed his protest. He pressed the matter no further.

Marital jealousy is similarly soft-pedalled. They do not meet adultery with violence. A usual response on the plains to the wife's adultery was to cut off the fleshy part of her nose. This was done even in the Southwest by non-Pueblo tribes like the Apache. But in Zuñi the unfaithfulness of the wife is no excuse for violence. The husband does not regard it as a violation of his rights. If she is unfaithful, it is normally a first step in changing husbands, and their institutions make this sufficiently easy so that it is a really tolerable procedure. They do not contemplate violence.

Wives are often equally moderate when their husbands are known to be unfaithful. As long as the situation is not unpleasant enough for relations to be broken off, it is ignored. The season before one of Dr. Bunzel's visits in Zuñi one of the young husbands of the household in which she lived had been carrying on an extra-marital affair that became bruited about all over the pueblo. The family ignored the matter completely. At last the white trader, a guardian of morals, expostulated with the wife. The couple had been married a dozen years and had three children; the wife belonged to an important family. The trader set forth with great earnestness the need of making a show of authority and putting an end to her husband's outrageous conduct. 'So,' his wife said, 'I didn't wash his clothes. Then he knew that I knew that everybody knew, and he stopped going with that girl.' It was effective, but not a word was passed. There were no outbursts, no recriminations, not even an open recognition of the crisis.

Wives, however, are allowed another course of action which is not sanctioned in the case of deserted husbands. A wife may fall upon her rival and beat her up publicly. They call each other names and give each other a black eye. It never settles anything, and even in the rare cases when it occurs, it dies down as quickly as it has flared. It is the only recognized fist-fight in Zuñi. If on the other hand a woman remains peacefully with her husband while he conducts amour after amour, her family are angry and bring pressure to bear upon her to separate from him. 'Everybody says she must love him,' they say, and all her relatives are ashamed. She is disobeying the rules that are laid down for her.

For the traditional course is that of divorce. If a man finds his wife's female relatives uncongenial, he is free to return to his mother's household. It provides a means of avoiding domestic intimacy with individuals he dislikes, and he merely dissolves the relationships which he has found difficult to handle amicably.

If the Pueblos provide institutions that effectively minimize the appearance of a violent emotion like jealousy, they are even more concerned to provide Apollonian techniques at death. Nevertheless there is a difference. Jealousy, it is evident from the practices of many different cultures, is one of the emotions that can be most effectively fostered by cultural arrangements, or it can be outlawed. But bereavement is not so easily escaped. The death of a near relative is the closest thrust that existence deals. It threatens the solidarity of the group, calls for drastic readjustments, especially if the dead individual is an adult, and often means loneliness and sorrow for the survivors.

The Pueblos are essentially realistic, and they do not deny sorrow at death. They do not, like some of the cultures we shall discuss, convert mourning for a near relative into an ambitious display or a terror situation. They treat it as loss, and as important loss. But they provide detailed techniques for getting past it as quickly and with as little violence as possible. The emphasis is upon making the mourner forget. They cut a lock of hair from the deceased and make a smudge to purify those who grieve too much. They scatter black cornmeal with the left hand — associated with death — to 'make their road black'; that is, to put darkness between themselves and their grief. In Isleta, on the evening of the fourth day, before the relatives separate after the death, the officiating priest makes a ground altar on which they put the prayer-sticks for the dead, the dead man's bow and arrow, the hairbrush used to prepare the body for burial, and articles of the dead man's clothing. There are, besides, the bowl of medicine water, and a basket of food to which everyone has contributed. On the floor, from the house door to the altar, the priests make a road of meal for the deceased to come in by. They gather to feed the dead man for the last time and send him away. One of the priests sprinkles everyone from the medicine bowl, and then opens the house door. The chief speaks to the dead man, bidding him to come and eat. They hear the footsteps outside and his fumbling at the door. He enters and eats. Then the chief sprinkles the road for him to leave by, and the priests 'chase him out of the village.' They take with them the prayer-sticks for the dead, the pieces of his clothing and his personal possessions, the hairbrush and the bowl of food. They take them outside the village and break the hairbrush and the bowl, burying everything out of sight. They return on a run, not looking behind them, and bolt the door against the dead by scratching a cross upon it with a flint knife to prevent his entrance. It is the formal breach with the dead. The chief speaks to the people telling them that they shall not remember any more. 'It is now four years he is dead.' In ceremonial and in folklore they use often the idea that the day has become the year or the year the day. Time has elapsed to free them of grief. The people are dismissed, and the mourning is over.

Whatever the psychological bent of a people, however, death is a stubbornly inescapable fact, and in Zuñi the Apollonian discomfort at not being able to outlaw the upheaval of death on the part of the nearest of kin is very clearly expressed in their institutions. They make as little of death as possible. Funeral rites are the simplest and least dramatic of all the rites they possess. None of the elaboration that goes into their calendric ceremonials is to be found on this occasion. The corpse is interred at once, and no priests officiate.

But a death that touches an individual closely is not so easily disposed of even in Zuñi. They conceptualize this persistence of grief or discomfort by the belief that the surviving spouse is in great danger. His dead wife may 'pull him back'; that is, in her loneliness she may take him with her. It is exactly the same for a wife whose husband has died. If the survivor grieves he is the more liable to the danger. Therefore he is treated with all the precautions with which the person who has taken life is surrounded. He must isolate himself for four days from ordinary life, neither speak nor be spoken to, take an emetic for purification every morning, and go outside the village to offer black cornmeal with his left hand. He swings it four times around his head and casts it from him to 'take off the bad happening,' they say. On the fourth day he plants his prayer-sticks to the dead and prays her, in the one prayer in Zuñi that is addressed to an individual, either human or supernatural, to leave him at peace, not to drag him down with her, and to grant him

> All of your good fortune whatsoever,
> Preserving us along a safe road.

The danger that is upon him is not considered over for a year. During that time his dead wife will be jealous if he approaches a woman. When the year is up he has intercourse with a stranger and gives her a gift. With the gift goes the danger that has haunted him. He is free again, and he takes another wife. It is the same with a wife whose husband has died.

On the western plains mourning behaviour was at the furthest remove from such an anxiety display. It was a Dionysian indulgence in uninhibited grief. All their behaviour stressed rather than avoided the despair and upheaval that is involved in death. The women gashed their heads and their legs, and cut off their fingers. Long lines of women marched through the camp after the death of an important person, their legs bare and bleeding. The blood on their heads and the calves of their legs they let cake and did not remove. As soon as the corpse was taken out for burial, everything in the lodge was thrown on the ground for anyone to possess himself of. The possessions of the dead were not thought to be polluted, but all the property of the household was given away because in its grief the family could have no interest in things they owned and no use for them. Even the lodge was pulled down and given to another. Nothing was left to the widow but the blanket around her. The dead man's favourite horses were led to his grave and killed there while all the people wailed.

Excessive individual mourning also was expected and understood. After the interment a wife or a daughter might insist upon staying at the grave, wailing and refusing to eat, taking no notice of those who tried to urge her back to the camp. A woman, especially, but sometimes a man, might go out wailing alone in dangerous places and sometimes received visions that gave supernatural power. In some tribes women often went to the graves and wailed for years, and in later years still went on pleasant afternoons to sit beside them without wailing.

The abandon of grief for children is especially characteristic. The extremity of the parents' grief could be expressed among the Dakota by their coming naked into the camp, wailing. It was the only occasion on which such a thing could happen. An old writer says of his experience among another Plains tribe, 'Should anyone offend the parent during this time [of mourning] his death would most certainly follow, as the man, being in profound sorrow, seeks something on which to wreak his revenge, and he soon after goes to war, to kill or to be killed, either being immaterial to him in that state.' They courted

death as the Pueblos pray to be delivered from the awful
possibility of it.

These two attitudes at death are familiar types of contrasted behaviour, and most individuals recognize the
congeniality of one or the other. The Pueblos have institutionalized the one, and the Plains the other. This does
not mean, of course, that violent and uninhibited grief is
called up in each member of a bereaved family on the
western plains, or that in the pueblos after being told to
forget he adjusts himself with only such discomfort as
finds expression in breaking a hairbrush. What is true is
that in one culture he finds the one emotion already
channelled for him, and in the other the other. Most human beings take the channel that is ready made in their
culture. If they can take this channel, they are provided
with adequate means of expression. If they cannot, they
have all the problems of the aberrant everywhere.

There is another death situation that is much more
fully provided with ritual techniques in these cultures —
the situation of the man who has killed another. In Zuñi a
slayer is treated just as a surviving spouse is treated, only
his retreat is in the ceremonial kiva, supervised by the
priests, and the removal of the discomfort that rests upon
him is more elaborately accomplished. It consists in his
initiation into the war society. His retreat, which like the
widower's involves sitting without movement, neither
speaking nor being spoken to, taking emetics, and ab-
staining from food, is the retreat of his initiation into the
society. Any initiate into any society observes analogous
tabus, and in Zuñi the restrictions that fall upon a man
who has taken life are thought of as an initiatory retreat.
His release from restrictions is his entrance upon his new
social responsibilities as a member of the war society. The

war chiefs function for life, not only in war, but more especially as guards and emissaries on ceremonial and public
occasions. They are the arm of the law wherever any formal arrangements must be made. They have charge of the
scalp-house where the scalps are kept, and they are especially efficacious in bringing rain.

The scalp throughout the long and elaborate ceremonial
of the war dance is the symbol of the man who has been
killed. The purpose of the ceremony is both to signalize
the initiation of the new member of the war society and to
convert the scalp into one of the Zuñi rain-making supernaturals. It must be honored by the dance and must be
adopted into the pueblo by the usual adoption rites.
These rites, at any adoption or marriage, consist essentially of the washing of the newcomer's head by the elder
women of the father's family. So also the scalp is washed
in clear water by the aunts of the slayer and adopted into
the tribe by the same procedures by which the initiate
was adopted at marriage into the family of his bride. The
scalp-dance prayers are very explicit. They describe the
transformation of the valueless enemy into a sacred fetish
of the people and the joy with which the people acknow-
ledge the new blessing.

> For indeed the enemy
> Even though on rubbish
> He lived and grew to maturity,
> By virtue of the corn priests' rain prayers,
> [He has become valuable.]
> Indeed the enemy,
> Though in his life
> He was a person given to falsehood,
> He has become one to foretell
> How the world will be,
> How the days will be....

Even though he was without value,
Yet he was a water being,
He was a seed being;
Desiring the enemy's waters,
Desiring his seeds,
Desiring his wealth,
Eagerly you shall await his days.'
When with your clear water
You have bathed the enemy,[2]
When in the corn priests' water-filled court
He has been set up,[3]
All the corn priest's children
With the song sequences of the fathers
Will be dancing for him.
And whenever all his days are past,
Then a good day,
A beautiful day,
A day filled with great shouting,
With great laughter,
A good day,
With us, your children,
You will pass.

So the scalp becomes a supernatural thing to which to pray, and the slayer a life member of the important war society.

In Dionysian cultures the whole situation is handled differently. Very often they made of it a terrible danger crisis. The slayer was in supernatural danger, and as among the Pima he was purified for twenty days, sitting in a small round pit dug in the ground. He was fed by a ceremonial father at the end of a six-foot pole, and released from his danger only upon being thrown, bound hand and foot, into the river.

[1] Of the scalp dance.
[2] Adoption rite of washing the scalp.
[3] On the scalp-pole in the plaza.

On the western plains, however, their violence did not capitalize these supernatural contaminations. The man who had killed another was not a person who needed salvation, he was a victor, and the most envied of all victors. All their Dionysian excitement was achieved in the celebration of an uninhibited triumph, a gloating over the enemy who had been worsted. It was a completely joyous occasion. The returning war party fell upon its own home camp in a surprise mock attack at daybreak, their faces blackened in triumph,

> ... shooting off their guns and waving the poles on which were the scalps that had been taken. The people were excited and welcomed them with shouts and yells. All was joy. The women sang songs of victory.... In the front rank were those who had... counted coups.... Some threw their arms around the successful warriors. Old men and women sang songs in which their names were mentioned. The relatives of those who rode in the first rank... testified to their joy by making gifts to friends or to poor people. The whole crowd might go to where some brave man lived or to where his father lived, and there dance in his honour. They were likely to prepare to dance all night, and perhaps to keep up this dancing for two days and two nights.

Everyone joined in the scalp dance, but it was no religious occasion. No medicine men officiated. In keeping with its social character it was in charge of men-women, transvestites who had adopted the female life and who were in this tribe recognized as matchmakers and 'good company.' They called out the dances and carried the scalps. Old men and women came out as clowns, and some of them even dressed to represent the very warriors whose scalps were the centre of the ceremony.

No one who has seen the two dances can doubt the way in which they stand contrasted: the scalp dance of the

Pueblos with its formal sets alternating in balanced programme before the elaborate ground altar set with the
great war medicine bundles, and the scalp dance of the
Cheyenne, with its physical vigour and its celebration of
the pride of victory, its imitation of the movements of
hand-to-hand conflict, its zest in having found oneself the
better man. In the Pueblo dance all is sobriety and group
action, as befits an occasion upon which the cloud is being
lifted from the slayer by his induction into an important
and valuable society and the installation of the scalp of an
unremarkable enemy as one of the rain-making supernaturals. In the dance on the plains, even though the
dancers come out in groups, each of them is nevertheless a
solo dancer, following his own inspiration in expressing
through every movement of his trained body the glory of
physical encounter. It is all individualism, all exultation
and triumph.

The Apollonian attitude of the Pueblos toward death
cannot outlaw the death of relatives nor the killing of
enemies; it can at its best only make them sources of
blessing and provide means of getting past them with the
least violence. Homicide, the taking of life within the
group, occurs so seldom that there are hardly even tales
remembered of it, but if it occurs, it is settled without ado
by payment arranged between the kin groups. The taking of one's own life, however, is entirely outlawed. Suicide is too violent an act, even in its most casual forms,
for the Pueblos to contemplate. They have no idea what
it could be. Pressed to match stories, the Zuñi tell of a
man who had been heard to say that he would like to die
with a beautiful woman. One day he was called to cure a
sick woman, and his medicine involved the chewing of
one of their wild medicinal plants. In the morning he was

found dead. It is as close as they can come to the idea of the act, and it does not occur to them that he could have taken his life. Their story is only of a man whose death occurred in the form he had been heard to wish for.

The situation that to us parallels our practice of suicide occurs only in folktales. A deserted wife in the tales occasionally asks the Apache to come in four days to destroy the pueblo and hence her spouse and his paramour. She herself cleanses herself ritually and puts on her best clothing. On the appointed morning she goes out to meet the enemy and be the first to fall before them. This, of course, falls within our category of suicide, though they think only of the ritual revenge. 'Of course we would not do that now,' they say; 'she was mean.' They do not get beyond the fact of her vengefulness. She was destroying her fellow villagers' possibilities of happiness, from which she felt herself shut out. In particular she was spoiling her husband's newfound pleasure. The rest of the tale is not really imagined in Zuñi; it is beyond their experience, like the supernatural messenger she gets to carry her message to the Apaches. The more particularly you illustrate the practice of suicide to a Zuñi audience, the more politely and smilingly incredulous they become. It is very strange, the things that white people do. But this is most laughable of all.

The Plains Indians, on the other hand, did far more with the idea of suicide than we do. In many of the tribes a man who saw nothing ahead that looked more attractive to him could take a year's suicide pledge. He assumed a peculiar badge, a buckskin stole some eight feet long. At the end where it dragged behind upon the ground it had a long slit, and the pledger as he took his pledged place in the forefront of their guerrilla warfare was staked to his position through the slit in his insignia. He could not retreat. He could advance, for the staking did not, of course, hamper his movement. But if his companions fell back, he must stay in his foremost position. If he died, he at least died in the midst of the engagements in which he delighted. If he survived the year, he had won by his courting of death all the kinds of recognition that the Plains held dear. To the end of his life, when great men publicly recounted their exploits in the constant, recognized boasting contests, he could name his exploits and the year of his pledge. He could use the counts he acquired in joining societies and in becoming a chief. Even a person who did not despair of his life at all might be so tempted by the honours that were attainable in this fashion that he would take the pledge. Or a society might try to pledge an unwilling member. The warrior's pledge was by no means the only way in which suicide was recognized on the plains. It was not a common act among them as it is in some primitive regions, but tales of suicide for love often recur. They could well understand the violent gesture of flinging away one's life.

There is still another way in which the Apollonian ideal expresses itself in Pueblo institutions. They do not culturally elaborate themes of terror and danger. They have none of the Dionysian will to create situations of contamination and fear. Such indulgences are very common in mourning all over the world — burial is an orgy of terror, not of grief. In Australian tribes the nearest of kin fall upon the skull and pound it to bits that it may not trouble them. They break the bones of the legs that the ghost may not pursue them. In Isleta, however, they break the hairbrush, not the bones of the corpse. The Navajo, the people closest to the Pueblos, burn the lodge and everything in it at death. Nothing the dead man has owned can pass casually to another. It is contaminated. Among the Pueblos only his bow and arrow and his mili, the medicine man's fetish of a perfect corn ear, are buried with the dead, and the mili is denuded first of all its valuable macaw feathers. They throw away nothing at all. The Pueblos in all their death institutions are symbolizing the ending of this man's life, not the precautions against the contamination of his corpse, or against the envy and vindictiveness of his ghost.

All the life crises are treated in some civilizations as terror situations. Birth, the onset of puberty, marriage, and death are constantly recurring occasions for this behaviour. Just as in mourning the Pueblos do not capitalize terror in death, so they do not upon the other occasions. Their handling of menstruation is especially striking because all about them are tribes who have at every encampment small houses for the menstruating woman. Usually she must cook for herself, use her own set of dishes, isolate herself completely. Even in domestic life her contact is defiling, and if she should touch the implements of the hunter their usefulness would be destroyed. The Pueblos not only have no menstrual huts, but they do not surround women with precautions at this time. The catamenial periods make no difference in a woman's life.

The great fear situation of surrounding tribes is their institution of sorcery. Sorcery is a label that is usually kept to describe African and Melanesian practices, but the fear, the suspicion, the hardly controlled antagonism to the medicine man in North America that extends from Alaska through the Shoshonean people of the Great Basin to the Pima of the Southwest and is widely associated with the Midewiwin Society to the east, is thoroughly characteristic of sorcery. Any Dionysian society values supernatural power not only because it is powerful, but because it is dangerous. The common drive for capitalizing dangerous experiences had free passage in the tribal attitude toward the medicine man. He had power to harm more particularly than he had power to help. Their attitude toward him was compounded of fear, of hatred, and of suspicion. His death could not be avenged, and if he failed in his cures and suspicion came to rest upon him, he was commonly killed by the people.

The Mojave, a non-Pueblo tribe of the Southwest, carried this attitude to great lengths. 'It is the nature of doctors to kill people in this way just as it is in the nature of hawks to kill little birds for a living,' they say. All those whom a medicine man killed were in his power in the after life. They constituted his band. Of course it was to his interest to have a large, rich company. A medicine man would say quite openly, 'I don't want to die yet. I haven't got a large enough band ready.' With a little more time he would have command of a company he could be proud of. He would hand a stick to a man as a token and say, 'Don't you know I killed your father?' Or he would come and tell a sick person, 'It is I who am killing you.' He did not mean that he was using poison or that he had killed the young man's father with a knife. It was supernatural killing, a blame- and terror-situation open and declared.

Such a state of affairs is impossible to imagine in Zuñi. Their priests are not the object of veiled hatred and suspicion. They do not embody in themselves the characteristic Dionysian double aspects of supernatural power, so that they must be at once death-bringers and saviours from disease. Even ideas of witchcraft that are omnipresent in the pueblos today, for all that they are full of European detail, do not constitute a genuine situation of sorcery. Witchcraft in Zuñi is not an exercise of a daring man's will to supernatural power. I doubt whether any-one has any specific witch techniques which he makes a practice of using. All their descriptions of witch behaviour are folkloristic, like the owl's eyes the witch substitutes in his head after laying his own on a niche in the wall. They are not the gruesome details of actually practised malice that are characteristic of other areas. Witchcraft among the Pueblos, like so many of their situations, is an anxiety complex. They vaguely suspect one another; and if a man is sufficiently disliked, witchcraft is sure to be attributed to him. There is no concern with witchcraft allegations at an ordinary death. It is only in time of epidemic that they pursue witches, when the general anxiety takes this form of expressing itself. They do not make a situation of overshadowing terror out of the power of their holy men.

In the pueblos, therefore, there is no courting of excess in any form, no tolerance of violence, no indulgence in the exercise of authority, or delight in any situation in which the individual stands alone. There are none of the situations that the Dionysian counts most valuable. Nevertheless they have a religion of fertility, and by de-finition we regard fertility cults as Dionysian. Dionysus was the god of fertility, and in most of the world we have no reason to separate the two traits; the pursuit of excess and the cult of procreative power have merged over and over again in the most distant parts of the globe. The way in which the Apollonian Pueblos pursue this same cult of fertility, therefore, makes doubly vivid the basic tenets of their life.

The vast majority of their fertility ceremonies are without any use of sex symbolism. Rain is induced by the monotonous repetitiveness of the dance that forces the clouds up the sky. Productiveness of the cornfield is ensured by burying in it objects which have been made powerful by having been placed on the altars or used by supernatural impersonations. Sex symbolism is much more in evidence in the near-by pueblo of Hopi than it is in Zuñi. In Hopi there is very common ceremonial use of small black cylinders associated with small reed circlets or wheels. The cylinders are a male symbol and the circlets female. They are tied together and thrown into the sacred spring.

In the Flute Society ceremony, a boy comes in with two girls to bring rain, and they are given in anticipation, the boy a cylinder, and the girls each a reed circlet. On the last day of the ceremony these children, attended by certain priests, carry these objects to the sacred spring and smear them with the fertile mud scooped from the spring floor. Then the procession starts back toward the pueblo. Four ground paintings such as are used for altars have been made along the return route, and the children advance, leading the rest, and throwing, the boy his cylinder, the girls their circlets, upon each ground painting in turn. Finally they are deposited in the dance shrine in the plaza. It is a decorous and sober performance, formal and unemotional to the last degree.

This kind of ceremonial sex symbolism is constantly used in Hopi. In the dances of the women's societies — Zuñi, on the other hand, has no women's societies — it is especially popular. In one of these ceremonies, while the girls, with cornstalks in their hands are dancing in a circle, four maidens come out dressed as men. Two of them represent archers and two represent lancers. The archers have each a bundle of vines and a bow and arrow and they advance shooting their arrows into the vine bundles. The lancers have each a long stick and a circlet and throw the lance into the rolling hoop. When they reach the dance circle they throw their sticks and hoops over the dancers into the circle. Later they throw little balls of dampened cornmeal out from the centre of the dancing girls to the spectators, who scramble to possess themselves of them. The symbolism is sexual, and the object is fertility, but the behaviour is at the opposite pole from the cult of Dionysus.

In Zuñi this kind of symbolism has not flourished. They have ceremonial races which, as everywhere in the pueblos, are run for fertility. One of them is between men and women, the men at one end of the line with their kick-sticks, the women at the other with their hoops, which they kick with their toes as the men their sticks. Sometimes women run these races with the masked clowns. In any case the women must win or the race would be to no purpose. In Peru when similar races were run for the same purpose every man ran naked and violated every woman he overtook. The same petition is symbolized in Zuñi and in Peru, but Zuñi's is an Apollonian refashioning of the Dionysian symbolism of Peru.

Nevertheless the association of licence with fertility ceremonial is not entirely lacking even in Zuñi. On two occasions, at the ceremonial rabbit hunt and at the scalp dance, laxness is countenanced to the extent that it is said that children conceived on these nights are exceptionally vigorous. There is a relaxation of the usual strict chaperonage of girls, a 'boys will be boys' attitude. There is no promiscuity and no hint of anything orgiastic. In addition the medicine-bundle cult that has control of snow and cold weather is said to have formerly held certain observances when for one night the priestesses of the bundle received lovers and collected a thumb's length of turquoise from their partners to add to the decorations of the bundle. The practice is no longer observed, and it is impossible to tell to what degree license was recognized.

Sex is not well understood in the pueblos. Little realistic attention, in Zuñi at least, is directed toward it, and there is a tendency, familiar enough to us in our own cultural background, to explain sex symbolism by some inappropriate substitution. The wheels and the cylinders which the Hopi use in constant and specific sex symbolism, they will tell you, represent the small clay rolls that the rain forms in the washes. The shooting of husk bundles with arrows they say represents the lightning striking the cornfield. Even more extreme substitutions are to be found in the explanations of the most honest informants. It is an unconscious defence which they carry to the point of absurdity.

A similar defence seems to have obliterated all traces of the cosmological tales of the origin of the universe in the sex act. Even so late as fifty years go, Cushing recorded in Zuñi a reference to this tale which is the fundamental cosmology of the non-Pueblo Yuman tribes of the Southwest and is known in many neighbouring regions. The sun cohabited with the earth, and out of her womb life came — the inanimate objects men use, as well as men and animals. In Zuñi since Cushing's time origin myths have been recorded from different societies, different priesthoods, and from laymen, and life is still said to begin in the fourth underground world, but they do not recognize it as earth's womb in which life has been stirred by the sky father. Their imaginations do not turn in that direction.

The attitude toward sex in Zuñi parallels certain standards we know in our civilization as Puritanical, but the contrasts are quite as striking as the parallels. The Puritan attitude toward sex flows from its identification as sin, and the Zuñi have no sense of sin. Sin is unfamiliar to them, not only in sex but in any experience. They do not suffer from guilt complexes, and they do not consider sex as a series of temptations to be resisted with painful efforts of the will. Chastity as a way of life is regarded with great disfavour, and no one in their folktales is criticized more harshly than the proud girls who resist marriage in their youth. They stay in and work, ignoring the occasions when they should legitimately be admired by the young men. But the gods do not take the steps they were supposed to take in Puritan ethics. They come down and contrive in spite of obstacles to sleep with them, and teach them delight and humility. By these 'amiable disciplinary means' they bring it about that the girl shall embrace in marriage the proper happiness of mortals.

Pleasant relations between the sexes are merely one aspect of pleasant relations with human beings. Where we make a fundamental distinction, their phrase of commendation is, 'Everybody likes him. He is always having affairs with women.' Or, 'Nobody likes him. He never has trouble over women.' Sex is an incident in the happy life.

Their cosmological ideas are another form in which they have given expression to their extraordinarily consistent spirit. The same lack of intensity, of conflict, and of danger which they have institutionalized in this world, they project also upon the other world. The supernaturals, as Dr. Bunzel says, 'have no animus against man. Inasmuch as they may withhold their gifts, their assistance must be secured by offerings, prayers and magical practices.' But it is no placation of evil forces. The idea is foreign to them. They reckon, rather, that the supernaturals like what men like, and if men like dancing so will the supernaturals. Therefore they bring the supernaturals back to dance in Zuñi by donning their masks, they take out the medicine bundles and 'dance' them. It gives them pleasure. Even the corn in the storeroom must be danced. 'During the winter solstice, when all ritual groups are holding their ceremonies, the heads of households take six perfect ears of corn and hold them in a basket while they sing to them. This is called "dancing the corn" and is performed that the corn may not feel neglected during the ceremonial season.' So too the great Dance of the Corn, now no longer performed, culminated in this enjoyment they had the means of sharing with the corn ears.

They do not picture the universe, as we do, as a conflict of good and evil. They are not dualistic. The European notion of witchcraft, in becoming domesticated in the pueblos, has had to undergo strange transformation. It derives among them from no Satanic majesty pitted against a good God. They have fitted it into their own scheme, and witch power is suspect not because it is given by the devil, but because it 'rides' its possessors, and once assumed, cannot be laid aside. Any other supernatural power is assumed for the occasion calling it forth. One indicates by planting prayer-sticks and observing the tabus that one is handling sacred things. When the occasion is over, one goes to one's father's sisters to have one's head washed and is again upon a secular footing. Or a priest returns his power to another priest that it may

rest until it is called for again. The idea and techniques
of removing sacredness are as familiar to them as those of
removing a curse were in mediæval times. In Pueblo
witchcraft no such techniques of freeing oneself of supernatural power are provided. One cannot be quit of the
uncanny thing, and for that reason witchcraft is bad and
threatening.

It is difficult for us to lay aside our picture of the universe as a struggle between good and evil and see it as the
Pueblos see it. They do not see the seasons, nor man's
life, as a race run by life and death. Life is always present,
death is always present. Death is no denial of life. The
seasons unroll themselves before us, and man's life also.
Their attitude involves 'no resignation, no subordination
of desire to a stronger force, but the sense of man's one-
ness with the universe.' When they pray they say to
their gods,

> We shall be one person.

They exchange intimate relationship terms with them:

> Holding your country,
> Holding your people,
> You will sit down quietly for us.
> As children to one another
> We shall always remain.
> My child,[1]
> My mother,[1]
> According to my words
> Even so may it be.

They speak of exchanging breath with their gods:

> Far off on all sides
> I have as my fathers life-giving priests [2]

[1] Gods are here addressed as the children of mortals no less than their parents.
[2] Supernatural beings; gods.

128

> Asking for their life-giving breath,
> Their breath of old age,
> Their breath of waters,
> Their breath of seeds,
> Their breath of riches,
> Their breath of fecundity,
> Their breath of strong spirit,
> Their breath of power,
> Their breath of all good fortune
>         with which they are possessed,
> Asking for their breath,
> Into our [1] warm bodies taking their breath,
> We shall add to your [2] breath.
> Do not despise the breath of your fathers,
> But draw it into your body....
> That we may finish our roads together.
> May my father bless you with life;
> May your road be fulfilled.

The breath of the gods is their breath, and by their common sharing all things are accomplished.

Like their version of man's relation to other men, their version of man's relation to the cosmos gives no place to heroism and man's will to overcome obstacles. It has no sainthood for those who,

> Fighting, fighting, fighting,
> Die driven against the wall.

It has its own virtues, and they are singularly consistent. The ones that are out of place they have outlawed from their universe. They have made, in one small but long-established cultural island in North America, a civilization whose forms are dictated by the typical choices of the Apollonian, all of whose delight is in formality and whose way of life is the way of measure and of sobriety.

[1] The medicine man's.    [2] The patient's.

# V

---

*Dobu*

---

DOBU ISLAND lies in the d'Entrecasteaux group off the southern shore of eastern New Guinea. The Dobuans are one of the most southerly of the peoples of northwestern Melanesia, a region best known through the many publications of Dr. Bronislaw Malinowski on the Trobriand Islands. The two groups of islands lie so near that the people of Dobu sail to the Trobriands on trading expeditions. But they are people of another environment and another temperament. The Trobriands are fertile low-lying islands which provide an easy and bountiful living. The soil is rich and the quiet lagoons full of fish. The Dobuan islands, on the other hand, are rocky volcanic upcroppings that harbour only scanty pockets of soil and allow little fishing. Population presses hard upon the possible resources, even though the tiny scattered villages in their most prosperous days numbered only about twenty-five people and now are cut to half, while the Trobriands' dense population lives at ease in large closely set communities. The Dobuans are known to all the white recruiters as easy marks in the area. Risking hunger at home, they sign up readily for indentured labour; being used to coarse and scanty fare, the rations they receive as work-boys do not cause mutiny among them.

The reputation of the Dobuans in the neighbouring

islands, however, does not turn on the fact of their poverty. They are noted rather for their dangerousness. They are said to be magicians who have diabolic power and warriors who halt at no treachery. A couple of generations ago, before white intervention, they were cannibals, and that in an area where many peoples eat no human flesh. They are the feared and distrusted savages of the islands surrounding them.

The Dobuans amply deserve the character they are given by their neighbours. They are lawless and treacherous. Every man's hand is against every other man. They lack the smoothly working organization of the Trobriands, headed by honoured high chiefs and maintaining peaceful and continual reciprocal exchanges of goods and privileges. Dobu has no chiefs. It certainly has no political organization. In a strict sense it has no legality. And this is not because the Dobuan lives in a state of anarchy, Rousseau's 'natural man' as yet unhampered by the social contract, but because the social forms which obtain in Dobu put a premium upon ill-will and treachery and make of them the recognized virtues of their society.

Nothing could be further from the truth, however, than to see in Dobu a state of anarchy. Dobuan social organization is arranged in concentric circles, within each of which specified traditional forms of hostility are allowed. No man takes the law into his own hands except to carry out these culturally allowed hostilities within the appropriate specified group. The largest functioning Dobuan grouping is a named locality of some four to twenty villages. It is the war unit and is on terms of permanent international hostility with every other similar locality. Before the days of white control no man ventured into an alien locality except to kill and to raid. One service, however, the localities exact of each other. In cases of death and serious illness, when it is necessary to find out by divination the person who is responsible, a diviner is brought from an enemy locality. Diviners within the locality are thus not called upon to face the dangers attendant upon divining a culprit, and a practitioner is called in to whom distance gives a certain immunity.

Danger indeed is at its height within the locality itself. Those who share the same shore, those who go through the same daily routine together, are the ones who do one another supernatural and actual harm. They play havoc with one's harvest, they bring confusion upon one's economic exchanges, they cause disease and death. Everyone possesses magic for these purposes and uses it upon all occasions, as we shall see. The magic is indispensable for dealings within one's locality, but its force is thought not to maintain itself outside one's known and familiar circle of villages. People with whom one associates daily are the witches and sorcerers who threaten one's affairs.

At the centre of this local group, however, is a group within which a different behaviour is required. Throughout life one may turn to it for backing. It is not the family, for it does not include the father nor his brothers and sisters nor a man's own children. It is the firm undissolving group of the mother's line. Living, they own their gardens and their house-sites in a common village. Dead, they are buried in a common plot on ancestral land. Every village has at its core a graveyard overgrown with the brilliant-leaved croton shrubs. In it lie the distaff line of one's mother, male and female, the owners of the village during their lives, buried now at its centre. Around it are grouped the platform houses of the living owners, the matrilineal line. Within this group inheritance passes and co-operation exists. It is called the 'mother's milk,' the susu, and consists of a female line of descent and the brothers of these women in each generation. The children of these brothers are not included; they belong to their mother's villages, groups toward which there is usually a major enmity.

The susu lives, often with closely related susu, in its own village, the privacy of which is strictly observed. There is no casual coming and going in Dobu. A path leads around the outskirts of each village, and those who are privileged to approach so near, skirt the settlement by this path. As we shall see, after their father's death the children of the men of that village have not even this privilege of approach. If the father is still living, or if it is the village of their spouse, they may enter by invitation. All others pass around by the by-path. They may not stop. Not even religious ceremonies nor harvest feasts nor tribal initiations call people together promiscuously, for Dobu does not specialize in such occasions. In the centre of the village a graveyard takes the place of the open communal dance plaza of the Trobriands. Dobuans are too aware of the dangers of strange places to go afield for social or religious observances. They are too aware of the dangers of jealous sorcery to tolerate strangers in their stronghold.

Marriage, of course, must be with someone outside this trusted circle. It remains within the locality, and therefore it allies two villages between which enmity runs high. Marriage brings with it no amelioration of hostility. From its beginning the institutions that surround it make for conflict and hard feeling between the two groups. Marriage is set in motion by a hostile act of the mother-in-law. She blocks with her own person the door of her house within which the youth is sleeping with her daughter, and he is trapped for the public ceremony of betrothal. Before this, since the time of puberty, the boy has slept each night in the houses of unmarried girls. By custom his own house is closed to him. He avoids entanglements for several years by spreading his favours widely and leaving the house well before daylight. When he is trapped at last, it is usually because he has tired of his roaming and has settled upon a more constant companion. He ceases to be so careful about early rising. Nevertheless he is never thought of as being ready to undertake the indignities of marriage, and the event is forced upon him by the old witch in the doorway, his future mother-in-law. When the villagers, the maternal kin of the girl, see the old woman immobile in her doorway, they gather, and under the stare of the public the two descend and sit on a mat upon the ground. The villagers stare at them for half an hour and gradually disperse, nothing more; the couple are formally betrothed.

From this time forward the young man has to reckon with the village of his wife. Its first demand is upon his labour. Immediately his mother-in-law gives him a digging-stick with the command, 'Now work.' He must make a garden under the surveillance of his parents-in-law. When they cook and eat, he must continue work, since he cannot eat in their presence. He is bound to a double task, for when he has finished work on his father-in-law's yams he has still to cultivate his own garden on his own family land. His father-in-law gets ample satisfaction of his will to power and hugely enjoys his power over his son-in-law. For a year or more the situation continues. The boy is not the only one who is caught in this affair, for his relatives also are loaded with obligations. So heavy are the

burdens upon his brothers in providing the necessary garden stuff and the valuables for the marriage gift that
nowadays young men at their brother's betrothal escape
from the imposition by signing up with the white recruiter
for indentured labour.

When the marriage valuables have finally been ac-
cumulated by the members of the groom's susu, they carry
them formally to the village of the bride. The party is
made up of the groom's brothers and sisters, his mother
and her brothers and sisters. His father is excluded, as
are also the husbands and wives of the party, and the
children of all the men. They present the gifts to the
bride's susu. There is, however, no friendly mingling of
the two parties. The bride's party await them at the further end of their ancestral village. The visitors remain at
the end near their own village. They appear sedulously
unaware of each other's existence. A wide space separates
them. If they must notice the other party, they glare with
hostility.

Every move in the marriage play is managed with
similar dour formality. The bride's susu must go to the
groom's village and formally sweep it throughout, meanwhile taking with them a considerable gift of uncooked
food. Next day the groom's kin return again with a reciprocal gift of yams. The marriage ceremony itself consists
in the groom's receiving from his mother-in-law in her
village a mouthful of food of her cooking, and the bride's
similarly receiving food from her mother-in-law in the
village of her husband. In a society where eating together
is one of the institutional intimacies the rite is thoroughly
appropriate.

For marriage sets up a new grouping within which
intimacy and common interests are respected. Dobu does

not solve its marital problems by ignoring marriage alliances in the fashion of many tribes of Dutch New Guinea who have strong clans like Dobu. In these tribes the maternal line lives together, harvests together, and shares economic undertakings. The women's husbands visit them secretly at night or in the bush. They are the 'visiting husbands' and in no way disturb the self-sufficiency of the matrilineal line.

Dobu, however, provides common house-room for the husband and wife and jealously safeguards their privacy in their own house. The pair also provide garden food for themselves and their children in common. But in making these two requirements which seem so elementary to a person brought up in Western civilization, Dobu must face most difficult problems. All its strongest loyalties are to the susu. If an inviolably private house and garden is provided for the married pair, on whose home ground and under whose hostile eyes shall they lie — the susu of the wife or the susu of the husband? The problem is solved logically enough, but in a way which is understandably uncommon. From marriage until death the couple live in alternate years in the village of the husband and the village of the wife.

Each alternate year one spouse has the backing of his own group and commands the situation. The alternate year the same spouse is a tolerated alien who must efface himself before the owners of his spouse's village. Dobuan villages are divided by this rift into two groups which stand always over against each other: on the one hand those who are of the matrilineal lineage and are called Owners of the Village; on the other those who are married into it and those who are the children of the men owners. The former group is always dominant and can put at disadvantage those who are merely resident for the year because of the exigencies of married life. The owners present a solid front; the group of the outsiders has little coherence. Dobuan dogma and practice both are against uniting two villages by a number of marital alliances. The more widely alliances are spread among the various villages, the more heartily the arrangements are approved. Therefore the spouses who are married-in have no bonds of common susu allegiance. There is a totemic category also which overpasses the bonds of the 'locality,' but it is an empty classification in Dobu without functions or importance, and need not be considered, for it does not effectively ally the unco-ordinated individuals who have married into the village.

By all the traditional means at its command Dobuan society demands that during the year in the spouse's village the spouse who is on alien territory play a rôle of humiliation. All the owners of the village may call him by his name. He may never use the name of any one of them. There are several reasons why personal names are not used in Dobu as in our own civilization, but when personal names are used it signifies that important liberties may be taken by the namer. It denotes prestige in relation to the person named. Whenever the village makes or receives gifts in betrothal, in the exchange of marriage gifts which is renewed year after year, or at death, the spouse who is married-in and resident there for the year must absent himself. He is a perpetual outsider.

These are, however, the least of the indignities of his position. There is tension of a more important sort. The village in which the couple are living at the moment is seldom satisfied with the behaviour of the spouse who has married in. Because of the marital exchanges between

137

the two villages, which continue with much the same formalities from the wedding till the death of one of the spouses, the marriage is an important investment of the susu. The men of the mother's line have an economic right to play an active rôle in it. It is easy for the spouse who is on home ground to turn to his susu, especially to the mother's brother, for support in the marital quarrels that recur constantly in Dobu. The mother's brother is usually only too willing to lecture the outsider publicly or send him or her packing from the village with obscene abuse.

Tension of an even more intimate kind is also present. Faithfulness is not expected between husband and wife, and no Dobuan will admit that a man and woman are ever together even for the shortest interval except for sexual purposes. The outsider spouse of the year is quick to suspect unfaithfulness. Usually he has grounds. In the suspicion-ridden atmosphere of Dobu the safest liaison is with a village 'brother' or a village 'sister.' During the year when one is in one's own village circumstances are propitious and supernatural dangers at a minimum. Public opinion strongly disapproves of marriage between such classificatory 'brothers' and 'sisters.' It would disrupt the village to have obligatory marital exchanges between two parts of the settlement. But adultery within this group is a favourite pastime. It is celebrated constantly in mythology, and its occurrence in every village is known to everyone from early childhood. It is a matter of profoundest concern to the outraged spouse. He (it is as likely to be she) bribes the children for information, his own or any in the village. If it is the husband, he breaks his wife's cooking-pots. If it is the wife, she maltreats her husband's dog. He quarrels with her violently, and no quarrel can go unheard in the close set, leaf-thatched houses of Dobu. He throws himself out of the village in a fury. As a last resort of impotent rage he attempts suicide by one of several traditional methods, no one of which is surely fatal. He is usually saved and by this means he enlists his wife's susu; in fear of what his relatives might do if the outraged spouse succeeded in his attempts at suicide, they are moved to a more conciliatory behavior. They may even refuse to take any further steps in the matter, and the partners to the marriage may remain sullenly and angrily together. The next year the wife can retaliate similarly in her own village.

The Dobuan requirement that a husband and wife maintain a common domicile is therefore by no means the simple matter it seems to us in our civilization. The circumstances make of it an institution of such difficulty that it continuously threatens the marriage and commonly destroys it. Broken marriages are excessively common, fully five times as frequent as, for example, in Manus, another Oceanic culture which Dr. Fortune has described. The second requirement exacted of Dobuan partners in marriage is rendered equally difficult by the cultural institutions: that they provide garden food in common for themselves and their children. This requirement comes into conflict with basic privileges and magical prerogatives.

The fierce exclusiveness of ownership in Dobu is nowhere more violently expressed than in the beliefs about hereditary proprietorship of yams. The line of yams descends within the susu as surely as the blood in the veins of its members. The seed yams are not pooled even in the gardens of the married pair. Each of them cultivates his own garden, planted with seed yams of his hereditary line, and they are made to grow by magical incantations owned individually and secretly in his susu line. The universal dogma of their society is that only yams of one's own blood line will grow in one's garden, brought to fruition by the magical incantations that have descended with the seed. The exception that custom allows in practice we shall describe later. No exception is allowed in so far as the conjugal gardens are concerned. Individually husband and wife save their seed from the preceding crop, plant their hereditary yams, and are responsible for the final yield. Food is never sufficient in Dobu, and everyone goes hungry for the last few months before planting if he is to have the requisite yams for seed. The greatest Dobuan delinquency is the eating of one's seed yams. The loss is never made up. It would be impossible for the husband or wife to make it good, for yams not of the matrilineal line would not grow in one's garden. Even one's own susu does not make up so flagrant a bankrupcy as a loss of seed. One who would fall so low as to eat his yams for planting is a bad bet backed not even by his own clan. He is for life the Dobuan beachcomber.

The garden of the wife and the garden of the husband, therefore, are inevitably separate. The seed yams are separately owned in perpetuity, and they are grown with magical incantations also separately handed down and not pooled. The failure of either's garden is deeply resented and becomes the basis of marital quarrels and divorce. Nevertheless work in the gardens is shared by the two; their gardens are as inviolably private to the husband and wife and the children as the house is; and the food supply from the gardens is pooled for their common use.

As soon as the marriage is dissolved by death, or whenever the father dies even though the father and mother have separated years before, all food from the father's village, every bird or fish or fruit, becomes strictly tabu to his children. Only during his lifetime they eat it without hurt, a difficult concession in Dobu to the fact that children are reared by their two parents. In similar fashion, at the father's death the children are forbidden entry into his village. That is, as soon as the exigencies of the marital alliance no longer have to be considered, the mother's village claims them to the exclusion of any contact with the outlawed line. When as adults or old people they must carry food to the village of their father in a ritual exchange, on the outskirts they stand motionless with bowed head while others take their burdens into the village. They wait till the party returns, and then head the procession back to their mother's village. The village of one's father is called 'the place of bowing one's head.' Even more stringent is the tabu upon approaching the village of one's dead spouse. One must stop short still further off or find one's way circuitously past it. The concessions so insecurely granted to a marital alliance have been rescinded with redoubled restrictions.

The jealousy, the suspicion, the fierce exclusiveness of ownership that are characteristic of Dobu are all in the foreground of Dobuan marriage, but it is impossible to give them full weight until we have considered also their manner of life in other respects. The motivations that run through all Dobuan existence are singularly limited. They are remarkable because of the consistency with which the institutions of the culture embody them and the lengths to which they are carried. In themselves they have the simplicity of mania. All existence is cut-throat competition, and every advantage is gained at the expense of a defeated rival. This competition, however, is not like that we shall describe upon the Northwest Coast, where rivalry is in the full glare of publicity and conflict is arrogant and aboveboard. In Dobu it is secret and treacherous. The good man, the successful man, is he who has cheated another of his place. The culture provides extravagant techniques and elaborate occasions for such behaviour. In the end all existence in Dobu is brought under the domination of these purposes.

The violence of Dobuan regard for ownership and the degree to which it involves the victimizing of others and their reciprocating suspicion and ill-will are grossly reflected in their religion. The whole region of Oceania adjacent to Dobu is one of the world's strongholds of magical practices, and those students of religion who define religion and magic as mutually exclusive and opposed to one another would have to deny religion to the Dobuans. Anthropologically speaking, however, magic and religion are complementary ways of handling the supernatural, religion depending upon setting up desirable personal relations with that world, and magic using techniques which automatically control it. In Dobu there is no propitiation of supernatural beings, no gifts or sacrifices to cement co-operation between gods and petitioners. The supernatural beings that are known in Dobu are a few secret magical names, the knowledge of which, like the discovery of the name 'Rumpelstilchen' in the folktale, gives the power of command. Therefore the names of supernaturals are unknown to large numbers of Dobuans. No man knows any except those for which he has paid or which have come to him by inheritance. The important names are never spoken aloud, but mumbled under the breath to prevent anyone else's hearing. All the beliefs connected with them are related to name-magic rather than to religious propitiation of the supernatural.

# DOBU

Every activity has its relevant incantations, and one of the most striking of all Dobuan beliefs is that no result in any field of existence is possible without magic. We have seen how large a part of Zuñi life is passed over by their religion. There all religious practices are said to be for rain, and even allowing for the exaggeration of the traditional dogma, there are great areas of existence that are not provided with religious techniques. On the Northwest Coast, as we shall see, religious practices impinge very slightly upon the important activity of their lives, the consolidating of status. It is otherwise in Dobu. For any result of any kind one is dependent upon the magic one knows. Yams cannot grow without their incantations, sex desire does not arise without love-magic, exchanges of valuables in economic transactions are magically brought about, no trees are protected from theft unless malevolent charms have been placed upon them, no wind blows unless it is magically called, no disease or death occurs without the machinations of sorcery or witchcraft.

The magical incantations, therefore, are of incomparable importance. The violence with which success is coveted is faithfully reflected in the fierce competition for magical formulæ. These are never owned in common. There are no secret societies whose prerogative they are. There are no groups of brothers to all of whom they descend. Even co-operation within the susu never extends so far as to give its members joint benefit in the powers of an incantation. The susu merely channels the strict individual inheritance of magic. One has a claim upon the formulæ of one's mother's brother, but each incantation can be taught to only one of the clan. It can never be taught to two sons of the possessor's sister, and the owner of the formula makes his own choice among the possible heirs. Often he chooses the eldest son, but if another son has been closer to him or more helpful, he passes over the eldest son and the latter has no redress. For life he may be without important formulæ such as those of the yams and the economic exchanges. It is a handicap which it is an insult for anyone to mention, and one which usually allows of no amelioration. Every man and woman, however, possesses some charms. Disease-causing incantations and love-magic are widely held. Today work-boys away from home may even sell a charm without reference to inheritance, and the wages of four months of indentured labour is still passed between them for a single incantation even though the principals in the transaction have been servants of the white man and to some degree alienated from native culture. The amount of the payment is a slight indication of their value.

Dobuans of the small island of Tewara where Dr. Fortune lived denied categorically that the whites or the native Polynesian teachers of the missions on Dobu Island had been able to maintain gardens. It was impossible, they said, without magic. They did not avail themselves of that universal primitive alibi, that the native rules hold good only for the native. In Dobu reliance upon magic, and upon magic only, is too strong to allow the admission that whites or Polynesians are freed from its necessity.

The bitterest conflict for the possession of magical incantations is between the sister's sons, who rightfully claim the magic of their mother's brother, and the latter's own sons, whose close association with their father in the household and common cause with him in gardening make a counter-claim strong enough to secure recognition in Dobuan practice. Dobuan dogma insists always that only the yam-magic which descends in the clan with the seed can grow that seed. Seed, as we have seen, is never alienated from the clan. Nevertheless the garden incantations are taught also to the owner's sons. It is another surreptitious concession to the strength of the group resulting from marriage, and is, of course, a flagrant violation of Dobuan dogma, which secures to each individual his exclusive right of ownership.

The incantations are 'like a doctor's practice or a business place's goodwill or a peer's title and lands. A doctor that alienated the one and the same practice by selling it or bequeathing it to two different people who are not partners but business antagonists would hardly have his sale legally supported. The same is true of a business goodwill. A sovereign who gave two men the same peerage and lands in feudal days would have had rebellion at his gates. Yet in Dobu where [the two heirs] are not partners or close friends or sharers in common property but more apt to be antagonistic, the same practice is made legal enough. The one and the same goodwill is given to both.' If the son, however, has obtained more of the father's magic at his death than the sister's son, the latter, the rightful owner according to Dobuan orthodox teaching, claims his rights from the son and must be taught by him without fee. If the balance lies in the other direction the son has no corresponding claims.

The magical incantations of Dobu must be word-perfect to be effective, and there are often specific leaves or woods that must be used with them with symbolic actions. They are most of them examples of sympathetic magic and depend upon the technique of mentioning bush-growing water plants to the new-leafed yam that it may imitate their luxuriance, or describing the hornbill's rending of a tree stump to ensure the ravages of gangosa. The incantations

are remarkable for their malevolence and for the degree
to which they embody the Dobuan belief that any man's
gain is another's loss.

The ritual of the garden begins when the earth is prepared for the planting of the seed yams and continues
until the harvesting. The planting charms describe the
yams just planted as of huge varieties and already grown.
The charms required during the early growth picture the
twining of the vines under the image of the web-spinning
of the large spider kapali:

> Kapali, kapali,
> twisting around,
> he laughs with joy.
> I with my garden darkened with foliage,
> I with my leaves.
> Kapali, kapali,
> twisting around,
> he laughs with joy.

During all this time no magical watch has been set upon
the yams, no magical thieving has been undertaken. But
now that they are somewhat grown it is necessary to root
them solidly in one's own place. For yams are conceived
as persons and are believed to wander nightly from garden
to garden. The vines remain behind but the tubers are
gone. Toward the middle of the morning they normally
return. For this reason yams are not dug early in the
morning when garden work is usually done; it would be in
vain. Their return must be compliantly awaited. Also
when the yams are growing they resent too early curtail-
ment of their freedom; therefore the husbanding incantations are not begun until the plants have reached a certain
stage of growth. These incantations lure the roaming
yams to remain in one's own garden at the expense of the

garden in which they were planted. Gardening in Dobu is as competitive as the struggle for an inheritance. A man has no notion that another gardener can plant more yams than he can or make more yams grow from his seed tubers. Whatever harvest his neighbour has in excess of his own is thought to have been magically thieved from his own or someone else's garden. Therefore physical guard is mounted by the man over his own garden from this time until harvesting, he uses whatever charms he knows to attract his neighbour's yams, and he opposes the charms of his neighbours by counter-charms. These counter-charms root the yam tuber firmly in the earth where it was planted and safeguard it for the owner's harvesting:

> Where stands the kasiara palm? [1]
> In the belly of my garden
> at the foot of my house platform
> he stands.
> He will stand inflexible, unbending,
> he stands unmoved.
> The smashers of wood smash,
> the hurlers of stone hurl,
> they remain unmoved.
> The loud stampers of earth stamp,
> they remain unmoved.
> He remains, he remains
> inflexible, unbending.
> The yam kulia, [2]
> he remains inflexible, unbending.
> He remains, he remains unmoved
> in the belly of my garden.

The privacy of the garden is respected to such a degree that by custom man and wife have intercourse within it.

---

[1] The hardest wood in the bush. It stands erect in a storm that bends all other trees.

[2] A variety of yam. The whole stanza is repeated for all the varieties.

A good crop is a confession of theft. It is supposed to have been alienated from the gardens even of one's own susu by dangerous sorcery. The amount of the harvest is carefully concealed and reference to it is an insult. In all the surrounding islands of Oceania harvest is the occasion for a great ritual display of yams, an ostentatious parade that is a high point in the year's ceremonial. In Dobu it is as secret as theft. The man and his wife convey it little by little to the storehouse. If their harvest is good they have reason to fear the spying of others, for in case of disease or death the diviner commonly attributes the calamity to a good harvest. Someone is thought to have resented the successful crop so much that he put sorcery upon the successful gardener.

The disease-charms have a malevolence all their own. Every man and woman in the Tewara village owns from one to five. Each is a specific for a particular disease, and the person who owns the incantation owns also the incantation for removing the same affliction. Some persons have a monopoly of certain diseases and hence are sole owners of the power to cause it and the power to cure it. Whoever has elephantiasis or scrofula in the locality, therefore, knows at whose door to lay it. The charms make the owner powerful and are greatly coveted.

The incantations give their possessors an opportunity for the most explicit expression of malignity the culture allows. Ordinarily such expression is tabu. The Dobuan does not risk making a public challenge when he wishes to injure a person. He is obsequious and redoubles the shows of friendship. He believes that sorcery is made strong by intimacy, and he waits the opportunity for treachery. But in placing his disease-charm upon his enemy and in teaching his charm to his sister's son he has full licence for malevolence. It is an occasion out of reach of his enemy's eye or ear, and he lays aside his pretences. He breathes the spell into the excreta of the victim or into a creeper which he lays across the path of his enemy, biding near-by to see that the victim actually brushes against it. In communicating the spell the sorcerer imitates in anticipation the agony of the final stages of the disease he is inflicting. He writhes upon the ground, he shrieks in convulsion. Only so, after faithful reproduction of its effects, will the charm do its destined work. The diviner is satisfied. When the victim has brushed against the creeper he takes the bit of vine home with him and lets it wither in his hut. When he is ready for his enemy's death he burns it in his fire.

The charms themselves are almost as explicit as the action that accompanies them. Each line is punctuated with a vicious spitting of ginger upon the object which is to carry the charm. The following is the incantation for causing gangosa, the horrible disease which eats away the flesh as the hornbill, its animal patron from which the disease is named, eats the tree trunks with its great rending beak:

> Hornbill dweller of Sigasiga
> in the lowana tree top,
> he cuts, he cuts,
> he rends open,
> from the nose,
> from the temples,
> from the throat,
> from the hip,
> from the root of the tongue,
> from the back of the neck,
> from the navel,
> from the small of the back,

from the kidneys,
from the entrails,
he rends open,
he rends standing.
Hornbill dweller of Tokuku,
in the lowana tree top,
he [1] crouches bent up,
he crouches holding his back,
he crouches arms twined in front of him,
he crouches hands over his kidneys,
he crouches head bent in arms twined about it.
he crouches double twined.
Wailing, shrieking,
it [2] flies hither,
quickly it flies hither.

When a person finds himself the victim of a disease, he sends to the person who has put the disease upon him. There is no other way to ward off death. The disease can only be cured or ameliorated by the corresponding exorcism owned by the same sorcerer. Usually the sorcerer, if he is induced to exorcise the disease, does not himself visit the sufferer. He breathes the exorcism into a vessel of water brought him by a relative of the sick man. It is sealed, and the sufferer is bathed with the water in his own house. The exorcism is often thought to stave off death and permit deformity — a reflection of the fact that many of the common native diseases produce deformity rather than death. For the introduced diseases, tuberculosis, measles, influenza, and dysentery, though they have been known and fatal in Dobu for fifty years, there are no incantations.

The Dobuans use these disease-charms freely and for characteristic purposes. Their way of putting a simple

[1] The victim.

[2] The immaterial power of the charm.

property mark on goods or trees is to contaminate them by magic with their proprietary disease. The natives say, 'That is Alo's tree,' or 'That is Nada's tree,' meaning, 'That is the tree Alo has charmed with tertiary yaws,' or 'That is the tree upon which Nada has placed paralysis.' Everyone knows, of course, the possessors of these disease-charms, and whoever owns them uses them as property marks. The only way in which one can gather the fruit of one's own trees is first to exorcise the disease. Since the ownership of the exorcism is inseparable from the ownership of the disease-causing charm, safety from the original disease placed upon the tree can always be managed. The difficulty is that the possibility of theft from the disease-charmed tree must also be guarded against. A thief has placed a second disease upon the tree. He has run the risk of not exorcising the original disease by his own disease incantation, which may not be an exorcism specific to the disease with which the tree is contaminated. He recites his hereditary exorcism, inserting also mention of the disease he is concerned to remove from the tree, afterward placing his own hereditary disease-causing charm upon it. Therefore when the owner comes to harvest his tree it is possible that another disease may be gathered with the fruit. The exorcism he uses is always couched in the plural for safety's sake. The formula runs:

> *They* fly away,
> *they* go.

Suspicion, in Dobu, runs to paranoid lengths, and a counter-charm is always suspected. Actually the fear of the imposed disease is too great to allow such trifling except in the case of famine, when theft may be risked as an alternative to starvation. The fear with which the curse of disease laid upon property is regarded is overwhelming. The incantation is reserved for outlying trees; a curse upon trees of the village would kill the whole village. Everyone would move away if the dried coconut palm frond that signifies the imposition of the curse was found tied around a village tree. When Dr. Fortune, before he had been taught the gangosa charm, made as if to place it upon goods he wished to leave unprotected in an unfamiliar village, his house-boys bolted precipitously into the night. He found later that families living fifty or a hundred yards away abandoned their houses and went to their homes in the hills.

The power to inflict disease does not stop with these universally owned spells for specific diseases. Powerful sorcerers — rather, powerful men, since all men are sorcerers — have a still more extreme resource, vada. They can confront the victim himself, and such is the terror of the sorcerer's curse that he falls writhing to the ground. He never regains his wits and wastes away to a destined death. In order to inflict this curse a man bides his time and when he is ready to act chews great quantities of ginger to make his body hot enough to raise the power of the charm to a proper pitch. He abstains from sexual intercourse. He drinks great quantities of sea water to parch his throat, that he may not swallow his own evil charms with his saliva. Then he enlists a trusted relative as watchdog to climb a tree near the garden where the unsuspecting victim is at work alone. Together the two make themselves invisible by magical incantation, and the watcher takes up his position in the tree in order to be able to give the alarm if anyone approaches. The sorcerer crawls unheard till he faces his victim. He lets out the curdling shriek of the sorcerer, and the victim falls to the ground. With his charmed lime spatula the sorcerer removes the organs of his body, so they say, and closes the wound without scar. Three times he tests the victim: 'Name me.' It is a proof of his success that the man is beyond recognizing or naming anyone. He only mumbles meaninglessly and runs raving down the path. He never eats again. He is incontinent of urine, and his bowels are affected. He loses strength and dies.

This account was given by a trustworthy and intimately known native. Evidence of the native belief may be observed in the cases of those who are stricken in lingering death after the sorcerer's confrontation. Vada stresses in extreme form the malignity of Dobuan practices and the terror that makes possible its ultimate effects.

So far we have avoided mention of Dobuan economic exchanges. The passion for endless reciprocal commercial transactions that grips so much of Melanesia is present also in Dobu. The passionately desired and passionately resented success which lies closest to the heart of every Dobuan is sought primarily in two fields, the field of material possessions and the field of sex. Sorcery is another field, but in these connections it is an instrument rather than an end, a means toward attaining and defending success in the primary activities.

Material success in a community ridden with treachery and suspicion like Dobu must necessarily offer many contrasts to the economic goals that are recognized in our civilization. Accumulation of goods is ruled out at the beginning. Even one successful harvest spied out by others and never admitted by the gardener is occasion enough for the practice of fatal sorcery. Ostentatious display is likewise debarred. The ideal commercial technique would be a system of counters that pass through each man's hands but may not remain with him as a permanent possession. It is precisely the system that obtains in Dobu. The high point of life in these islands is an international exchange which includes a dozen islands that lie in a roughly drawn circle approximately one hundred and fifty miles in diameter. These islands constitute the Kula ring which Dr. Malinowski has described also for the Trobriands, the partners of Dobu to the north.

The Kula ring extends further than the Dobuan configuration of culture, and other cultures which participate in it have certainly given its procedures other motivations and satisfactions. The peculiar customs of the Kula which Dobu has made so coherent with the rest of its cultural pattern did not necessarily originate in these patterns or in the motivations that are now associated with them in Dobu. We shall discuss only the Dobuan exchange. Except for the Trobriands, we do not know the Kula customs of the other islands.

The Kula ring is a circle of islands around which one kind of valuable travels in one direction and another in the other in semi-annual exchange. The men of each island make long voyages across the open seas, carrying shell necklaces in clockwise direction and armshells counter-clockwise. Each man has his partner in the exchanging island to each direction and bargains for advantage by every means in his control. Eventually the valuables make full circle, and new ones of course may be added. The armshells and the necklaces are all named with personal names, and certain ones possess a traditional excessive value in proportion to their fame.

The matter is not so utterly fantastic as it sounds from the formal pattern of the procedure. Great parts of Melanesia and Papua are honeycombed with local specialization of industries. In the Kula ring one people polishes greenstone, one makes canoes, another makes pottery, another carves wood, and still another mixes paints. Exchange of all these articles goes on under cover of the ritual bargaining for the major valuables. In a region where the passion for reciprocal exchanges has been enormously cultivated, the system of ceremonial exchange institutionalized in the Kula does not seem so extreme as it necessarily does to observers from a culture which lacks the equivalent substructure. Even the seemingly arbitrary direction in which the armshells and the necklaces move has its basis in the exigencies of the situation. The armshells are made of trocus shell, which is found only in the northern region of the Kula ring, and the necklaces are fashioned of spondylus shell, which is imported from the south into the most southern islands of the group. Therefore in the trading of the western islands of the ring, which overbalance those to the east, the northern valuables go south and the southern valuables go north. At the present time the valuables are old and traditional and new importations of small importance. But the pattern remains.

Every year during the lull in gardening operations after the yams are planted and before they must be magically guarded to keep them at home, the canoes of Dobu go on the Kula expedition to the north and to the south. Every man has Kula valuables from the south to promise in exchange for the Kula valuables he is to receive from the north.

The peculiar character of Kula exchange depends upon the fact that each island goes to receive the valuables in the island of its partners. The voyaging island takes gifts in solicitation and receives the valuables, promising return of those in its possession when the hosts return the visit. Therefore Kula exchange is never a market transaction, each man spreading out his valuables and arranging the acceptable exchange. Each man receives his prize on the basis of the gift of solicitation and a promise, a promise which is supposed to be of a valuable he has already in his possession but has left at home ready to give at the appropriate moment.

The Kula is not a group exchange. Each man exchanges individually, and with all the forms of courtship, with an individual partner. The charms for success in the Kula are love-charms. They magically dispose the partner to favour the suit of the petitioner. They make the petitioner irresistible in his bodily beauty, smoothing his skin, clearing it of the scars of ringworm, reddening his mouth, and scenting him with perfumes and unguents. In the extravagant ideology of Dobu only the equivalent of physical passion can make credible the spectacle of a peaceful and advantageous exchange of valuables.

The men of each canoe-load gather together their solicitory gifts of food and manufactured objects. Only the owner of the canoe and his wife have used any magic incantations before the sailing. All other magic is reserved until the Kula is actually under way. The owner of the canoe has risen at dawn to charm the mat which is to cover the valuables on the return voyage and to ensure magically its covering a great pile of wealth. His wife also has an incantation she must use to exalt the expedition of her husband, his coming like thunder over the sea, his rousing a quivering eagerness not only in the body of his partner but in that of his wife and of his children, their dreams full of the great man, her husband. When all the preparations are completed, however propitious the wind, a ritual halt must be observed for the remainder of the day. It should be observed on a desolate and uninhabited fore-shore away from all contamination by women, children, dogs, and everyday involvements. But when the canoes go south there is no such island available, and the ritual halt is observed on the beach, every man going back to the village at night, remarking, however contrary to fact, that the wind had been impossible. It is a form of ritual suspicion that is never allowed to lapse. Next morning the canoe owner packs the canoe, using his second incantation, the last that has any communal application. Even in this, as in his wife's previous incantation, he names himself pre-eminently. The food he is taking as gifts of solicitation he converts magically into the Kula valuables themselves and describes the partners to whom they are to go as waiting for their arrival as for the new moon, watching from the edge of their house platforms for them, for the canoe owner himself.

The Dobuans are bad sailors, hugging the reef and dis-embarking every night. The seasons for the Kula trips are the seasons of the long calms. They use wind-charms, calling upon the desired northwest wind to take in wedlock their sail of fine pandanus leaf, to clutch it, her misbehaving child, to come quickly to prevent another's stealing her husband from her. They believe about wind, as they believe about all other events of existence, that it arises from no other source than magic.

When at last the canoes have arrived at the islands of their destination, they select a barren coral reef and dis-embark for the great Kula preparatory rites. Each man, by magic and by personal decoration, makes himself as beautiful as possible. The incantations are private pro-perty in true Dobuan fashion, and each man uses his magic for his strictly personal benefit. Those who know no incantation are under the greatest handicaps. They must make shift for themselves, using such substitutes as suggest themselves to them. As a matter of fact, in spite of the inviolable secrecy in which the possession of these charms is held, the men of each canoe-load not knowing who among them possesses the charms, in the cases that have been observed the men who know them are those who handle the largest Kula exchanges. Their self-confidence gives them a sufficient advantage over their companions. Those who know charms and those who do not alike take the physical pains that prepare one for the Kula arrival; they scent themselves with the perfumed leaf that is used in courtship, they put on a fresh pubic leaf, they paint their faces and their teeth, they anoint their bodies with coconut oil. Only so are they ready to present themselves to their partners.

Each man's transactions are conducted as private business. Sharp dealings are important and highly valued, and true to the Dobuan dogma that it is the closely associated person who is the dangerous threatener of your life, retaliation upon the successful Kula trader is in the hands of his unsuccessful canoe partner or at least in those of another man from his locality, not a matter to be settled between the internationals themselves. It is said of the Kula valuables, in Homeric refrain, 'many men died because of them.' But the deaths were not brought about by the anger of outraged partners in exchange, Dobuan against Trobriander, or man of Tubetube against Dobuan. It is always unsuccessful Dobuan against a successful man of his own locality.

The most prolific source of bad feeling is the sharp practice known as wabuwabu.

# DOBU

To wabuwabu is to get many spondylus shell necklaces from different places to the south on the security of one arm-shell left at home in the north; or vice versa, many armshells from the north on a security that cannot meet them, promising the one valuable which one possesses to many different persons in return for their gifts that are being solicited. It is sharp practice, but it is not entirely confidence trickstering.

'Suppose I, Kisian of Tewara, go to the Trobriands and secure an armshell named Monitor Lizard. I then go to Sanaroa and in four different villages secure four different shell necklaces, promising each man who gives me a shell necklace Monitor Lizard in later return. I, Kisian, do not have to be very specific in my promise. Later when four men appear in my home at Tewara each expecting Monitor Lizard, only one will get it. The other three are not defrauded permanently, however. They are furious, it is true, and their exchange is blocked for the year. Next year, when I, Kisian, go again to the Trobriands I shall represent that I have four necklaces at home waiting for those who give me four armshells. I obtain more armshells than I obtained previously and pay my debts a year late.

'The three men who did not get Monitor Lizard are at a disadvantage in my place, Tewara. Later when they return to their homes they are too far off to be dangerous to me. They are likely to use sorcery to attempt to kill their successful rival who got the armshell Monitor Lizard. That is true enough. But that is their own business. I have become a great man by enlarging my exchanges at the expense of blocking theirs for a year. I cannot afford to block their exchange for too long or my exchanges will never be trusted by anyone again. I am honest in the final issue.

To wabuwabu successfully is a great achievement, one of the most envied in Dobu. The great mythical hero of the Kula was an expert in it. Like all Dobuan practices it stresses one's own gains at the expense of another's loss. It allows one to reap personal advantage in a situation in which others are victimized. The Kula is not the only undertaking in which a man may risk wabuwabu. The term covers also the victimizing of others in the marital exchanges. The series of payments that are set up between two villages during betrothal involve considerable property. A man who dares to run the risk may enter into an engagement in order to reap the economic profits. When the balance of the exchanges is heavily on his side, he breaks off the betrothal. There is no redress. A person who gets away with it proves thereby that his magic is stronger than the magic of the village he has outraged, which will, of course, attempt his life. He is an enviable person.

Wabuwabu in this latter instance differs from that in the Kula because the exchange itself is within the locality. The enmity that is inseparable from relations within this group sets over against each other the two parties to the exchange instead of setting by the ears the commercial associates travelling in the same canoe, as in the Kula. Wabuwabu in the two cases has in common the fact that it is an advantage taken of another person of the locality.

The attitudes that we have discussed, those involved in marriage, magic, gardening, and economic exchange, are all expressed in the strongest terms in behaviour at the time of death. Dobu, in Dr. Fortune's words, 'cowers under a death as under a whipping,' and looks about immediately for a victim. True to Dobuan dogma, the victim is the person nearest to the dead; that is, the spouse. They believe that the person with whom one shares the bed is the person to charge with one's fatal illness. The husband has used his disease-causing incantations, and the wife has used witchcraft. For though women also may know the disease-charms, a special form of power is always attributed to them by men, and death and desolation are by a common convention of speech universally laid at their doors. The diviner, when he is called in to determine the murderer, is not bound by this convention, and lays the death as often at the door of a man as of a woman. The convention reflects sex antagonism more faithfully probably than it reflects attempted murder. At any rate, men attribute to women a special technique of villainy, one that strangely resembles the European tradition of witches on their broomsticks. Dobuan witches leave their bodies sleeping beside their husbands and fly through the air to cause accident — a man's fall from a tree or a canoe's drifting from its moorings are due to flying witches — or to abstract the soul from an enemy, who will thereupon weaken and die. Men are in terror of these machinations of their women, so much so that, believing that Trobriand women do not practise witchcraft, they put on in the Trobriands a self-confident manner which they do not assume at home. In Dobu the wife is at least as much feared by her husband as the husband by his wife.

In the event that either of the married couple falls seriously ill, the two must move immediately to the village of the afflicted person if they are living for the year in the village of the other spouse. Death must occur there if possible, where the surviving spouse is in the power of the susu of the bereaved. He is the enemy within the camp, the witch or the sorcerer who has caused the breach in the opposing ranks. The susu presents a solid front around the body of its dead. Only they can touch the corpse or perform any of the duties of burial. Only they can give the mourning cries. It is most strictly prohibited that the spouse be within sight of any of these proceedings. The dead is displayed upon the house platform and the body is adorned with valuables if he was rich; large yams are put about it if he was a good gardener. The maternal kin raise their voices in the traditional keening. That night or the next day the children of the sister of the deceased carry the body away for burial.

The house of the dead is left empty and abandoned. It will not be used again. Under the raised floor of the house an enclosure is walled in by plaited mats, and into it the owners of the village marshal the surviving spouse. His body is blackened with charcoal from the fires, and the black looped rope, the badge of mourning, is hung around his neck. The first month or two he spends seated on the ground in the dark enclosure. Later he works in the gardens of his parents-in-law under their surveillance as he did during the period of betrothal. He works also the gardens of his dead wife and of her brothers and sisters. He receives no recompense, and his own gardens must be worked for him by his own brothers and sisters. He is not allowed to smile, nor to take part in any exchange of food. When the skull is taken from the grave and the sister's children of the deceased dance with it, he must not look upon the dancers. The skull is kept by the sister's son and the spirit ceremonially sent upon its way to the land of the dead.

His own kin not only have to work his gardens during the time of his mourning. They have much heavier burdens. After the burial they must bring payment for it to the village of the dead. They present cooked yams to the sister's sons who have performed the actual services, and a large gift of uncooked yams, which are displayed in the village of the dead and distributed to the relatives of the deceased within the village, the members of the susu receiving the large share.

A widow is similarly in subjection to the kin of her dead

husband. Her children have special duties laid upon them, for throughout the year they must cook a mash of bananas and taro and take it to the susu of the dead 'to pay for their father.' 'Did he not hold us in his arms?' They are the outsiders paying the close kin group of their father, to which they do not belong, for one of their number who has done well by them. They are discharging an obligation, and there is no repayment for these services.

The mourner must be released from subjection by further payments by his own clan to the clan of the deceased. They bring the gift of uncooked yams as before and the kinsmen of the dead cut his rope badge of mourning and wash the charcoal from his body. There is dancing, and his relatives lead him back again to his own village. The year of his penance is ended. He never enters the village of his spouse again. If it is a widower who is released from mourning, his children of course remain behind in the village of their true kin, the village their father may never re-enter. The song that is sung at the termination of mourning celebrates the farewell that is obligatory between them. It is addressed to the father whose last day of penance has come:

> Lie awake, lie awake and talk
> at the midnight hour.
> First lie awake and talk,
> lie awake and talk.

> Maiwortu, your charcoal body smear
> by Mwaniwara below.
> Dawn breaks the black of night.
> First lie awake and talk.

Maiwortu is the widower to whom there remains this one last night when he may talk with his children. Tomorrow his charcoal smear will be washed from him. As 'dawn breaks the black of night' his body will appear again un-blackened. He and his children will not talk together again.

The respective clans of the spouses are not the only ones who are involved in mutual recriminations at the time of mourning. The surviving spouse is not only a representative of the enemy village who is by traditional formula chargeable with the death of the deceased. He is also a representative of all those who have married into the village of the dead person. As we have seen, this group is drawn from as many villages as possible, since it is re-garded as bad policy for a village to have several marital alliances in the same village. These spouses of the owners are those who will eventually, if their marriages continue in force, be in like case with the spouse who is now serving his time. At the beginning of the mourning they have a right to place a prohibition upon the fruit trees of the vil-lage owners and even, with a great show of anger, to cut down some of them. To remove the tabu, some weeks later they arm themselves with spears and descend upon the village as upon a village they mean to overpower in warfare. They carry with them a large pig and throw it down rudely before the hut of the dead's nearest of kin. With a rush they swarm up the betel palms of the village, strip them bare of nuts, and rush away again almost be-fore people have realized what is happening. The two attacks are ritual expression of resentment against a group who can eventually exact penance in mourning. Traditionally the fat pig was a human victim. At any rate, the villagers, once the invaders have rushed out of sight, are frenzied with excitement over the boar. It is cooked and becomes the basis for a series of feasts offered to all the villages of the spouses, a gift of cooked food which is offered in the most insulting fashion possible. The donors take the liquid lard and pour it over a respected older man of the village of the recipients. They smear and plaster him. Immediately the man springs forward in the most threatening attitudes, dancing with imaginary spear and affronting his hosts with traditional insults. He is allowed the privilege of giving expression, as earlier in the tree tabu, to the resentment of the spouses against the clan of the dead which can exact penance from them in mourning. One of the susu of the dead takes up a threatening attitude against the old man, but does not say anything very insulting, and the other eventually washes and eats heartily. If the village of the dead takes cooked mash instead of pig to the villages of its spouses, the mash is similarly poured over the recipient and similarly resented in a public dance. The tension between these two groups is ended by one of the largest feasts of Dobu, a feast given at the village of the dead and distributed with insult to the guests from the villages related by marriage. 'Tawa, your share! He who is dead had many domestic pigs. Your sows are barren.' 'Togo; your share! He who is dead was a master of fish nets. This is how *you* catch fish.' 'Kopu, your share! He who was dead was a great gardener. He came from his work at dusk. You creep home exhausted at noon.' As Dr. Fortune says, 'In this happy manner the locality pulls together its forces whenever death has stricken it.'

The traditional suspicion between the village of the survivor and the village of the dead does not mean, of course, that the surviving spouse is specifically regarded as the murderer. He may be, but diviners are quick to seize upon any conspicuous success of the dead in any field and charge the death to jealousy aroused by that

165

event. 'More often than not,' however, the mourning observances are no mere ritual form, but the expression 'of sullen suspicion on the one hand and of resentment of suspicion on the other.' They are in any case characteristic projections of sentiments that run riot in Dobu.

Murder may be done by non-magical means as well as magical. Poison is as universally suspected as sorcery or witchcraft. No woman leaves her cooking-pot a moment untended lest someone gain access to it. Individuals own various poisons which they try out as they do their magical incantations. After these poisons have been proved to kill, they are useful in a serious encounter.

'"My father told me of it, it is budobudo. Plenty of it grows by the sea. I wanted to try it out. We drew the sap from it. I took a coconut, drank from it, squeezed the sap into the remainder, and closed it up. Next day I gave it to the child saying, 'I have drunk of it, you may drink.' She fell ill at midday. In the night she died. She was my father's village sister's daughter. My father poisoned her mother with the budobudo. I poisoned the orphan later."

'"What was the trouble?"

'"She bewitched my father. He felt weak. He killed her and his body grew strong again."'

The formula that corresponds to our thank-you upon receiving a gift is, 'If you now poison me, how should I repay you?' That is, they seize upon the occasion to remark by formula to the giver that it is not to his advantage to use the universal weapon against one who is under obligations to him.

Dobuan conventions exclude laughter and make dourness a virtue. 'The root of laughter, they,' they say in scorn of a less malevolent neighbouring people. One of the prime obligations in important observances like gardening and the Kula is to refrain from pleasurable activities or expressions of happiness. 'In the gardens we do not play, we do not sing, we do not yodel, we do not relate legends. If in the garden we behave so, the seed yams say, "What charm is this? Once it was a good charm, but this, what is this?" The seed yams mistake our speech. They will not grow.' The same tabu is in force during the Kula. One man crouching on the outskirts of a village of the Amphletts where the people were dancing, indignantly repudiated the suggestion that he might join: 'My wife would say I had been happy.' It is a paramount tabu.

This dourness which is a valued virtue bears also upon the lengths to which jealousy and suspicion are carried in Dobu. As we have seen, trespassing in a neighbour's house or garden is forbidden. Each person is left in possession. Any meeting between man or woman is regarded as illicit, and in fact a man by convention takes advantage of any woman who does not flee from him. It is taken for granted that the very fact of her being alone is licence enough. Usually a woman takes an escort, often a small child, and the chaperonage protects her from accusation as well as from supernatural dangers. Therefore a husband normally mounts guard at the entrance to the garden in the seasons of women's work, amusing himself talking to a child, perhaps, and seeing that his wife speaks to no one. He keeps track of the length of time she absents herself in the bush for the natural functions and may even, in extreme cases, accompany her there in spite of the terrible prudery of Dobu. It is significant that prudery should be as extreme in Dobu as it was among our Puritan ancestors. No man uncovers himself before another. Even in a male crew travelling in a canoe, a man goes over the

side out of sight in the stern, even to urinate. Any uncovering of one's sex life is tabu also; one may not refer to
it except when one indulges in obscene abuse. Therefore
a convention of speech refers to the prenuptial courtship
as chaste, though the dance songs that dramatize it are
full of explicit passion and the facts are a matter of the
past experience of every adult.

The deep-seated prudery of Dobu is familiar enough
to us in our own cultural background, and the dourness of
Dobuan character that is associated with it accompanied
also the prudery of the Puritans. But there are differences.
We are accustomed to associate this complex with a
denial of passion and a lesser emphasis upon sex. The
association is not inevitable. In Dobu dourness and prudery go along with prenuptial promiscuity and with a high
estimation of sex passion and techniques. Men and
women alike rate sex satisfaction high and make achievement of it a matter of great concern. There is no convention of indifference or absorption in a masculine world that
supports a man whose wife he suspects of betraying him.
The vicissitudes of passion are exploited, whereas in Zuñi,
for instance, they are moderated by the tribal institutions.
The stock sex teaching with which women enter marriage
is that the way to hold their husbands is to keep them as
exhausted as possible. There is no belittling of the physical
aspects of sex.

The Dobuan, therefore, is dour, prudish, and passionate,
consumed with jealousy and suspicion and resentment.
Every moment of prosperity he conceives himself to have
wrung from a malicious world by a conflict in which he has
worsted his opponent. The good man is the one who has
many such conflicts to his credit, as anyone can see from
the fact that he has survived with a measure of prosperity.

It is taken for granted that he has thieved, killed children and his close associates by sorcery, cheated whenever he dared. As we have seen, theft and adultery are the object of the valued charms of the valued men of the community. One of the most respected men on the island gave Dr. Fortune an incantation for making the spellbinder invisible with the recommendation: 'Now you can go into the shops in Sydney, steal what you like and get away with it unseen. I have many times taken other persons' cooked pig. I joined their group unseen. I left unseen with my joint of pig.' Sorcery and witchcraft are by no means criminal. A valued man could not exist without them. The bad man, on the other hand, is the one who has been injured in fortune or in limb by the conflicts in which others have gained their supremacy. The deformed man is always a bad man. He carries his defeat in his body for all to see.

It is a further and most unusual development of this cut-throat warfare that the usual forms of legality are absent in Dobu. There are, of course, many different kinds of validation by which legality is achieved in different cultures. We shall see how on the Northwest Coast of America no word-perfect knowledge of the ritual or meticulous acquaintance with the accompanying acts could constitute legal ownership, but killing the owner gave one instantly the legal ownership, otherwise unobtainable. One could not steal a ritual by eavesdropping, but the legally validating act is one that we should pronounce thoroughly illegal in our civilization. The point is that there is a legally validating act. In Dobu there is none. Eavesdropping is constantly feared because knowledge of an incantation obtained in this way is as good as knowledge obtained in any other. Anything that one can get away with is respected. Wabuwabu is an institutionalized

169

practice, but even sharp practice to which no convention gives approval is not socially dealt with in Dobu. A few thick-skinned individuals do not submit to the mourning for the spouse. A woman can only evade it if a man is willing to let her elope with him, and in this case the village of her dead husband come to the village to which she has escaped and litter it with leaves and limbs of trees. In case a man walks out, nothing is done. It is his public avowal that his magic is so good that the village into which he has married is powerless against him.

The same absence of social legality is behind the lack of chieftainship or the investiture of any individual with recognized authority. In one village a conjunction of circumstances gave to Alo a degree of recognized authority. 'A great deal of Alo's power was due not only to his force of personality and his inheritance of magic by primogeniture, but also to the fact that his mother had been prolific and his grandmother before her. He was the eldest of the eldest line, and his blood brothers and sisters formed the village majority. On such rare circumstances as the combination of a strong personality with inheritance of magic in a family conspicuous for its magical knowledge, and with prolific descendants, does the barest show of legality in Dobu depend.'

The treacherous conflict which is the ethical ideal in Dobu is not palliated by social conventions of what constitutes legality. Neither is it ameliorated by ideals of mercy or kindness. The weapons with which they fight carry no foils. Therefore they do not waste breath and risk interference with their plans by indulging in challenge and insult. Only in the one ritual feast of which we have spoken is insult traditionally indulged. In ordinary converse the Dobuan is suave and unctuously polite. 'If we wish to kill a man we approach him, we eat, drink, sleep, work and rest with him, it may be for several moons. We bide our time. We call him friend.' Therefore when the diviner weighs the evidences in determining the murderer, suspicion falls upon anyone who has sought out his company. If they were together for no reason that appeared customary, the matter is regarded as proved. As Dr. Fortune says, 'The Dobuans prefer to be infernally nasty or else not nasty at all.'

Behind a show of friendship, behind the evidences of co-operation, in every field of life, the Dobuan believes that he has only treachery to expect. Everyone else's best endeavours, according to their institutions, are directed toward bringing his own plans to confusion and ruin. Therefore when he goes on the Kula, he uses a charm 'to shut the mouth of him who stays at home.' It is taken for granted that those left behind are working against him. Resentment is constantly referred to as a motivation which will bring anything to pass. Their magical techniques in many cases follow a pattern according to which an incantation is said only over the first yams planted or the first food and solicitory gifts packed in the Kula canoes. Dr. Fortune asked a magician about it. '"Yams are like persons," he explained. "They have understood. One says, 'That yam he charms. What about me?' Oh, he is angry, and he shoots up strongly."' What is relied upon in dealings with men is relied upon also in dealings with supernaturals.

The resentful human, however, has one resource no Dobuan attributes to the supernaturals. He may attempt suicide or cut down the tree from which fruit has been stolen. It is a final resource which saves the face of the humiliated and is supposed to rally the support of his own susu. Suicide, as we have seen, is usually attempted in marital quarrels and does actually rouse the clan to support the resentful spouse who has attempted his life. The institution of cutting down one's fruit trees from which fruit has been taken is less obvious. People who have no disease-causing charms to place upon their trees name them for a fatal accident or serious illness of a near relative, and the person who steals from the tree is liable to this calamity. If someone braves the curse, the owner descends upon his tree and cuts it down. It is similar to behaviour at the taking of life in attempted suicide, but it makes it clear that the appeal in both cases is not to the pity and support even of one's relatives. Rather, in the extremity of humiliation, the Dobuan projects upon himself and his possessions the maliciousness and the will to destroy which are required in all his institutions. He is limited to the same technique, though he uses it in these instances against himself.

Life in Dobu fosters extreme forms of animosity and malignancy which most societies have minimized by their institutions. Dobuan institutions, on the other hand, exalt them to the highest degree. The Dobuan lives out without repression man's worst nightmares of the ill-will of the universe, and according to his view of life virtue consists in selecting a victim upon whom he can vent the malignancy he attributes alike to human society and to the powers of nature. All existence appears to him as a cut-throat struggle in which deadly antagonists are pitted against one another in a contest for each one of the goods of life. Suspicion and cruelty are his trusted weapons in the strife and he gives no mercy, as he asks none.

# VI

## The Northwest Coast of America

THE Indians who lived on the narrow strip of Pacific
seacoast from Alaska to Puget Sound were a vigorous and
overbearing people. They had a culture of no common
order. Sharply differentiated from that of the surrounding
tribes, it had a zest which it is difficult to match among
other peoples. Its values were not those which are commonly recognized, and its drives not those frequently
honoured.

They were a people of great possessions as primitive
peoples go. Their civilization was built upon an ample
supply of goods, inexhaustible, and obtained without
excessive expenditure of labour. The fish, upon which
they depended for food, could be taken out of the sea in
great hauls. Salmon, cod, halibut, seal, and candlefish
were dried for storage or tried out for oil. Stranded whales
were always utilized, and the more southern tribes went
whaling as well. Their life would have been impossible
without the sea. The mountains abutted sharply upon
their shore territory; they built upon the beaches. It was
a country wonderfully suited to the demands they put
upon it. The deeply indented coast was flanked with
numberless islands which not only trebled the shoreline,
but gave great sheltered areas of water and protected
navigation from the unbroken sweep of the Pacific. The

sea life that haunts this region is proverbial. It is still the great spawning ground of the world, and the tribes of the Northwest Coast knew the calendar of the fish runs as other peoples have known the habits of bears or the season for putting seed into the earth. Even in the rare cases when they depended upon some product of the earth, as when they cut the great trees that they split into boards for their houses or hollowed with fire and adzes for canoes, they held close to the waterways. They knew no transportation except by water, and every tree was cut close enough to a stream or inlet so that it could be floated down to the village.

They kept up constant intercommunication by means of seagoing canoes. They were adventurous, and expeditions pushed far to the north and south. Marriages, for persons of prestige, were arranged with the nobility of other tribes, and invitations to great feasts, the potlatches, were sent hundreds of miles up the coast and answered by canoe-loads of the distant tribes. The languages of these peoples belonged to several different stocks, and it was necessary therefore for most people to speak a number of unrelated languages. Certainly the differences in language formed no obstacle to the diffusion of minute details of ceremonial or of whole bodies of folklore the fundamental elements of which they shared in common.

They did not add to their food supply by means of agriculture. They tended small fields of clover or cinquefoil, but that was all. The great occupation of the men, aside from hunting and fishing, was woodworking. They built their houses of wooden planks, they carved great totem poles, they fashioned the sides of boxes of single boards and carved and decorated them, they dug out seagoing canoes, they made wooden masks and household furniture and utensils of all kinds. Without metal for axes or saws they felled the great cedars, split them into boards, transported them by sea without any use of the wheel to the villages and made of them their great many-family houses. Their devices were ingenious and admirably calculated. They guided accurately the split of the logs into planks, raised tremendous tree trunks as house-posts and house-beams, knew how to sew wood through slanted awl-holes so that no sign of the joining remained upon the surface, and out of single cedars constructed canoes capable of navigating the open sea and of carrying fifty or sixty men. Their art was bold and exotic, and as competent as any that a primitive people has achieved.

The culture of the Northwest Coast fell into ruin during the latter part of the last century. Our first-hand knowledge of it therefore as a functioning civilization is limited to those tribes that were described a generation ago, and it is only the Kwakiutl of Vancouver Island whose culture we know in great detail. For the most part, therefore, the description of this culture will be that of the Kwakiutl, supplemented by the contrasting details that are known from other tribes and by the memories of old men who once took part in what is now a vanished civilization.

Like most of the American Indians, except those of the Southwest pueblos, the tribes of the Northwest Coast were Dionysian. In their religious ceremonies the final thing they strove for was ecstasy. The chief dancer, at least at the high point of his performance, should lose normal control of himself and be rapt into another state of existence. He should froth at the mouth, tremble violently and abnormally, do deeds which would be terrible in a normal state. Some dancers were tethered by four ropes held by attendants, so that they might not do irreparable damage in their frenzy. Their dance songs celebrated this madness as a supernatural portent:

> The gift of the spirit that destroys man's reason,
>> O real supernatural friend,[1] is making people afraid.
>
> The gift of the spirit that destroys man's reason,
>> O real supernatural friend, scatters the people who are in the house.[2]

The dancer meanwhile danced with glowing coals held in his hands. He played with them recklessly. Some he put in his mouth, others he threw about among the assembled people, burning them and setting fire to their cedar-bark garments. When the Bear Dancers danced, the chorus sang:

> Great is the fury of this great supernatural one.
> He will carry men in his arms and torment them.
> He will devour them skin and bones, crushing flesh and bone with his teeth.

All dancers who made mistakes in their performances must always fall down as if dead, and the Bear impersonators fell upon them and tore them to pieces. Sometimes this was a pretence, but according to the traditional teaching for certain errors there was no mitigation of the penalty. The Bears were dressed for their great ceremonies completely in black bearskins, and even on lesser occasions they wore upon their arms the skins of the bear's forelegs with all the claws displayed. The Bears danced around the fire, clawing the earth and imitating the motions of angry bears, while the people sang the song of a Bear dancer:

[1] That is, Cannibal at North End of the World, the supernatural patron of the dancer, in whose power he dances.

[2] That is, they flee in fear.

# NORTHWEST COAST OF AMERICA

How shall we hide from the bear that is moving
all around the world?
Let us crawl underground! Let us cover our backs
with dirt that the terrible great bear from
the north of the world may not find us.

These dances of the Northwest Coast were the performances of religious societies into which individuals
were initiated by the supernatural patrons of the society.
The experience of meeting the supernatural spirit was
closely related to that of the vision, the experience which
in so many parts of North America gave to the suppliant,
fasting in isolation and often torturing himself, the guardian spirit who aided him for life. On the Northwest Coast
the personal encounter with the spirit had become a formal matter, nothing more than a way of phrasing the right
to join a coveted secret society. But in proportion as the
vision had become an empty form, the emphasis had been
placed upon the divine madness incumbent upon one who
had a right to supernatural power. The Kwakiutl youth
about to become a member of one of their religious societies
was snatched away by the spirits, and remained in the
woods in isolation for the period during which he was said
to be held by the supernaturals. He fasted that he might
appear emaciated, and he prepared himself for the demonstration of frenzy which he must give upon his return.
The whole Winter Ceremonial, the great Kwakiutl series
of religious rites, was given to 'tame' the initiate who returned full of 'the power that destroys man's reason' and
whom it was necessary to bring back to the level of secular
existence.

The initiation of the Cannibal Dancer was peculiarly
calculated to express the Dionysian purport of Northwest
Coast culture. Among the Kwakiutl the Cannibal Society

outranked all others. Its members were given the seats of highest honour at the winter dances, and all others must hold back from the feast till the Cannibals had begun to eat. That which distinguished the Cannibal from the members of all other religious societies was his passion for human flesh. He fell upon the onlookers with his teeth and bit a mouthful of flesh from their arms. His dance was that of a frenzied addict enamoured of the 'food' that was held before him, a prepared corpse carried on the outstretched arms of a woman. On great occasions the Cannibal ate the bodies of slaves who had been killed for the purpose.

This cannibalism of the Kwakiutl was at the furthest remove from the epicurean cannibalism of many tribes of Oceania or the customary reliance upon human flesh in the diet of many tribes of Africa. The Kwakiutl felt an unmitigated repugnance to the eating of human flesh. As the Cannibal danced trembling before the flesh he was to eat, the chorus sang his song:

> Now I am about to eat,
> My face is ghastly pale.
> I am about to eat what was given me by Cannibal
> at the North End of the World.

Count was kept of the mouthfuls of skin the Cannibal had taken from the arms of the onlookers, and he took emetics until he had voided them. He often did not swallow them at all.

Much greater than the contamination of flesh bitten from living arms was reckoned that of the flesh of the prepared corpses and of the slaves killed for the cannibal ceremonies. For four months after this defilement the Cannibal was tabu. He remained alone in his small inner sleeping-room, a Bear dancer keeping watch at the door. He used special utensils for eating and they were destroyed at the end of the period. He drank always ceremonially, never taking but four mouthfuls at a time, and never touching his lips to the cup. He had to use a drinking-tube and a head-scratcher. For a shorter period he was forbidden all warm food. When the period of his seclusion was over, and he emerged again among men, he feigned to have forgotten all the ordinary ways of life. He had to be taught to walk, to speak, to eat. He was supposed to have departed so far from this life that its ways were unfamiliar to him. Even after his four months' seclusion was ended, he was still sacrosanct. He might not approach his wife for a year, nor gamble, nor do any work. Traditionally he remained aloof for four years. The very repugnance which the Kwakiutl felt toward the act of eating human flesh made it for them a fitting expression of the Dionysian virtue that lies in the terrible and the forbidden.

During the time when the Cannibal initiate was secluded alone in the woods, he procured a corpse from a tree where it had been disposed. The skin had already been dried by exposure, and he especially prepared it for his 'food' in the dance. In the meantime the period of his seclusion was drawing to an end and the tribe were preparing for the Winter Dance which was primarily his initiation as a member of the Cannibal Society. The people of the tribe, according to their ceremonial prerogatives, made themselves sacred. They called among them the spirits of the Winter Dance, and those who had a right to do so gave demonstrations of their supernatural frenzy. The greatest effort and meticulousness of observance were necessary because their power must be great enough to call back the Cannibal from his sojourn with the supernaturals. They called him by strong dances and by the exercise of inherited powers, but at first all their efforts were in vain.

At last all the Cannibal Society by their combined frenzy roused the new initiate, who all of a sudden was heard upon the roof of the house. He was beside himself. He shoved aside the boards of the roof and jumped down among all the people. In vain they tried to surround him. He ran around the fire and out again by a secret door, leaving behind him only the sacred hemlock branches he had worn. All the societies followed him toward the woods, and presently he was seen again. Three times he disappeared, and the fourth an old man went out ahead, 'the bait,' as he was called. The Cannibal rushed upon him, seized his arm, and bit it. The people caught him in the act and brought him to the house where the ceremonial was to be held. He was out of his senses and bit those whom he laid hold of. When they came to the ceremonial house he could not be made to enter. At last the woman co-initiate whose duty it was to carry the prepared body across her arms appeared naked with the corpse. She danced backward, facing the Cannibal, enticing him to enter the house. He still could not be prevailed upon, but at length he again climbed the roof and jumped down through the displaced boards. He danced wildly, not able to control himself, but quivering in all his muscles in the peculiar tremor which the Kwakiutl associate with frenzy.

The dance with the corpse was repeated during the Cannibal's period of ecstasy. Perhaps the most striking Dionysian technique of the Winter Ceremonial is that which finally tames the Cannibal and ushers in his four-month period of tabu. According to the ideas that are current in their culture it expresses in the most extreme manner the supernatural power that lies in the horrible and the forbidden.

The rite was led by four priests with inherited supernatural powers of taming the Cannibal. The initiate was beside himself. He ran about wildly while the attendants tried to hold him. He could not dance, for he was too far gone in frenzy. By different rites of exorcism they tried to 'reach' the Cannibal in his ecstasy. They tried first the fire exorcism, swinging burning cedar bark over his head until he was prostrated. Then they tried a water exorcism, ceremonially heating stones in the fire with which to warm water in a water box, and putting the water ritually upon the head of the initiate. Next they made a figure of cedar bark to represent the Cannibal in frenzy and burned it upon the fire.

The final exorcism, however, was that which was performed with menstrual blood. Upon the Northwest Coast menstrual blood was polluting to a degree hardly excelled in the world. Women were secluded during this period, and their presence rendered any shamanistic practice impotent. They could not step across any brook nor go near the sea lest the salmon take offence. Deaths which occurred in spite of shamanistic cures were regularly laid to the unsuspected presence in the house of cedar bark upon which there was a trace of menstrual blood. For the final exorcism of the Cannibal, therefore, the priest took cedar bark upon which there was menstrual blood of four women of the highest rank, and smoked the face of the Cannibal. As the exorcism took effect the dancing of the Cannibal became more sober, until upon the fourth dance he was tamed and quiet, his frenzy gone from him.

The Dionysian slant of Northwest Coast tribes is as

violent in their economic life and their warfare and mourning as it is in their initiations and ceremonial dances.
They are at the opposite pole from the Apollonian Pueblos,
and in this they resemble most other aborigines of North
America. The pattern of culture which was peculiar to
them, on the other hand, was intricately interwoven out
of their special ideas of property and of the manipulation
of wealth.

The tribes of the Northwest Coast had great possessions,
and these possessions were strictly owned. They were
property in the sense of heirlooms, but heirlooms, with
them, were the very basis of society. There were two
classes of possessions. The land and sea were owned by a
group of relatives in common and passed down to all its
members. There were no cultivated fields, but the relationship group owned hunting territories, and even wild-
berrying and wild-root territories, and no one could tres-
pass upon the property of the family. The family owned
fishing territories just as strictly. A local group often had
to go great distances to those strips of the shore where
they could dig clams, and the shore near their village
might be owned by another lineage. These grounds had
been held as property so long that the village-sites had
changed, but not the ownership of the clam-beds. Not
only the shore, but even deep-sea areas were strict property. For halibut fishing the area belonging to a given
family was bounded by sighting along double landmarks.
The rivers, also, were divided up into owned sections for
the candlefish hauls in the spring, and families came from
great distances to fish their own section of the river.

There was, however, still more valued property that
was owned in a different fashion. It was not in the ownership of the means of livelihood, however far that was

carried, that Kwakiutl proprietorship chiefly expressed itself. Those things which were supremely valued were prerogatives over and above material well-being. Many of these were material things, named house-posts and spoons and heraldic crests, but the greater number were immaterial possessions, names, myths, songs, and privileges which were the great boast of a man of wealth. All these prerogatives, though they remained in a blood lineage, were nevertheless not held in common, but were owned for the time being by an individual who singly and exclusively exercised the rights which they conveyed.

The greatest of these prerogatives, and the basis of all others, were the nobility titles. Each family, each religious society, had a series of titular names which individuals assumed according to their rights of inheritance and financial ability. These titles gave them the position of nobility in the tribe. They were used as personal names, but they were names that according to tradition had not been added to nor subtracted from since the origin of the world. When a person took such a name he assumed in his own person all the greatness of his ancestors who had in their lifetime borne the name, and when he gave it to his heir he necessarily laid aside all right to use it as his own.

The assumption of such a name did not depend on blood alone. In the first place, these titles were the right of the eldest born, and youngest sons were without status. They were scorned commoners. In the second place, the right to a title had to be signalized by the distribution of great wealth. The women's engrossing occupation was not the household routine, but the making of great quantities of mats, baskets, and cedar-bark blankets, which were put aside in the valuable boxes made by the men for the same purpose. Men likewise accumulated canoes, and the shells or dentalia they used as money. Great men owned or had out at interest immense quantities of goods, which were passed from hand to hand like bank notes to validate the assumption of the prerogatives.

These possessions were the currency of a complex monetary system which operated through the collection of extraordinary rates of interest. One hundred per cent interest was usual for a year's loan. Wealth was counted in the amount of property which the individual had out at interest. Such usury would have been impossible except for the fact that sea food was abundant and easy to secure, their supply of shells for money was constantly augmented from the sea, and that fictitious units of great values were used, the 'coppers.' These were etched sheets of native copper valued as high as ten thousand blankets and more. They had, of course, very small intrinsic worth and were valued according to the amount that had been paid for them when they last changed hands. Besides, the amassing of the return payments was never the work of one individual in any of the great exchanges. The entrepreneurs were figureheads of the entire local group, and, in intertribal exchanges, of the entire tribe, and commanded for the occasion the goods of all the individuals of their group.

Every individual of any potential importance, male or female, entered this economic contest as a small child. As a baby he had been given a name which indicated only the place where he was born. When it was time for him to assume a name of greater importance, the elders of his family gave him a number of blankets to distribute, and upon receiving the name he distributed this property among his relatives. Those who received the child's gifts made it a point to repay him promptly and with excessive interest.

Whenever a chief who was one of these beneficiaries distributed property at a public exchange soon after, he gave the child treble what he had received. At the end of the year the boy had to repay with one hundred per cent interest those who had originally financed him, but he retained the remainder in his own name and this was the equivalent of the original stock of blankets. For a couple of years he distributed these, and collected interest, until he was ready to pay for his first traditional potlatch name. When he was ready, all his relatives gathered and all the elders of the tribe. In the presence of all the people and before the chief and the old men of the tribe his father then gave up to him a name which designated his position in the tribe.

From this time the boy had a traditional position among the titled men of the tribe. Thereafter at the potlatches he gave or took part in he took still greater and greater names. A person of any importance changed names as snakes change their skins. The names indicated his family connections, his riches, his status in the tribal structure. Whatever the occasion of the potlatch, whether it was a marriage, the coming-of-age of his grandchild, or an intertribal challenge to a rival chief, the host used the occasion to validate the assumption of a new name and its prerogatives, either for himself or for an heir.

Among the Kwakiutl marriage played the most important rôle in this acquisition of status. To the north of them other tribes of the Northwest Coast were matrilineal, and position descended in the female line, though it was the men who were the actual incumbents. The Kwakiutl, on the other hand, originally lived in local bands and men set up their households in the villages of their fathers. They did not wholly lay aside this old basis of their society, even in modifying it greatly. They compromised. Most prerogatives they came to transfer by marriage; that is, a man gave his privileges to the man who married his daughter. But they were only controlled by the son-in-law and did not become his individual property. They were held in trust for his relatives, and especially for the donor's daughter's children. In this way matrilineal inheritance was secured, though there were no matrilineal groups.

Prerogatives and property were given to the son-in-law upon the birth of children, or upon their coming-of-age, as a return upon the property which had been given by his family as the bride price. In other words, a wife was obtained exactly after the manner of a copper. Just as in any economic exchange, there was a down payment which validated the transaction. The greater the amount of the bride-price at marriage, the more glory the clan of the groom could claim, and this payment had to be returned with great interest at a return potlatch usually held at the birth of the first child. As soon as this payment was made, the wife was said to have been recovered by her own family, and her marriage was called 'staying in the house [of her husband] for nothing.' Therefore the husband made another payment to retain her, and the wife's father transferred wealth to him in return. In this way all through life, at the birth or maturity of offspring, the father-in-law transferred his prerogatives and wealth to the husband of his daughter for the children who were the issue of the marriage.

Among the Kwakiutl the religious organization duplicated the secular. Just as the tribe was organized in lineages which had in their possession the titles of nobility, so it was organized also in societies with supernatural powers, the Cannibals, the Bears, the Fools, and the like. In the same way as the families, they also had ranking titles at their disposal, and no man had great position without a place among the leaders of the religious hierarchy as well as of the secular. The year was divided into two parts. In the summer the secular organization of the tribe was in force, and every man took precedence according to the respective rank of the title of nobility which he held. In the winter all this was laid aside. From the moment the whistles of the supernatural powers of the Winter Ceremonial were heard, it was tabu to refer to a man by his secular name. The whole structure of society which was built around these titles was put aside, and for the winter months the members of the tribe were grouped according to the spirits who had initiated them into the supernatural societies. For the period of the Winter Ceremonial a man had rank according to the greatness of the name he held as a member of the Cannibal, the Bear, the Fool, or some other society.

The contrast, however, was not so great as we might suppose. Just as titles of secular nobility were inherited within the lineage, so also were the high titles in the religious societies. They were a chief item in the promised dowry upon marriage. The initiation into the Cannibal Society, or the Fool Society, was the acquisition of prerogatives to which one had a right by birth or marriage, and they were validated like any other by the distribution of property. The season during which the tribe was organized according to religious affiliations, therefore, was not a period during which the great families laid aside their inherited position, but only a period during which they demonstrated their second set of privileges, privileges analogous to those which they held in the secular organization of the tribe.

It was this game of validating and exercising all the prerogatives and titles that could be acquired from one's various forbears, or by gift or by marriage, which chiefly engrossed the Indians of the Northwest Coast. Everyone in his degree took part in it, and to be shut out from it was the chief stigma of the slave. Manipulation of wealth in this culture had gone far beyond any realistic transcription of economic needs and the filling of those needs. It involved ideas of capital, of interest, and of conspicuous waste. Wealth had become not merely economic goods, even goods put away in boxes for potlatches and never used except in exchange, but even more characteristically prerogatives with no economic functions. Songs, myths, names of chiefs' house-posts, of their dogs, of their canoes, were wealth. Valued privileges, like the right to tie a dancer to a post, or to bring in tallow for the dancers to rub on their faces, or shredded cedar bark for them to wipe it off again, were wealth and were passed down in family lines. Among the neighbouring Bella Coola, family myths became such exceedingly valued and cherished property that it became the custom for the nobility to marry within the family so that such wealth should not be dissipated among those not born to hold it.

The manipulation of wealth on the Northwest Coast is clearly enough in many ways a parody on our own economic arrangements. These tribes did not use wealth to get for themselves an equivalent value in economic goods, but as counters of fixed value in a game they played to win. They saw life as a ladder of which the rungs were the titular names with the owned prerogatives that were vested in them. Each new step upward on the ladder called for the distribution of great amounts of wealth, which nevertheless were returned with usury to make possible the next elevation to which the climber might aspire.

This primary association of wealth with the validation of nobility titles is, however, only a part of the picture. The distribution of property was rarely so simple as this. The ultimate reason why a man of the Northwest Coast cared about the nobility titles, the wealth, the crests and the prerogatives lays bare the mainspring of their culture: they used them in a contest in which they sought to shame their rivals. Each individual, according to his means, constantly vied with all others to outdistance them in distributions of property. The boy who had just received his first gift of property selected another youth to receive a gift from him. The youth he chose could not refuse without admitting defeat at the outset, and he was compelled to cap the gift with an equal amount of property. When the time came for repayment if he had not double the original gift to return as interest he was shamed and demoted, and his rival's prestige correspondingly enhanced. The contest thus begun continued throughout life. If he was successful he played with continually increasing amounts of property and with more and more formidable rivals. It was a fight. They say, 'We do not fight with weapons. We fight with property.' A man who had given away a copper had overcome his rival as much as if he had overcome him in battle array. The Kwakiutl equated the two. One of their dances was called 'bringing blood into the house,' and the hemlock wreaths the men carried were said to represent heads taken in warfare. These they threw into the fire, calling out the name of the enemies they represented and shouting as the fire flared up to consume them. The wreaths, however, represented the coppers they had given away, and the names they called

out were the names of the rivals whom they had van-
quished by the distribution of property.

The object of all Kwakiutl enterprise was to show oneself superior to one's rivals. This will to superiority they
exhibited in the most uninhibited fashion. It found expression in uncensored self-glorification and ridicule of all
comers. Judged by the standards of other cultures the
speeches of their chiefs at their potlatches are unabashed
megalomania.

I am the great chief who makes people ashamed.
I am the great chief who makes people ashamed.
Our chief brings shame to the faces.
Our chief brings jealousy to the faces.
Our chief makes people cover their faces by what he is con-
    tinually doing in this world,
Giving again and again oil feasts to all the tribes.

\* \* \*

I am the only great tree, I the chief!
I am the only great tree, I the chief!
You are my subordinates, tribes.
You sit in the middle of the rear of the house, tribes.
I am the first to give you property, tribes.
I am your Eagle, tribes!

\* \* \*

Bring your counter of property, tribes, that he may try in vain
    to count the property that is to be given away by the
    great copper maker, the chief.
Go on, raise the unattainable potlatch-pole,
For this is the only thick tree, the only thick root of the tribes.
Now our chief will become angry in the house,
He will perform the dance of anger.
Our chief will perform the dance of fury.

\* \* \*

I am Yaqatlenlis, I am Cloudy, and also Sewid; I am great Only
One, and I am Smoke Owner, and I am Great Inviter. These are

the names which I obtained as marriage gifts when I married the daughters of the chiefs of the tribes wherever I went. Therefore I feel like laughing at what the lower chiefs say, for they try in vain to down me by talking against my name. Who approaches what was done by the chiefs my ancestors? Therefore I am known by all the tribes over all the world. Only the chief my ancestor gave away property in a great feast, and all the rest can only try to imitate me. They try to imitate the chief, my grandfather, who is the root of my family.

* * *

I am the first of the tribes,
I am the only one of the tribes.
The chiefs of the tribes are only local chiefs.
I am the only one among the tribes.
I search among all the invited chiefs for greatness like mine.
I cannot find one chief among the guests.
They never return feasts,
The orphans, poor people, chiefs of the tribes!
They disgrace themselves,
I am he who gives these sea otters to the chiefs, the guests, the chiefs of the tribes.
I am he who gives canoes to the chiefs the guests, the chiefs of the tribes.

These hymns of self-glorification were sung by the chief's retainers upon all great occasions, and they are the most characteristic expressions of their culture. All the motivations they recognized centred around the will to superiority. Their social organization, their economic institutions, their religion, birth and death, were all channels for its expression. As they understood triumph, it involved ridicule and scorn heaped publicly upon one's opponents, who were, according to their customs, also their invited guests. At a potlatch the host's party carved mocking life-sized figures of the chief who was to receive the copper. His poverty was symbolized by his protruding

ribs, and his insignificance by some undignified posture.
The chief who was the host sang songs holding his guests
up to contempt:

Wa, out of the way,
Wa, out of the way.
Turn your faces that I may give way to my anger by striking
    my fellow-chiefs.
They only pretend; they only sell one copper again and again
    and give it away to the little chiefs of the tribes.
Ah, do not ask for mercy,
Ah, do not ask in vain for mercy and raise your hands, you
    with lolling tongues.
I only laugh at him, I sneer at him who empties [the boxes of
    property] in his house, his potlatch house, the inviting
    house where we are made hungry.

\* \* \*

This is the cause of my laughter,
The cause of my laughter at the one who is hard up,
The one who points about for his ancestors that are chiefs.
The puny ones have no ancestors who were chiefs,
The puny ones have no names coming from their grandfathers,
The puny ones who work,
The puny ones who work hard,
Who make mistakes, who come from insignificant places in the
    world.
This only is the cause of my laughter.

\* \* \*

I am the great chief who vanquishes,
I am the great chief who vanquishes.
Oh, go on as you have done!
Only at those who continue to turn around in this world,
Working hard, losing their tails (like salmon), I sneer,
At the chiefs under the true great chief.
Ha! have mercy on them! put oil on their dry brittle-haired
    heads,

The heads of those who do not comb their hair.
I sneer at the chiefs under the true great chief,
I am the great chief who makes people ashamed.

The whole economic system of the Northwest Coast was bent to the service of this obsession. There were two means by which a chief could achieve the victory he sought. One was by shaming his rival by presenting him with more property than he could return with the required interest. The other was by destroying property. In both cases the offering called for return, though in the first case the giver's wealth was augmented, and in the second he stripped himself of goods. The consequences of the two methods seem to us at the opposite poles. To the Kwakiutl they were merely complementary means of subduing a rival, and the highest glory of life was the act of complete destruction. It was a challenge, exactly like the selling of a copper, and it was always done in opposition to a rival who must then, in order to save himself from shame, destroy an equal amount of valuable goods.

The destruction of goods took many forms. Great potlatch feasts in which quantities of candlefish oil were consumed were reckoned as contests of demolition. The oil was fed lavishly to the guests, and it was also poured upon the fire. Since the guests sat near the fire, the heat of the burning oil caused them intense discomfort, and this also was reckoned as a part of the contest. In order to save themselves from shame, they had to lie unmoved in their places, though the fire blazed up and caught the rafters of the house. The host also must exhibit the most complete indifference to the threatened destruction of his house. Some of the greatest chiefs had a carved figure of a man upon the roof. It was called the vomiter, and a trough was so arranged that a steady stream of the valuable candlefish oil poured out of the figure's open mouth into the house fire below. If the oil feast surpassed anything the guest chief had ever given, he must leave the house and begin preparations for a return feast that would outstrip the one given by his rival. If he believed that it had not equalled a feast that he had previously given, he heaped insults upon his host, who then took some further way of establishing his greatness.

For this purpose the host might send his messengers to break in pieces four canoes and bring the pieces to heap upon the fire. Or he might kill a slave. Or he might break a copper. By no means all of the coppers that were broken at potlatches were lost to the owner as wealth. There were many gradations in the destruction of a copper. A chief who did not feel the occasion great enough for the gift of his valuable copper might cut out a section of it, and it was then necessary for his rival to cut out a section from an equally valuable copper. The return of goods followed the same course as if the whole copper had been given. In contests with different rivals a copper might be scattered many hundreds of miles along the coast. When at last a great chief succeeded in acquiring the scattered pieces, he had them riveted, and the copper had then a greatly increased value.

According to Kwakiutl philosophy, the actual demolition of the copper was only a variant of this practice. The great chief would summon his tribe and declare a potlatch. 'Furthermore such is my pride, that I will kill on this fire my copper Dandalayu which is groaning in my house. You all know how much I paid for it. I bought it for four thousand blankets. Now I will break it in order to vanquish my rival. I will make my house a fighting place for you, my tribe. Be happy, chiefs, this is the first time that so great a potlatch has been given.' The chief put his copper upon the fire and it was consumed, or from some great headland he cast it into the sea. He was then stripped of his wealth, but he had acquired unparalleled prestige. He had gained the final advantage over his rival, who had to destroy a copper of equal value or retire in defeat from the contest.

The behaviour which was required of the chief was arrogant and tyrannical to a degree. There were necessarily cultural checks upon too despotic an interpretation of a chief's rôle. He was not free to destroy property to the utter impoverishment of his people or to engage in contests which were ruinous to them. The great social check that acted to keep his activity within limits they phrased as a moral tabu: the tabu on overdoing. Overdoing was always dangerous, and a chief must keep within bounds. These boundaries exacted by custom allowed, as we shall see, many extreme courses, but the check was always in readiness if a chief overreached his claims on tribal support. Good fortune, they believed, abandoned the man who went too far, and he was no longer supported by his followers. Society set limits, though the limits seem to us fantastic.

This will to superiority which was allowed such latitude on the Northwest Coast was expressed in every detail of their potlatch exchanges. For great potlatches invitations were sent out a year or more in advance, and great boat-loads of nobles came from distant tribes. The host opened the sale of a copper with self-glorifying speeches and claims as to the greatness of his name and of his copper. He challenged his guests to bring out the property which they had ready for the return gift. The guests began modestly, offering the merest fraction of the proper value, and working gradually toward the climax. The party of the seller received each added increment with scorn: 'Did you think you had finished? You were not provident when you resolved to buy this great copper. You have not finished; you will give more. The price of the copper will correspond to my greatness. I ask four hundred more.' The purchaser answered him, 'Yes, chief, you have no pity,' and sent immediately for the blankets that had been demanded of him. His counter of blankets counted them aloud and addressed the assembled tribes: 'Ya, tribes. Do you see our way of buying blankets? My tribe are strong when they buy coppers. They are not like you. There are sixteen hundred blankets in the pile I carry here. These are my words, chiefs of the Kwakiutl, to those who do not know how to buy coppers.' When he had finished, his chief rose and addressed the people: 'Now you have seen my name. This is my name. This is the weight of my name. This mountain of blankets rises through our heavens. My name is the name of the Kwakiutl, and you cannot do as we do, tribes. Look out, later on I shall ask you to buy from me. Tribes, I do not look forward to the time when you shall buy from me.'

But the sale of the copper had only begun. A chief of the seller's party rose and recounted his greatness and his privileges. He told his mythological ancestry and he said: 'I know how to buy coppers. You always say you are rich, chief. Did you not give any thought to this copper? Only give a thousand blankets more, chief.' In this fashion the price of the copper was increased until three thousand two hundred blankets had been counted out in payment. Next the valuable boxes to put them in were demanded of the purchaser. They were brought. Then more gifts were necessary 'to adorn the owner of the copper.' The purchaser acceded and presented them, saying, 'Listen, chiefs. Adorn yourselves with this canoe the value of which is fifty blankets, and with this canoe the value which is fifty blankets, and with this canoe the value of of which is fifty blankets, and with these two hundred blankets. Now there are four thousand blankets. It is done.' The owner answered, 'I take the price.' But it was not done. The purchaser now addressed the owner of the copper, saying: 'Why, have you taken the price, chief? You take the price too soon. You must think poorly of me, chief. I am a Kwakiutl, I am one of those from whom all your tribes all over the world took their names. You give up before I have finished trading with you. You must always stand beneath us.' He sent his messengers to call his sister, his princess, and gave to his rivals two hundred blankets more, 'the clothes of his princess.' This made two hundred blankets of the fifth thousand.

This was a more or less routine purchase of a copper. In the contests between great chiefs the violence and the rivalry that were the heart of this culture found free scope. The story of the conflict of Fast Runner and of Throw Away, chiefs of the Kwakiutl, shows the way in which these contests become open enmity. The two chiefs were friends. Throw Away invited the clan of his friend to a feast of salmon berries and carelessly served the grease and berries in canoes that had not been cleaned sufficiently to do them honour. Fast Runner chose to take this as a gross insult. He refused the food, lying down with his black bear blanket drawn over his face, and all his relatives, seeing he was displeased, followed his example. The host urged them to eat, but Fast Runner had his speaker address him, complaining of the indignity: 'Our chief will not eat the dirty things you have offered, O dirty man.' Throw Away scornfully replied: 'Let it be as you say. You speak as if you were a person of very great wealth.' Fast Runner replied, 'Indeed I am a person of great wealth,' and he sent his messengers to bring his copper Sea Monster. They gave it to him, and he pushed it under the fire, 'to put out the fire of his rival.' Throw Away sent also for his copper. His attendants brought him Looked at Askance and he pushed it also under the fire in the feasting-place, 'to keep the fire burning.' But Fast Runner had also another copper, Crane, and he sent for that and placed it upon the fire 'to smother it.' Throw Away had no other copper, so he could not add more fuel to keep his fire going and was defeated in the first round.

The following day Fast Runner returned the feast and sent his attendants to invite Throw Away. Throw Away meanwhile had pledged property enough to borrow another copper. Therefore when the crabapples and grease were set before him, he refused in the words which Fast Runner had used the day before, and sent his attendants to bring the copper Day Face. With this he extinguished his rival's fire. Fast Runner rose and addressed them: 'Now is my fire extinguished. But wait. Sit down again, and see the deed that I shall do.' He put on the excitement of the Dance of the Fools, of whom he was a member, and destroyed four canoes of his father-in-law's. His attendants brought them to the feasting-house and heaped them on the fire to take away the shame of having had their fire extinguished by Throw Away's copper. His guests at all costs had to remain where they were or admit defeat. The black bear blanket of Throw Away was scorched, and below his blanket the skin of his legs was blistered, but he held his ground. Only when the blaze had begun to die down, he arose as if nothing had happened and ate of the feast in order to show his complete indifference to the extravagance of his rival.

Fast Runner and Throw Away were now in open enmity. They chose, therefore, to give rival initiations into the secret societies, using their religious privileges rather than their secular. Throw Away secretly planned to give this Winter Ceremonial, and Fast Runner, hearing of it through his informers, determined to outdo him. Throw Away initiated a son and a daughter, but Fast Runner two sons and two daughters. Fast Runner now had outdistanced his rival, and when his four children were brought back from their seclusion and the excitement of the dance was at its height, he had a slave scalped and butchered by the Fool dancers and the Grizzly Bear Society and the flesh eaten by the Cannibals. The scalp he gave to Throw Away, who clearly could not match this mighty deed.

Fast Runner had still another triumph. His daughters were being initiated as war dancers, and they asked to be put upon the fire. A great wall of firewood was raised about the fire, and the daughters were tied to boards ready to be committed to the flames. Instead, two slaves dressed like true war dancers and similarly tied to boards were put into the fire. For four days the daughters of Fast Runner remained in hiding, and then, from the ashes of the slaves which had been preserved, they apparently returned to life. Throw Away had nothing to match this great demonstration of privilege, and he and his men went off to fight the Nootka. Only one man returned to tell of the defeat and death of the war party.

This is told as a true story, and there are eye-witness accounts of other contests that vary only in the acts which the rival chiefs performed to demonstrate their greatness. On one occasion within the lifetime of men now living, the chief tried to 'put out' the fire of his rival with seven canoes and four hundred blankets, while his host poured oil upon the fire in opposition. The roof of the house caught fire and the whole house was nearly destroyed, while those who were concerned kept their places with assumed indifference and sent for more possessions to heap upon the fire. 'Then those who went to get the two hundred blankets returned, and they spread them over the fire of the host. Now they "put it out." Then the host took more salal berries and crabapples, and the copper his daughter was carrying when she danced, and he pushed it under the feast-fire. The four young men who ladled the oil poured the ladleful into the fire, and the oil and the blankets were burning together. The host took the oil and poured it about among his rivals.'

Such contests were the peak of ambition. Their picture of the ideal man was drawn up in terms of these contests, and all the motivations proper to them were reckoned as virtue. An old chieftainess, addressing her son at a potlatch, admonished him: 'My tribe, I speak particularly to my son. Friends, you all know my name. You knew my father, and you know what he did with his property. He was reckless and did not care what he did. He gave away or killed slaves. He gave away or burned his canoes in the fire of the feast-house. He gave away sea-otter skins to his rivals in his own tribe or to chiefs of other tribes, or he cut them to pieces. You know that what I say is true. This, my son, is the road your father laid out for you, and on which you must walk. Your father was no common man. He was a true chief among the Koskimo. Do as your father did. Either tear up the button blankets or give them to the tribe which is our rival. That is all.' Her son answered: 'I will not block the road my father laid out for me. I will not break the law my chief laid down for me. I give these blankets to my rivals. The war that we are having now is sweet and strong.' He distributed the blankets.

The occasions upon which distribution of property took this form on the Northwest Coast were legion. Many of them were events which seem at the furthest remove from economic exchange, and the behaviour proper among the Kwakiutl at marriage, or death, or upon an accident is unintelligible until we understand the peculiar psychology that underlay them. The relations between the sexes, religion, and even misfortune were elaborated in this culture in proportion as they offered occasion for demonstrating superiority by the distribution or destruction of property. The chief occasions were those of the investiture of an heir, of marriage, and of acquisition and demonstration of religious powers, of mourning, of warfare, and of accident.

The investiture of an heir was an obvious occasion for uncensored claims to greatness. Every name, every privilege, had to be bestowed upon a man's successor, and such bestowal had to be validated by the characteristic distribution and destruction of property. 'An armour of wealth' had to be buckled upon the new incumbent. Potlatches of this kind were important and complicated affairs, but the essential features of the proceedings were nevertheless fairly simple. The following potlatch 'for the greatness of his prince's name Tlāsotiwalis' is a characteristic one. It was a feast for all the tribes of the lineage, and when they were assembled, the chief, the father of Tlāsotiwalis, gave a dramatic representation of privileges to which he was entitled by the family myth, and proclaimed his son's change of name. The heir was now to assume one of the traditional prince's names, and the property was ready to distribute in his honour. At the height of the dancing the chorus sang, in his father's name, the song composed for him:

Make way and let him have this [copper] with which I am always trying to strike my rival chiefs.
Do not ask for mercy, tribes, putting out your tongues and pressing back your hands.

And the young prince came out from the inner room carrying the copper Dentalayu. His father addressed him with goading admonitions: 'Ah, you are great, chief Tlāsotiwalis! Do you really wish it? Is it really your great wish to let it lie dead by the side of the fire, this copper that has a name, this Dentalayu? Live up to your prerogatives! For indeed you are descended from extravagant chiefs who did thus with coppers that had names' (i.e., broke them). His son broke the copper with all attendant ceremony, and distributed it among his rivals, saying to the guests: 'I am following the road made by my chief, my father, the road to walk on, extravagant, merciless chief, the chief who is afraid of nothing. I mean this, chiefs, I have danced to pieces Dentalayu for you, tribes!' He distributed all the remainder of the property, and assumed his father's chieftainship.

A variant of this type of potlatch was that which was given upon the adolescence of the woman of highest rank in the family of a chief, either his younger sister or his daughter. The greatness of the names had to be validated like the investiture of an heir, though by a lesser display. A great quantity of property other than blankets and coppers were gathered for distribution. There were articles of women's clothing, women's clam-digging canoes, gold and silver bracelets and earrings and basket hats and abalone ornaments. The distribution gave the chief a right to claim that he had mounted another step upon the ladder of the full-fledged chief; in their phrase, 'the chief who had gone through.'

Potlatching for an heir on the Northwest Coast, in spite of the opportunities for self-congratulation and display which it provided, was not directly a contest with a rival and was never, therefore, as full and congenial an expression of the culture of the people as the potlatching that centred around marriage. Marriage was dramatized, like the purchase of a copper, as a warfare. An important man about to contract a marriage called his relatives and associates together as for a war party and announced to them: 'Now we shall make war upon the tribes. Help me to bring my wife into the house.' Preparations were immediately undertaken, but the weapons with which they fought were the blankets and the coppers which were in their possession. The warfare consisted essentially in the interchange of goods.

The bride-price the bridegroom paid for the bride was bid up and up as in the case of the purchase of a copper. The bridegroom and his retainers went in a party to the house of the father of the bride. Each of the nobles brought forward a part of his property 'to lift the bride from the floor' and 'to make a seat for the bride.' More and more blankets were counted out, to overpower the family of the father-in-law, and to show the greatness of the bridegroom. The conflict between the two groups was given other expressions. The groom's party might arm themselves and rush upon the village of the bride, and the bride's village fall upon the attackers in turn. The fight might get out of hand and people be killed in the conflict. Or the father-in-law might draw up his men in a double line armed with burning brands turned inward, and the son-in-law's party had to run the gauntlet. Other families owned as their prerogative the right of building a tremendous fire in the feasting-house beside which the groom's party must sit without flinching till they were burned. Meanwhile, out of the mouth of the carved sea monster which might be another heraldic prerogative of the bride's family were vomited seven skulls, while the father of the bride mocked the groom's party: 'Beware, Gwatsenox! These are the bones of the suitors who came to marry my daughters and who ran away from my fire.'

As we have already seen, what was bought upon this occasion was not properly the bride, but the prerogatives which she had a right to pass on to her children. The bride-price, like any Northwest Coast transaction, was an obligation upon the father-in-law which he must return many-fold. The occasions for these return payments were the birth and maturity of offspring. At such times the father of the wife gave to his son-in-law not only many times the amount of material property that he had received, but also, and more importantly, the names and prerogatives which it was his right to pass on to his daughters' children. These became the property of the son-in-law, but only to the extent that he could pass them on to heirs whom he might choose, and who were sometimes not the children of the wife through whom the inheritance had come. They were not his property in the sense that he could use the names and the privileges in his own potlatching exploits. Among the greatest families these return payments upon the bride-price were delayed many years after the marriage, until the eldest son or daughter of the marriage was of an age to be initiated into the preeminent Cannibal Society. On these occasions the son-in-law, now about to receive this great return payment from his father-in-law, undertook to give the great Winter Ceremonial and to be responsible for the large disperse-ment of property it involved, and the father-in-law's re-turn payment financed him in his expenditure. The cere-monial turned upon the initiation of the child of the son-in-law into the Cannibal Society, and the name and the privileges which the young man or woman assumed at this time were the return upon the parents' wedding payment, the most valued possessions which were involved in the marriage transaction.

The amount of the return payment and the times upon which it was given were determined by the importance of the families, the number of offspring, and many other considerations that varied for each marriage. The cere-mony, however, was fixed and dramatic. The father-in-law prepared for years in advance. When the time came for the return payment he called in all his debts and ac-cumulated food in abundance, blankets, boxes, dishes, spoons, kettles, bracelets, and coppers. The bracelets were tied to sticks, ten to each stick, and the spoons and dishes attached to long ropes, the 'anchor lines of the canoe.' The relatives of the father-in-law gathered to sup-port him and to contribute to the display, and the rela-tives of the son-in-law assembled in all their festival array upon the platform of the son-in-law's house overlooking the beach. The father-in-law's party made the 'canoe' upon the beach. It was a square some hundred feet in each direction laid down upon the sand and formed of the lids of heirloom ceremonial boxes painted with animal faces and inset with sea-otter teeth. Down to this canoe they carried all the goods the father-in-law had collected. From the front ends of the canoe they tied to the son-in-law's house platform the anchor lines to which the carved wooden dishes and valuable spoons made of mountain-goat horn had been attached. All the relatives of the father-in-law entered the canoe and they and the son-in-law's party alternately sang their valuable songs. The wife of the son-in-law, the woman whose bride-price was that day being repaid, was in the canoe with her parents, loaded with ornaments which she was conveying to her husband. The great dance of the occasion was hers when she displayed her jewelry, an abalone shell nose-ring so enormous that it had to be tied to her ears for support, and earrings so heavy they were tied to the locks of her hair. After she had danced, the father-in-law rose and gave the title to all the property in the canoe to his son-in-law. The chief property was in a small box which contained the tokens of the privileges of the religious society memberships and of the names which he was transferring to his son-in-law for the use of his children.

As soon as the title to all the property had been given to the son-in-law, his friends rushed down upon the canoe with axes in their hands and split one of the box covers that formed the canoe, shouting, 'Now our loaded canoe is broken,' while the son-in-law responded, 'Let us be glad.' It was called sinking the canoe, and it signified the fact that the son-in-law would immediately distribute all the wealth contained in it among the tribe. That is, he would place it out at interest to augment his property further. It was a climax in the career of any man, and the song that belonged to the son-in-law on this occasion expressed the triumph of a chief at the apex of his power:

> I will go and tear in pieces Mount Stevens.
> I will use it for stones for my fire.
> I will go and break Mount Katstais,
> I will use it for stones for my fire.

Through four marriages an ambitious man sought to accumulate the title to more and more valuable prerogatives and to collect the return payments upon the bride-price. If an alliance of this kind was considered desirable and there was no marriageable daughter, the transfer might still take place. The son-in-law married, so they said, 'the left foot' of his father-in-law or his 'right arm' or some other part of his body. That is, a pretended marriage was performed with the same ceremonies as the real one, and by this means the privileges were transferred. If it is clear in such cases that marriage had become on the Northwest Coast a formal method of transferring privileges, it is even more striking in many of the accounts of intertribal marriages that resulted in jealous warfare. The marriage of a noblewoman into another group lost to the people of her tribe dances and privileges they might be very loath to have pass from them. In one such case the tribe from which the father-in-law had originally obtained the dance were outraged at a marriage by which the dance passed to a rival chieftain. They pretended to give a feast and invited the father-in-law and his tribe. When all were assembled, they fell upon them and killed the father-in-law and many of his friends. In this way they prevented the title to the dance from passing to the rival chief who had contracted the marriage and who would have obtained it upon the return of the bride-price. The chief, however, who by the death of his father-in-law had lost the right to the dance he coveted, was not to be so easily put off. He contracted another marriage with the daughter of the man who had killed his father-in-law and had therefore claimed the dance for his own, and he thus obtained the dance he had set out to acquire in his first marriage.

# PATTERNS OF CULTURE

In every possible way marriage on the Northwest Coast was a business transaction and followed the same peculiar rules. A woman who had borne a child so that the bride-price had been repaid with sufficient goods was regarded as having been redeemed by her blood kin. To allow her 'to stay in his house for nothing,' was of course beneath his dignity. Therefore he paid his father-in-law anew for her that he might not be the recipient of any unpaid-for favour.

In case there was dissatisfaction between the two parties to the marriage exchange, open conflict might break out between the son-in-law and his father-in-law. In one case the father-in-law gave blankets and a name to his son-in-law for the initiation of his youngest child, and the son-in-law, instead of distributing the blankets among the rival local groups, passed them off among his own relatives. This was a deadly insult, for it implied that the gift had been negligible, too small for the greatness of his name. The father-in-law retaliated and for the shame put upon him took back to his own village his daughter and her two children. The father-in-law intended this as a crushing blow, but by assuming indifference and abandoning his wife and children, the son-in-law turned the tables upon him. 'Then his father-in-law was shamed because his son-in-law would not pay to see his own children.' The son-in-law took another wife and continued on his career.

In another case the chief whose father-in-law had unduly delayed the return gift became impatient. He carved an image representing his wife and invited all the tribe to a feast. In the presence of all the people he put a stone around the neck of the image and threw it into the sea. To wipe out such an indignity it would have been necessary

208

for the father-in-law to distribute and destroy far more property than he possessed, so that by this means the son-in-law destroyed the high rank of his wife and through her that of his father-in-law. Of course the marriage was dissolved.

A man who did not himself inherit nobility titles could hope to gain standing by a marriage with a woman of a higher rank. He was usually a younger son who was barred from high status by the practice of primogeniture. If he married well and acquired wealth by an able manipulation of his debts, he was sometimes able to establish himself among the great men of the tribe. But the way was hard. It was a disgrace to the woman's family to have her united to a commoner, and the usual exchange of property at marriage was impossible, for the groom was unable to assemble the necessary goods. A marriage unrecognized by a potlatch was said to be 'a sticking together like dogs,' and the children of such a marriage were scorned as illegitimate. If his wife gave him nobility titles that were in her possession, a man was said to have obtained them for nothing, and it was a cause of shame to the family. 'Their name was disgraced and became a bad name because she had a common man for her husband.' Even though he accumulated property and validated the right to his names, the shame was remembered by the tribes and the chiefs might unite against him and break down his pretensions by worsting him in a potlatch. In one case in which the commoner husband of a noblewoman had attained high standing through the use of money earned from the whites, the chiefs brought together all their coppers to overcome him. According to the story in which they perpetuated his shame, they broke three coppers, of values of twelve thousand blankets, of nine thousand blankets, and of eighteen thousand blankets, and the pretender could not get together thirty-nine thousand blankets to buy enough coppers to match those that had been broken. He was defeated and his children assigned to other families that they, being half-noble, might not share in his disgrace.

Marriage was not the only way in which it was possible to acquire prerogatives. The means which was most honoured was the murder of the owner. The man who killed another took his name, his dances, and his crests. Tribes which because of the antagonism of the owners were not able to obtain the title to coveted dances and masks could still waylay a travelling canoe in which one man was known to own the ceremonial. The slayer then had the right to the dance, which he put at the disposal of his chief or elder brother who initiated his nephew or his son and gave to him the name and dance of the dead man. Such a means of transfer implied, of course, that the whole ceremony, with the words of the songs, the steps of the dances, and the use of the sacred objects, was known to the owner before he had killed its possessor. It was not knowledge of the ceremony he acquired. It was the title to it as property. The fact that the prerogatives of a victim in warfare could be claimed by the slayer undoubtedly reflects earlier historical conditions when the characteristic Northwest Coast prestige conflict was carried on chiefly by warfare, and the contest with property was of lesser importance.

Not only from human beings could privileges be obtained on the Northwest Coast by killing the owner; this was also a favourite means of obtaining power from the gods. A man who met and killed a supernatural being gained from him his ceremony and mask. All peoples are likely to use toward the supernaturals the behaviour they place most reliance upon in human relations, but it is not often that homage is so little regarded and that so far from awe being the required attitude toward the supernaturals the most rewarding behaviour is to kill or to shame them. It was accepted practice upon the Northwest Coast.

By still another method a man could obtain certain prerogatives without inheriting them and without buying them. This was by becoming a religious practitioner. In becoming a shaman one was initiated by the supernatural beings, not by a father or an uncle, and one obtained the recognized names and privileges from the spiritual visitant. Shamans therefore owned and exercised prerogatives 'according to the order of spirits,' but the privileges which they owned were regarded in the same manner as the privileges which had been inherited, and they were used in the same fashion.

The traditional way in which one became a shaman was by a cure in severe illness. Not all who were cured of sickness were thereafter shamans, but only those who were put away by themselves in a house in the woods for the spirits to cure. If the supernatural beings came to a man there and gave him a name and instructions, he followed then the same course that was followed by any initiate inheriting prerogatives. That is, he came back in the power of the spirits and demonstrated his newly acquired privileges. He announced his name and showed his power by curing someone who was sick. Then he distributed property to validate his new name and entered upon his career as a shaman.

Shamans used their prerogatives in the same way that chiefs and nobles used theirs, in a contest of prestige. The shamans held up to ridicule the supernatural pretensions of their rivals and contested with them to show their superior power. Each shaman had a trick that differed slightly from those of his rivals, and his supporters exalted his procedures at the expense of those of other shamans. Some shamans sucked out illness, some rubbed, some restored lost souls. A favourite device was to produce the illness from the body of the patient in the form of a small 'worm.' In order to be prepared for this demonstration, the shaman carried a roll of bird's down between his teeth and his upper lip. When he was called upon to cure, he first rinsed his mouth with water. When he had thus proved that he had nothing in his mouth, he danced and sucked and finally bit his cheeks so that his mouth was full of bloody saliva. He spat out the roll of down into a bowl with the blood he had supposedly sucked also from the seat of illness, and when he had rinsed the 'worm,' he exhibited it as evidence that he had removed the cause of pain and illness. Often several shamans tried their powers in a single cure, and those whose performances were unsuccessful lost face in the same way as a chief who was worsted in a contest for a copper. They were overcome and died of shame, or they might band together and kill the successful competitor. It was considered likely enough that anyone who overcame in shamanizing would be killed by his defeated rivals. No shaman's death was avenged, for his power was supposed to be used to harm as well as to cure, and as a sorcerer he had no claim to protection.

In another direction also shamanism among the Kwakiutl had come to parallel the secular contest that centred around crests and the validating of titular names. Just as an initiation into the Cannibal Society was a dramatic performance put on for the occasion, and the vision which elsewhere was believed to be an experience of personal contact with the supernatural became a mere formal dogma, so also in shamanism the personal propitiation of the spirits was lost sight of in the acquiring of tricks and the training of accomplices for the dramatic validation of the medicine man's claims. Each shaman had a helper, who might better be called his spy. It was his duty to mix with the people and to report to his master in what part of the body sick people felt pain. If the shaman was then called to cure, he showed his supernatural power by directing all his attention to the ailing member. The spy reported likewise if anyone complained of lassitude. At any general curing, therefore, the shamans showed their power by divining that these persons' souls needed to be recovered. The spies went great distances by canoe carrying messages which were interpreted as inspirations from the spirits.

The subterfuges of the shamans and their spies were not a matter of indifference either to the shamans themselves or to their people. Many peoples regard supernatural power as expressing itself naturally through man-manipulated tricks. The Kwakiutl did not. Only a shaman driven to despair, like Good-over-all-the-Earth, admitted that he made his raven rattle bite his hand by a feat of jugglery. Then the people knew that 'he was common, for he had made up all that he did in shamanism.' He withdrew in shame and went crazy within the year. A shaman whose trick was detected was similarly defeated. One medicine man used to take a stuffed squirrel out of his neckband and make it run up his arm. After he had danced with it and demonstrated that he could make it come alive, his secret helper on the roof moved a plank so that he could let down a string which the shaman slipped over his squirrel and let it fly up to the roof. Then he called it down again. The audience noticed that he stood always in one place in the house to call his squirrel and someone went to the roof and discovered a place over which a thin shingle had been laid. The shaman gave up practising, he never went out any more, and like Good-over-all-the-Earth he also died of shame. Thus shamans among the Kwakiutl were accustomed to use underground means to put across their performances, and if they were discovered it was regarded as the equivalent of defeat in a potlatch contest.

Like any secular chief, a shaman had to validate his prerogatives by the distribution of property, and when he performed a cure he was rewarded according to the wealth and rank of the family of the sick person as in any distribution of property. Shamanism, the Kwakiutl say, was 'that which makes it easy to obtain property.' It was a way of obtaining without inheritance or purchase valuable privileges which could be used to raise one's status.

Inheritance and purchase might even, in Kwakiutl practice, be the means of acquiring shamanistic privileges, just as they were the means of acquiring all other prerogatives. It is obvious that the shamanistic tricks had to be taught and the shamans who taught them to novices certainly had to be paid. It is impossible to say how commonly supernatural powers were inherited. Men sometimes initiated their sons as shamans after they had retired to the woods for a period as the Cannibal dancers did. The great shaman Fool vomited up his quartz crystal from his body and threw it into the body of his son who became thereby a shaman of the highest degree. His father lost by this act, of course, all his rights to practise shamanism.

Behaviour on the Northwest Coast was dominated at every point by the need to demonstrate the greatness of the individual and the inferiority of his rivals. It was carried out with uncensored self-glorification and with gibes and insults poured upon the opponents. There was another side to the picture. The Kwakiutl stressed equally the fear of ridicule, and the interpretation of experience in terms of insults. They recognized only one gamut of emotion, that which swings between victory and shame. It was in term of affronts given and received that economic exchange, marriage, political life, and the practice of religion were carried on. Even this, however, gives only a partial picture of the extent to which this preoccupation with shame dominated their behaviour. The Northwest Coast carries out this same pattern of behaviour also in relation to the external world and the forces of nature. All accidents were occasions upon which one was shamed. A man whose axe slipped so that his foot was injured had immediately to wipe out the shame which had been put upon him. A man whose canoe had capsized had similarly to 'wipe his body' of the insult. People must at all costs be prevented from laughing at the incident. The universal means to which they resorted was, of course, the distribution of property. It removed the shame; that is, it re-established again the sentiment of superiority which their culture associated with potlatching. All minor accidents were dealt with in this way. The greater ones might involve giving a winter ceremonial, or head-hunting, or suicide. If a mask of the Cannibal Society was broken, to wipe out the count a man had to give a winter ceremonial and initiate his son as a Cannibal. If a man lost at gambling with a friend and was stripped of his property, he had recourse to suicide.

The great event which was dealt with in these terms was death. Mourning on the Northwest Coast cannot be understood except through the knowledge of the peculiar arc of behaviour which this culture institutionalized. Death was the paramount affront they recognized, and it was met as they met any major accident, by distribution and destruction of property, by head-hunting, and by suicide. They took recognized means, that is, to wipe out the shame. When a chief's near relative died, he gave away his house; that is, the planks of the walls and the roof were ripped from the framework and carried off by those who could afford it. For it was potlatching in the ordinary sense, and every board must be repaid with due interest. It was called 'craziness strikes on account of the death of a loved one,' and by means of it the Kwakiutl handled mourning by the same procedures that they used at marriage, at the attainment of supernatural powers, or in a quarrel.

There was a more extreme way of meeting the affront of death. This was by head-hunting. It was in no sense retaliation upon the group which had killed the dead man. The dead relative might equally have died in bed of disease or by the hand of an enemy. The head-hunting was called 'killing to wipe one's eyes,' and it was a means of getting even by making another household mourn instead. When a chief's son died, the chief set out in his canoe. He was received at the house of a neighbouring chief, and after the formalities he addressed his host, saying, 'My prince has died today, and you go with him.' Then he killed him. In this, according to their interpretation, he acted nobly because he had not been downed, but had struck back in return. The whole proceeding is meaningless without the fundamental paranoid reading of bereavement. Death, like all the other untoward accidents of existence, confounded man's pride and could only be handled in terms of shame.

There are many stories of this behaviour at death. A chief's sister and her daughter had gone up to Victoria, and either because they drank bad whiskey or because their boat capsized they never came back. The chief called together his warriors. 'Now I ask you, tribes, who shall wail? Shall I do it or shall another?' The spokesman answered, of course: 'Not you, chief. Let some other of the tribes.' Immediately they set up the war pole to announce their intention of wiping out the injury and gathered a war party. They set out and found seven men and two children asleep and killed them. 'Then they felt good when they arrived at Sebaa in the evening.'

A man now living describes an experience of his in the '70's when he had gone fishing for dentalia. He was staying with Tlabid, one of the two chiefs of the tribe. That night he was sleeping under a shelter on the beach when two men woke him, saying: 'We have come to kill Chief Tlabid on account of the death of the princess of our Chief Gagaheme. We have here three large canoes and we are sixty men. We cannot go home to our country without the head of Tlabid.' At breakfast, the visitor told Tlabid, and Tlabid said, 'Why, my dear, Gagaheme is my own uncle, for the mother of his father and of my mother are one; therefore he cannot do any harm to me.' They ate, and after they had eaten, Tlabid made ready and said he would go to get mussels at a small island outside of the village. The whole tribe forbade their chief to go mussel-gathering, but Tlabid laughed at what his tribe said. He took his cape and his paddle and went out of the door of his house. He was angry, and therefore none of his tribe spoke. He launched his canoe and when it was afloat his young son went aboard and sat in the bow with his father. Tlabid paddled away, steering away for a small island where there were many mussels. When he was halfway across three large canoes came in sight, full of men, and as soon as Tlabid saw them, he steered his canoe toward them. Now he did not paddle, and two of the canoes went landward of him and one canoe seaward, and the bows of all three canoes were in a line. The three canoes did not stop, and then the body of Tlabid could be seen standing up headless. The warriors paddled away, and when they were out of sight the tribe launched a small canoe and went to tow in the one in which Tlabid was lying dead. The child never cried, for 'his heart failed him on account of what had been done to his father.' When they arrived at the beach they buried the great chief.

A person whose death was determined upon to wipe out another's death was chosen for one consideration: that his rank was the equivalent of that of the dead. The death of a commoner wiped out that of a commoner, of a prince that of a princess. If, therefore, the bereaved struck down a person of equal rank, he had maintained his position in spite of the blow that had been dealt him.

The characteristic Kwakiutl response to frustration was sulking and acts of desperation. If a boy was struck by his father, or if a man's child died, he retired to his pallet and neither ate nor spoke. When he had determined upon a course which would save his threatened dignity, he rose and distributed property, or went head-hunting, or committed suicide. One of the commonest myths of the Kwakiutl is that of the young man who is scolded by his father or mother and who after lying for four days motionless upon his bed goes out into the woods intent on suicide. He jumps into waterfalls and from precipices, or tries to drown himself in lakes, but he is saved from death by a supernatural who accosts him and gives him power.

218

Thereupon he returns to shame his parents by his greatness.

In practice suicide was comparatively common. The mother of a woman who was sent home by her husband for unfaithfulness was shamed and strangled herself. A man whose son stumbled in his initiation dance, not being able to finance a second winter ceremonial, was defeated and shot himself.

Even if death is not taken into the hands of the shamed person in actual suicide, deaths constantly are regarded as due to shame. The shaman who was outjuggled in the curing dance, the chief who was worsted in the breaking of coppers, the boy worsted in a game, are all said to have died of shame. Irregular marriages take, however, the greatest toll. In these cases it was the father of the bridegroom who was most vulnerable, for it was the groom's prestige which was primarily raised by the marriage transfer of property and privileges, and his father therefore lost heavily in an irregular marriage.

The Kwakiutl tell of the death from shame of an old chief of one of their villages. His youngest son, years before, had gone with the daughter of respected slaves to a distant inlet. This was no matter for comment, for the younger sons were disregarded and of low caste. He and his wife had a beautiful daughter, and when she was of a marriageable age an elder brother of her father's saw her and obtained her in marriage without knowing her origin. They had a son and the elder brother gave his own noble name to his child. He took the family and his wife's parents home to his father, the old chief, who when he recognized his youngest son fell dead with shame; for his noble son had given his name to the offspring of the 'common little daughter of his youngest son.' Then the youngest son was happy because he had tricked his noble brother into marrying his daughter and had obtained one of the titular names for his grandchild.

The shame of the old chief at the marriage had in it no element of protest at the marriage of near kin. The marriage with the younger brother's daughter in case the younger brother was not outside the nobility altogether, was a traditionally approved marriage and very popular in some families. Aristocracy on the Northwest Coast had become so thoroughly associated with primogeniture that 'pride of blood,' which we associate with aristocracy, was not recognized.

The sulking and the suicides on the Northwest Coast are the natural complement of their major preoccupations. The gamut of the emotions which they recognized, from triumph to shame, was magnified to its utmost proportions. Triumph was an uninhibited indulgence in delusions of grandeur, and shame a cause of death. Knowing but the one gamut, they used it for every occasion, even the most unlikely.

All the rewards of their society they bestowed upon the person who could deal with existence in these terms. Every event, both the acts of one's fellows and the accidents dealt out by the material environment, threatened first and foremost one's ego security, and definite and specific techniques were provided to reinstate the individual after the blow. If he could not avail himself of these techniques, he had no recourse except to die. He had staked everything, in his view of life, upon a grandiose picture of the self, and when the bubble of his self-esteem was pricked, he had no security to fall back upon, and the collapse of his inflated ego left him prostrate.

His relation to his fellows was similarly dictated by this

same psychology. To maintain his own status he dealt out insults and ridicule to his neighbours. The object of his endeavours was to 'flatten' their pretensions by the weight of his own, to 'break' their names. The Kwakiutl carried this behaviour even into their dealings with their gods. The final insult they could use to a man was to call him a slave; hence when they had prayed for good weather and the wind did not change, they put upon their supernaturals the same affront. An old traveller writes of the Tsimshian: 'When calamities are prolonged or thicken, they get enraged against God and vent their anger against him, raising their eyes and hands in savage anger to heaven, stamping their feet on the ground and repeating, "You are a great slave." It is their greatest term of reproach.'

They did not suppose that supernatural beings were beneficent. They knew that hurricanes and avalanches were not, and they attributed to their gods the characteristics of the natural world. One of these, Cannibal at the North End of the River, employed a female slave to supply him with corpses. His guard, the Raven, ate their eyes, and another fabulous bird, his slave, fractured the skulls with his beak and sucked out the human brains. Supernatural beings were not supposed to have benevolent intentions. The first thing a canoe-builder had to do after he had adzed his canoe was to paint the face of a man on each side to frighten away the dead canoe-builders who would certainly cause it to split if they were not prevented. This is a far cry from the friendly and helpful relations that the priests of Zuñi count upon with those who have previously exercised their profession. On the Northwest Coast these were exactly the group whose hands were lifted against their living colleagues. As we have seen, a recognized way of obtaining blessings from the gods was to kill them. Then one triumphed and was rewarded by supernatural power.

The segment of human behaviour which the Northwest Coast has marked out to institutionalize in its culture is one which is recognized as abnormal in our civilization, and yet it is sufficiently close to the attitudes of our own culture to be intelligible to us and we have a definite vocabulary with which we may discuss it. The megalomaniac paranoid trend is a definite danger in our society. It faces us with a choice of possible attitudes. One is to brand it as abnormal and reprehensible, and it is the attitude we have chosen in our civilization. The other extreme is to make it the essential attribute of ideal man, and this is the solution in the culture of the Northwest Coast.

# VII

## *The Nature of Society*

THE three cultures of Zuñi, of Dobu, and of the Kwakiutl are not merely heterogeneous assortments of acts and beliefs. They have each certain goals toward which their behaviour is directed and which their institutions further. They differ from one another not only because one trait is present here and absent there, and because another trait is found in two regions in two different forms. They differ still more because they are oriented as wholes in different directions. They are travelling along different roads in pursuit of different ends, and these ends and these means in one society cannot be judged in terms of those of another society, because essentially they are incommensurable.

All cultures, of course, have not shaped their thousand items of behaviour to a balanced and rhythmic pattern. Like certain individuals, certain social orders do not subordinate activities to a ruling motivation. They scatter. If at one moment they seem to be pursuing certain ends, at another they are off on some tangent apparently inconsistent with all that has gone before, which gives no clue to activity that will come after.

This lack of integration seems to be as characteristic of certain cultures as extreme integration is of others. It is not everywhere due to the same circumstances. Tribes like those of the interior of British Columbia have incorporated traits from all the surrounding civilizations. They have taken their patterns for the manipulation of wealth from one culture area, parts of their religious practices from another, contradictory bits from still another. Their mythology is a hodge-podge of unco-ordinated accounts of culture heroes out of three different myth-cycles represented in areas around them. Yet in spite of such extreme hospitality to the institutions of others, their culture gives an impression of extreme poverty. Nothing is carried far enough to give body to the culture. Their social organization is little elaborated, their ceremonial is poorer than that in almost any other region of the world, their basketry and beading techniques give only a limited scope for activity in plastic arts. Like certain individuals who have been indiscriminately influenced in many different directions, their tribal patterns of behaviour are unco-ordinated and casual.

In these tribes of British Columbia the lack of integration appears to be more than a mere simultaneous presence of traits collected from different surrounding peoples. It seems to go deeper than that. Each facet of life has its own organization, but it does not spread to any other. At puberty great attention is paid to the magical education of children for the various professions and the acquisition of guardian spirits. On the western plains this vision practice saturates the whole complex of adult life, and the professions of hunting and warfare are dominated by correlated beliefs. But in British Columbia the vision quest is one organized activity and warfare is quite another. Similarly feasts and dances in British Columbia are strictly social. They are festive occasions at which the performers mimic animals for the amusement of the spectators. But it is strictly tabu to imitate animals who are counted as possible guardian spirits. The feasts do not have religious significance nor do they serve as opportunities for economic exchange. Every activity is segregated, as it were. It forms a complex of its own, and its motivations and goals are proper to its own limited field and are not extended to the whole life of the people. Nor does any characteristic psychological response appear to have arisen to dominate the culture as a whole.

It is not always possible to separate lack of cultural integration of this sort from that which is due more directly to exposure to contradictory influences. Lack of integration of this latter type occurs often on the borders of well-defined culture areas. These marginal regions are removed from close contact with the most characteristic tribes of their culture and are exposed to strong outside influences. As a result they may very often incorporate into their social organization or their art techniques most contradictory procedures. Sometimes they refashion the inharmonious material into a new harmony, achieving a result essentially unlike that of any of the well-established cultures with which they share so many items of behaviour. It may be that if we knew the past history of these cultures, we should see that, given a sufficient period of years, disharmonious borrowings tend to achieve harmony. Certainly in many cases they do. But in the cross-section of contemporary primitive cultures which is all that we can be sure of understanding, many marginal areas are conspicuous for apparent dissonance.

Other historical circumstances are responsible in other cases for a lack of integration in certain cultures. It is not only the marginal tribe whose culture may be unco-ordinated, but the tribe that breaks off from its fellows and takes up its position in an area of different civilization.

In such cases the conflict that is most apparent is between the new influences brought to bear upon the people of the tribe and what we may call their indigenous behaviour. The same situation occurs also to a people who have stayed at home, when a tribe with either great prestige or great numbers is able to introduce major changes in an area to which they have newly come.

An intimate and understanding study of a genuinely disoriented culture would be of extraordinary interest. Probably the nature of the specific conflicts or of the facile hospitality to new influences would prove more important than any blanket characterizations of 'lack of integration,' but what such characterizations would be we cannot guess. Probably in even the most disoriented cultures it would be necessary to take account of accommodations that tend to rule out disharmonious elements and establish selected elements more securely. The process might even be the more apparent for the diversity of material upon which it operated.

Some of the best available examples of the conflict of disharmonious elements are from the past history of tribes that have achieved integration. The Kwakiutl have not always boasted the consistent civilization which we have described. Before they settled on the coast and on Vancouver Island, they shared in general the culture of the Salish people to the south. They still keep myths and village organization and relationship terminology that link them with these people. But the Salish tribes are individualists. Hereditary privileges are at a minimum. Every man has, according to his ability, practically the same opportunity as any other man. His importance depends on his skill in hunting, or his luck in gambling, or his success in manipulating his supernatural claims as a doctor or diviner. There could hardly be a greater contrast than with the social order of the Northwest Coast.

Even this extreme contrast, however, did not militate against Kwakiutl acceptance of the alien pattern. They came to regard as private property even names, myths, house-posts, guardian spirits, and the right to be initiated into certain societies. But the adjustment that was necessary is still apparent in their institutions, and it is conspicuous at just those points where the two social orders were at odds; that is, in the mechanisms of the social organization. For though the Kwakiutl adopted the whole Northwest Coast system of prerogatives and potlatches, they did not similarly adopt the rigid matrilineal clans of the northern tribes which provided a fixed framework within which the privileges descended. The individual in the northern tribes fitted automatically into the title of nobility to which he had a right by birth. The individual among the Kwakiutl, as we have seen, spent his life bargaining for these titles, and could lay claim to any one that had been held in any branch of his family. The Kwakiutl adopted the whole system of prerogatives, but they left to the individual a free play in the game of prestige which contrasted with the caste system of the northern tribes, and retained the old customs of the south that the Kwakiutl had brought with them to the coast.

Certain very definite cultural traits of the Kwakiutl are the reflections of specific conflicts between the old and the new configurations. With the new emphasis on property, inheritance rules assumed a new importance. The interior Salish tribes were loosely organized in families and villages, and most property was destroyed at death. The rigid matrilineal clan system of the northern tribes, as we have seen, did not gain acceptance among the

Kwakiutl, but they compromised by stressing the right of the son-in-law to claim privileges from his wife's father, these privileges to be held in trust for his children. The inheritance, therefore, passed matrilineally, but it skipped a generation, as it were. In every alternate generation the prerogatives were not exercised but merely held in trust. As we have seen, all these privileges were manipulated according to the conventional potlatch techniques. It was an unusual adjustment and one which was clearly a compromise between two incompatible social orders. We have described in an earlier chapter how thoroughly they solved the problem of bringing two antagonistic social orders into harmony.

Integration, therefore, may take place in the face of fundamental conflicts. The cases of cultural disorientation may well be less than appear at the present time. There is always the possibility that the description of the culture is disoriented rather than the culture itself. Then again, the nature of the integration may be merely outside our experience and difficult to perceive. When these difficulties have been removed, the former by better field-work, the latter by more acute analysis, the importance of the integration of cultures may be even clearer than it is today. Nevertheless it is important to recognize the fact that not all cultures are by any means the homogeneous structures we have described for Zuñi and the Kwakiutl. It would be absurd to cut every culture down to the Procrustean bed of some catchword characterization. The danger of lopping off important facts that do not illustrate the main proposition is grave enough even at best. It is indefensible to set out upon an operation that mutilates the subject and erects additional obstacles against our eventual understanding of it.

Facile generalizations about the integration of culture are most dangerous in field-work. When one is mastering the language and all the idiosyncrasies of behaviour of an esoteric culture, preoccupation with its configuration may well be an obstacle to a genuine understanding. The field-worker must be faithfully objective. He must chronicle all the relevant behaviour, taking care not to select according to any challenging hypothesis the facts that will fit a thesis. None of the peoples we have discussed in this volume were studied in the field with any preconception of a consistent type of behaviour which that culture illustrated. The ethnology was set down as it came, with no attempt to make it self-consistent. The total pictures are therefore much more convincing to the student. In theoretical discussions of culture, also, generalizations about the integration of culture will be empty in proportion as they are dogmatic and universalized. We need detailed information about contrasting limits of behaviour and the motivations that are dynamic in one society and not in another. We do not need a plank of configuration written into the platform of an ethnological school. On the other hand, the contrasted goods which different cultures pursue, the different intentions which are at the basis of their institutions, are essential to the understanding both of different social orders and of individual psychology.

The relation of cultural integration to studies of Western civilization and hence to sociological theory is easily misunderstood. Our own society is often pictured as an extreme example of lack of integration. Its huge complexity and rapid changes from generation to generation make inevitable a lack of harmony between its elements that does not occur in simpler societies. The lack of integration is exaggerated and misinterpreted, however, in most studies because of a simple technical error. Primitive society is integrated in geographical units. Western civilization, however, is stratified, and different social groups of the same time and place live by quite different standards and are actuated by different motivations.

The effort to apply the anthropological culture area in modern sociology can only be fruitful to a very limited degree because different ways of living are today not primarily a matter of spatial distribution. There is a tendency among sociologists to waste time over the 'culture area concept.' There is properly no such 'concept.' When traits group themselves geographically, they must be handled geographically. When they do not, it is idle to make a principle out of what is at best a loose empirical category. In our civilization there is, in the anthropological sense, a uniform cosmopolitan culture that can be found in any part of the globe, but there is likewise unprecedented divergence between the labouring class and the Four Hundred, between those groups whose life centres in the church and those whose life centres on the race-track. The comparative freedom of choice in modern society makes possible important voluntary groups which stand for as different principles as the Rotary Clubs and Greenwich Village. The nature of the cultural processes is not changed with these modern conditions, but the unit in which they can be studied is no longer the local group.

The integration of culture has important sociological consequences and impinges upon several moot questions of sociology and social psychology. The first of these is the controversy over whether or not society is an organism. Most modern sociologists and social psychologists have argued elaborately that society is not and never can be anything over and above the individual minds that compose it. As part of their exposition they have vigorously attacked the 'group fallacy,' the interpretation which, they feel, would make thinking and acting a function of some mythical entity, the group. On the other hand, those who have dealt with diverse cultures, where the material shows plainly enough that all the laws of individual psychology are inadequate to explain the facts, have often expressed themselves in mystical phraseology. Like Durkheim they have cried, 'The individual does not exist,' or like Kroeber they have called in a force he calls the superorganic to account for the cultural process.

This is largely a verbal quarrel. No one of the so-called organicists really believes in any other order of mind than the minds of the individuals in the culture, and on the other hand even such a vigorous critic of the group-fallacy as Allport admits the necessity of the scientific study of groups, 'the province of the special science of sociology.' The argument between those who have thought it necessary to conceive of the group as more than the sum of its individuals and those who have not has been largely between students handling different kinds of data. Durkheim, starting from an early familiarity with the diversity of cultures and especially with the culture of Australia, reiterated, often in vague phraseology, the necessity of studies of culture. Sociologists, on the other hand, dealing rather with our own standardized culture, have attempted to demolish a methodology the need for which simply did not occur in their work.

It is obvious that the sum of all the individuals in Zuñi make up a culture beyond and above what those individuals have willed and created. The group is fed by tradition; it is 'time-binding.' It is quite justifiable to call it an organic whole. It is a necessary consequence of the animism embedded in our language that we speak of such a group as choosing its ends and having specific purposes; it should not be held against the student as an evidence of a mystic philosophy. These group phenomena must be studied if we are to understand the history of human behaviour, and individual psychology cannot of itself account for the facts with which we are confronted.

In all studies of social custom, the crux of the matter is that the behaviour under consideration must pass through the needle's eye of social acceptance, and only history in its widest sense can give an account of these social acceptances and rejections. It is not merely psychology that is in question, it is also history, and history is by no means a set of facts that can be discovered by introspection. Therefore those explanations of custom which derive our economic scheme from human competitiveness, modern war from human combativeness, and all the rest of the ready explanations that we meet in every magazine and modern volume, have for the anthropologist a hollow ring. Rivers was one of the first to phrase the issue vigorously. He pointed out that instead of trying to understand the blood feud from vengeance, it was necessary rather to understand vengeance from the institution of the blood feud. In the same way it is necessary to study jealousy from its conditioning by local sexual regulations and property institutions.

The difficulty with naïve interpretations of culture in terms of individual behaviour is not that these interpretations are those of psychology, but that they ignore history and the historical process of acceptance or rejection of traits. Any configurational interpretation of cultures also is an exposition in terms of individual psychology, but it depends upon history as well as upon psychology. It holds that Dionysian behaviour is stressed in the institutions of certain cultures because it is a permanent possibility in individual psychology, but that it is stressed in certain cultures and not in others because of historical events that have in one place fostered its development and in others have ruled it out. At different points in the interpretation of cultural forms, both history and psychology are necessary; one cannot make the one do the service of the other.

This brings us to one of the most hotly debated of all the controversies which impinge upon configurational anthropology. This is the conflict as to the biological bases of social phenomena. I have spoken as if human temperament were fairly constant in the world, as if in every society a roughly similar distribution were potentially available, and as if the culture selected from these according to its traditional patterns and moulded the vast majority of individuals into conformity. Trance experience, for example, according to this interpretation, is a potentiality of a certain number of individuals in any population. When it is honoured and rewarded, a considerable proportion will achieve or simulate it, but in our civilization where it is a blot on the family escutcheon the number will dwindle and those individuals be classified with the abnormal.

But there is also another possible interpretation. It has been vigorously contended that traits are not culturally selected but biologically transmitted. According to this interpretation the distinction is racial, and the Plains Indians seek visions because this necessity is transmitted in the chromosomes of the race. Similarly, the Pueblo cultures pursue sobriety and moderation because such conduct is determined by their racial heredity. If the biologi-

233

cal interpretation is true, it is not to history that we need to go to understand the behaviour of groups, but to physiology.

This biological interpretation, however, has never been given a firm scientific basis. In order to prove their point it would be necessary for those who hold this view to show physiological facts that account for even a small part of the social phenomena it is necessary to understand. It is possible that basal metabolism or the functioning of the ductless glands may differ significantly in different human groups and that such facts might give us insight into differences in cultural behaviour. It is not an anthropological problem, but when the physiologists and the geneticists have provided the material it may be of value to the students of cultural history.

The physiological correlations that the biologist may provide in the future, however, so far as they concern hereditary transmission of traits, cannot, at their best, cover all the facts as we know them. The North American Indians are biologically of one race, yet they are not all Dionysian in cultural behaviour. Zuñi is an extreme example of diametrically opposed motivations, and this Apollonian culture is shared by the other Pueblos, one group of which, the Hopi, are of the Shoshonean sub-group, a group which is widely represented among Dionysian tribes and to which the Aztec are said to be linguistically related. Another Pueblo group is the Tewa, closely related biologically and linguistically to the non-Pueblo Kiowa of the southern plains. Cultural configurations, therefore, are local and do not correlate with known relationships of the various groups. In the same way there is no biological unity in the western plains that sets these vision-seeking peoples off from other groups. The tribes who inhabit this region are drawn from the widespread Algonkian, Athabascan, and Siouan families, and each still retains the speech of their particular stock.[1] All these stocks include tribes who seek visions after the Plains fashion and tribes who do not. Only those who live within the geographical limits of the plains seek visions as an essential part of the equipment of every normal able-bodied man.

The environmental explanation is still more imperative, when instead of considering distribution in space, we turn to distribution in time. The most radical changes in psychological behaviour have taken place in groups whose biological constitution has not appreciably altered. This can be abundantly illustrated from our own cultural background. European civilization was as prone to mystic behaviour, to epidemics of psychic phenomena, in the Middle Ages, as it was in the nineteenth century to the most hard-headed materialism. The culture has changed its bias without a corresponding change in the racial constitution of the group.

Cultural interpretations of behaviour need never deny that a physiological element is also involved. Such a denial is based on a misunderstanding of scientific explanations. Biology does not deny chemistry, though chemistry is inadequate to explain biological phenomena. Nor is biology obliged to work according to chemical formulæ because it recognizes that the laws of chemistry underlie the facts it analyzes. In every field of science it is necessary to stress the laws and sequences that most adequately explain the situations under observation and nevertheless to insist that other elements are present, though they can be shown not to have had crucial importance in the final result. To

[1] The linguistic groupings in these cases correlate with biological relationship.

point out, therefore, that the biological bases of cultural behaviour in mankind are for the most part irrelevant is not to deny that they are present. It is merely to stress the fact that the historical factors are dynamic.

Experimental psychology has been forced to a similar emphasis even in studies dealing with our own culture. Recent important experiments dealing with personality traits have shown that social determinants are crucial even in the traits of honesty and leadership. Honesty in one experimental situation gave almost no indication whether the child would cheat in another. There turned out to be not honest-dishonest persons, but honest-dishonest situations. In the same way in the study of leaders there proved to be no uniform traits that could be set down as standard even in our own society. The rôle developed the leader, and his qualities were those that the situation emphasized. In these 'situational' results it has become more and more evident that social conduct even in a selected society is 'not simply the expression of a fixed mechanism that predetermines to a specific mode of conduct, but rather a set of tendencies aroused in variable ways by the specific problem that confronts us.'

When these situations that even in one society are dynamic in human behaviour are magnified into contrasts between cultures opposed to one another in goals and motivations to such a degree as Zuñi and the Kwakiutl, for instance, the conclusion is inescapable. If we are interested in human behaviour, we need first of all to understand the institutions that are provided in any society. For human behaviour will take the forms those institutions suggest, even to extremes of which the observer, deep-dyed in the culture of which he is a part, can have no intimation.

This observer will see the bizarre developments of behaviour only in alien cultures, not in his own. Nevertheless this is obviously a local and temporary bias. There is no reason to suppose that any one culture has seized upon an eternal sanity and will stand in history as a solitary solution of the human problem. Even the next generation knows better. Our only scientific course is to consider our own culture, so far as we are able, as one example among innumerable others of the variant configurations of human culture.

The cultural pattern of any civilization makes use of a certain segment of the great arc of potential human purposes and motivations, just as we have seen in an earlier chapter that any culture makes use of certain selected material techniques or cultural traits. The great arc along which all the possible human behaviours are distributed is far too immense and too full of contradictions for any one culture to utilize even any considerable portion of it. Selection is the first requirement. Without selection no culture could even achieve intelligibility, and the intentions it selects and makes its own are a much more important matter than the particular detail of technology or the marriage formality that it also selects in similar fashion.

These different arcs of potential behaviour that different peoples have selected and capitalized in their traditional institutions are only illustrated by the three cultures we have described. It is extremely improbable that the goals and motivations they have chosen are those most characteristic of the world. These particular illustrations were chosen because we know something about them as living cultures, and therefore can avoid the doubts that must always be present in the discussion of cultures it is no longer possible to check from observation. The culture of the Plains Indians is one, for instance, about which we have vast information and which is singularly consistent. Its psychological patterns are fairly clear from the native texts, the travellers' accounts, and the reminiscences and survivals of custom collected by ethnologists. But the culture has not been functioning for some time, and there is a reasonable doubt. One cannot easily tell how practice squared with dogma, and what expedients were common in adapting the one to the other.

Nor are these configurations we have discussed 'types' in the sense that they represent a fixed constellation of traits. Each one is an empirical characterization, and probably is not duplicated in its entirety anywhere else in the world. Nothing could be more unfortunate than an effort to characterize all cultures as exponents of a limited number of fixed and selected types. Categories become a liability when they are taken as inevitable and applicable alike to all civilizations and all events. The aggressive, paranoid tendencies of Dobu and the Northwest Coast are associated with quite different traits in these two cultures. There is no fixed constellation. The Apollonian emphases in Zuñi and in Greece had fundamentally different developments. In Zuñi the virtue of restraint and moderation worked to exclude from their civilization all that was of a different nature. Greek civilization, however, is unintelligible without recognizing the Dionysian compensations it also institutionalized. There is no 'law,' but several different characteristic courses which a dominant attitude may take.

Patterns of culture which resemble each other closely may not choose the same situations to handle in terms of their dominant purposes. In modern civilization the man who is ruthless in business competition is often a considerate husband and an indulgent father. The obsessive pursuit of success in Western civilization is not extended to family life to anything like the same degree that is developed in commercial life. The institutions surrounding the two activities are contrasted to an extent that is not true, for instance, in Dobu. Conjugal life in Dobu is actuated by the same motives as Kula trading. Even gardening in Dobu is an appropriation of other gardeners' yam tubers. But gardening is often a routine activity that is little affected whatever the pattern of the culture may be; it is a situation to which the dominant motives are not extended, or in which they are curtailed.

This unevenness in the extent to which behaviour is coloured by the dye of the cultural pattern is evident in Kwakiutl life. We have seen that the characteristic Kwakiutl reaction to the death of a noble adult was to carry out some plan for getting even, to strike back against a fate that had shamed them. But a young father and mother mourning for their baby need not behave in this fashion. The mother's lament is full of sorrow. All the women come to wail, and the mother holds her dead child in her arms, weeping over it. She has had carvers and doll-makers make all kinds of playthings, and they are spread about. The women wail, and the mother speaks to her child:

Ah, ah, ah, why have you done this to me, child? You chose me as your mother, and I tried to do everything for you. Look at all your toys and all the things I have had made for you. Why do you desert me, child? Is it because of something I did to you? I will try to do better when you come back to me, child. Only do this for me: get well right away in the place where you go, and as soon as you are strong come back to me. Please do not stay away. Have mercy on me who am your mother, child.

She is praying her dead child to return and be born again a second time from her body.

Kwakiutl songs also are full of grief at the parting of loved ones:

Oh, he is going far away. He will be taken to the pretty place named New York, my dear.
Oh, could I fly like a poor little raven by his side, my love.
Oh, could I fly by the side of my dear, my love.
Oh, could I lie down by the side of my dear, my pain.
The love for my dear kills my body, my master.
The words of him who keeps me alive kill my body, my dear.
For he said that he will not turn his face this way for two years, my love.
Oh, could I be the featherbed for you to lie down upon, my dear.
Oh, could I be the pillow for your head to rest upon, my dear.
Good-bye! I am downcast. I weep for my love.

However, even in these Kwakiutl songs grief is mingled with a sense of the shame that has been brought upon the sufferer, and then the sentiment turns to bitter mockery and the desire to even the scales again. The songs of jilted maidens and youths are not far from similar expressions that are familiar to us in our own culture:

Oh how, my lady love, can my thoughts be conveyed to you, my thoughts of your deed, my lady love?
It is the object of laughter, my lady love, it is the object of laughter, your deed, my lady love.
It is the object of contempt, my lady love, it is the object of contempt, your deed, my lady love.
Farewell to you, my lady love, farewell, mistress, on account of your deed, my lady love.

Or this one:

She pretends to be indifferent, not to love me, my true love, my
    dear.
My dear, you go too far, your good name is going down, my
    dear.
Friends, do not let us listen any longer to love songs that are
    sung by those who are out of sight.
Friends, it might be well if I took a new true love, a dear one.
I hope she will hear my love song when I cry to my new love,
    my dear one.

It is evident that grief turns easily into shame, but grief
nevertheless in certain limited situations is allowed expression. In the intimacies of Kwakiutl family life, also,
there is opportunity for the expression of warm affection
and the easy give-and-take of cheerful human relations.
Not all situations in Kwakiutl existence require equally
the motives that are most characteristic of their lives.

In Western civilization, as in Kwakiutl life, not all
aspects of life serve equally the will to power which is so
conspicuous in modern life. In Dobu and Zuñi, however,
it is not so easy to see what aspects of life are touched
lightly by their configurations. This may be due to the
nature of the cultural pattern, or it may be due to a genius
for consistency. At the present time it is not possible to
decide.

There is a sociological fact that must be taken into account in any understanding of cultural integration. This
is the significance of diffusion. A vast body of anthropological work has been devoted to plumbing the facts of
human imitativeness. The extent of the primitive areas
over which traits have diffused is one of the most startling
facts of anthropology. Traits of costume, of techniques,
of a ceremonial, of mythology, of economic exchange at

marriage, are spread over whole continents, and every tribe on one continent will often possess the trait in some form. Nevertheless, certain regions in these great areas have impressed distinctive goals and motivations upon this raw material. The Pueblos use the methods of agriculture, the magic devices, the widespread myths that belong to great sections of North America. An Apollonian culture on another continent would necessarily work with other raw material. The two cultures would have in common the direction in which they had modified the raw material that was available on each continent, but the available traits would be dissimilar. Comparable configurations in different parts of the world will therefore inevitably have different content. We can understand the direction in which Pueblo culture has moved by comparing it with other North American cultures, those which share the same elements but which use them in a different fashion. In a similar way we can best understand the Apollonian stress in Greek civilization by studying it in its local setting among the cultures of the eastern Mediterranean. Any clear understanding of the processes of cultural integration must take its point of departure from a knowledge of the facts of diffusion.

A recognition of these processes of integration, on the other hand, gives a quite different picture of the nature of widespread traits. The usual topical studies of marriage, or of initiation, or of religion, assume that each trait is a special area of behaviour which has generated its own motivations. Westermarck explains marriage as a situation of sex preference, and the usual interpretation of initiation procedures is that they are the result of puberty upheavals. Therefore all their thousand modifications are facts in a single series, and only ring the changes upon some one impulse or necessity that is implicit in the generic situation.

Very few cultures handle their great occasions in any such simple fashion. These occasions, whether of marriage or death or the invocation of the supernatural, are situations that each society seizes upon to express its characteristic purposes. The motivations that dominate it do not come into existence in the particular selected situation, but are impressed upon it by the general character of the culture. Marriage may have no reference to mating preferences, which are provided for in other ways, but accumulation of wives may be the current version of the accumulation of wealth. Economic practices may depart so far from their primary rôle of providing necessaries of food and clothing that all agricultural techniques may be directed toward piling up in lavish display many times the necessary food supply of the people and allowing it to rot ostentatiously for pride's sake.

The difficulty of understanding from the nature of the occasion even comparatively simple cultural responses has been clear over and over again in the description of the three cultures we have selected. Mourning, in terms of its occasion, is a grief or relief reaction to a loss situation. It happens that no one of the three cultures makes this type of response to its mourning institutions. The Pueblos come closest in that their rites treat the death of a relative as one of the important emergencies when society marshals its forces to put discomfort out of the way. Though grief is hardly institutionalized in their procedures, they recognize the loss situation as an emergency which it is necessary to minimize. Among the Kwakiutl, regardless of whether or not there may also be genuine sorrow, mourning institutions are special instances of a cultural paranoia

243

according to which they regard themselves as shamed by the death of their relatives and rouse themselves to get even. In Dobu the mourning institutions have much in common, but primarily they are punishments inflicted by the blood kin upon the spouse for having caused the death of one of their number. That is, the mourning institutions are again one of numberless occasions which Dobu interprets as treachery, and handles by selecting a victim whom it may punish.

It is an extraordinarily simple matter for tradition to take any occasion that the environment or the life-cycle provides and use it to channel purposes generically unrelated. The particular character of the event may figure so slightly that the death of a child from mumps involves the killing of a completely unimplicated person. Or a girl's first menstruation involves the redistribution of practically all the property of a tribe. Mourning, or marriage, or puberty rites, or economics are not special items of human behaviour, each with their own generic drives and motivations which have determined their past history and will determine their future, but certain occasions which any society may seize upon to express its important cultural intentions.

The significant sociological unit, from this point of view, therefore, is not the institution but the cultural configuration. The studies of the family, of primitive economics, or of moral ideas need to be broken up into studies that emphasize the different configurations that in instance after instance have dominated these traits. The peculiar nature of Kwakiutl life can never be clear in a discussion which singles out the family for discussion and derives Kwakiutl behaviour at marriage from the marriage situation. Similarly, marriage in our own civilization is a situation which can never be made clear as a mere variant on mating and domesticity. Without the clue that in our civilization at large man's paramount aim is to amass private possessions and multiply occasions of display, the modern position of the wife and the modern emotions of jealousy are alike unintelligible. Our attitudes toward our children are equally evidences of this same cultural goal. Our children are not individuals whose rights and tastes are casually respected from infancy, as they are in some primitive societies, but special responsibilities, like our possessions, to which we succumb or in which we glory, as the case may be. They are fundamentally extensions of our own egos and give a special opportunity for the display of authority. The pattern is not inherent in the parent-children situation, as we so glibly assume. It is impressed upon the situation by the major drives of our culture, and it is only one of the occasions in which we follow our traditional obsessions.

As we become increasingly culture-conscious, we shall be able to isolate the tiny core that is generic in a situation and the vast accretions that are local and cultural and man-made. The fact that these accretions are not inevitable consequences of the situation as such does not make them easier to change or less important in our behaviour. Indeed they are probably harder to change than we have realized. Detailed changes in the mother's nursery behaviour, for instance, may well be inadequate to save a neurotic child when he is trapped in a repugnant situation which is reinforced by every contact he makes and which will extend past his mother to his school and his business and his wife. The whole course of life which is presented to him emphasizes rivalry and ownership. Probably the child's way out lies through luck or detachment. In any case, the solution of the problem might well place less emphasis upon the difficulties inherent in the parent-child situation and more upon the forms taken in Western behaviour by ego-extension and the exploiting of personal relations.

The problem of social value is intimately involved in the fact of the different patternings of cultures. Discussions of social value have usually been content to characterize certain human traits as desirable and to indicate a social goal that would involve these virtues. Certainly, it is said, exploitation of others in personal relations and overweening claims of the ego are bad whereas absorption in group activities is good; a temper is good that seeks satisfaction neither in sadism nor in masochism and is willing to live and let live. A social order, however, which like Zuñi standardizes this 'good' is far from Utopian. It manifests likewise the defects of its virtues. It has no place, for instance, for dispositions we are accustomed to value highly, such as force of will or personal initiative or the disposition to take up arms against a sea of troubles. It is incorrigibly mild. The group activity that fills existence in Zuñi is out of touch with human life — with birth, love, death, success, failure, and prestige. A ritual pageant serves their purpose and minimizes more human interests. The freedom from any forms of social exploitation or of social sadism appears on the other side of the coin as endless ceremonialism not designed to serve major ends of human existence. It is the old inescapable fact that every upper has its lower, every right side its left.

The complexity of the problem of social values is exceptionally clear in Kwakiutl culture. The chief motive that the institutions of the Kwakiutl rely upon and which they share in great measure with modern society is the motive of rivalry. Rivalry is a struggle that is not centred upon the real objects of the activity but upon outdoing a competitor. The attention is no longer directed toward providing adequately for a family or toward owning goods that can be utilized or enjoyed, but toward outdistancing one's neighbours and owning more than anyone else. Everything else is lost sight of in the one great aim of victory. Rivalry does not, like competition, keep its eyes upon the original activity; whether making a basket or selling shoes, it creates an artificial situation: the game of showing that one can win out over others.

Rivalry is notoriously wasteful. It ranks low in the scale of human values. It is a tyranny from which, once it is encouraged in any culture, no man may free himself. The wish for superiority is gargantuan; it can never be satisfied. The contest goes on forever. The more goods the community accumulates, the greater the counters with which men play, but the game is as far from being won as it was when the stakes were small. In Kwakiutl institutions, such rivalry reaches its final absurdity in equating investment with wholesale destruction of goods. They contest for superiority chiefly in accumulation of goods, but often also, and without a consciousness of the contrast, in breaking in pieces their highest units of value, their coppers, and in making bonfires of their house-planks, their blankets and canoes. The social waste is obvious. It is just as obvious in the obsessive rivalry of *Middletown* where houses are built and clothing bought and entertainments attended that each family may prove that it has not been left out of the game.

It is an unattractive picture. In Kwakiutl life the rivalry is carried out in such a way that all success must be built upon the ruin of rivals; in *Middletown* in such a way that individual choices and direct satisfactions are reduced to a minimum and conformity is sought beyond all other human gratifications. In both cases it is clear that wealth is not sought and valued for its direct satisfaction of human needs but as a series of counters in the game of rivalry. If the will to victory were eliminated from the economic life, as it is in Zuñi, distribution and consumption of wealth would follow quite different 'laws.'

Nevertheless, as we can see in Kwakiutl society and in the rugged individualism of American pioneer life, the pursuit of victory can give vigor and zest to human existence. Kwakiutl life is rich and forceful in its own terms. Its chosen goal has its appropriate virtues, and social values in Kwakiutl civilization are even more inextricably mixed than they are in Zuñi. Whatever the social orientation, a society which exemplifies it vigorously will develop certain virtues that are natural to the goals it has chosen, and it is most unlikely that even the best society will be able to stress in one social order all the virtues we prize in human life. Utopia cannot be achieved as a final and perfect structure within which human life will reach a faultless flowering. Utopias of this sort should be recognized as pure day-dreaming. Real improvements in the social order depend upon more modest and more difficult discriminations. It is possible to scrutinize different institutions and cast up their cost in terms of social capital, in terms of the less desirable behaviour traits they stimulate, and in terms of human suffering and frustration. If any society wishes to pay that cost for its chosen and congenial traits, certain values will develop within this pattern, however 'bad' it may be. But the risk is great, and the social order may not be able to pay the price. It may break down beneath them with all the consequent wanton waste of revolution and economic and emotional disaster. In modern society this problem is the most pressing this generation has to face, and those who are obsessed with it too often imagine that an economic reorganization will give the world a Utopia out of their day-dreams, forgetting that no social order can separate its virtues from the defects of its virtues. There is no royal road to a real Utopia.

There is, however, one difficult exercise to which we may accustom ourselves as we become increasingly culture-conscious. We may train ourselves to pass judgment upon the dominant traits of our own civilization. It is difficult enough for anyone brought up under their power to recognize them. It is still more difficult to discount, upon necessity, our predilection for them. They are as familiar as an old loved homestead. Any world in which they do not appear seems to us cheerless and untenable. Yet it is these very traits which by the operation of a fundamental cultural process are most often carried to extremes. They overreach themselves, and more than any other traits they are likely to get out of hand. Just at the very point where there is greatest likelihood of the need of criticism, we are bound to be least critical. Revision comes, but it comes by way of revolution or of breakdown. The possibility of orderly progress is shut off because the generation in question could not make any appraisal of its overgrown institutions. It could not cast them up in terms of profit and loss because it had lost its power to look at them objectively. The situation had to reach a breaking-point before relief was possible.

Appraisal of our own dominant traits has so far waited till the trait in question was no longer a living issue. Religion was not objectively discussed till it was no longer the cultural trait to which our civilization was most deeply committed. Now for the first time the comparative study of religions is free to pursue any point at issue. It is not yet possible to discuss capitalism in the same way, and during wartime, warfare and the problems of international relations are similarly tabu. Yet the dominant traits of our civilization need special scrutiny. We need to realize that they are compulsive, not in proportion as they are basic and essential in human behaviour, but rather in the degree to which they are local and overgrown in our own culture. The one way of life which the Dobuan regards as basic in human nature is one that is fundamentally treacherous and safeguarded with morbid fears. The Kwakiutl similarly cannot see life except as a series of rivalry situations, wherein success is measured by the humiliation of one's fellows. Their belief is based on the importance of these modes of life in their civilizations. But the importance of an institution in a culture gives no direct indication of its usefulness or its inevitability. The argument is suspect, and any cultural control which we may be able to exercise will depend upon the degree to which we can evaluate objectively the favoured and passionately fostered traits of our Western civilization.

# VIII

## The Individual and the Pattern of Culture

THE large corporate behaviour we have discussed is nevertheless the behaviour of individuals. It is the world with which each person is severally presented, the world from which he must make his individual life. Accounts of any civilization condensed into a few dozen pages must necessarily throw into relief the group standards and describe individual behaviour as it exemplifies the motivations of that culture. The exigencies of the situation are misleading only when this necessity is read off as implying that he is submerged in an overpowering ocean.

There is no proper antagonism between the rôle of society and that of the individual. One of the most misleading misconceptions due to this nineteenth-century dualism was the idea that what was subtracted from society was added to the individual and what was subtracted from the individual was added to society. Philosophies of freedom, political creeds of *laissez faire,* revolutions that have unseated dynasties, have been built on this dualism. The quarrel in anthropological theory between the importance of the culture pattern and of the individual is only a small ripple from this fundamental conception of the nature of society.

In reality, society and the individual are not antagonists. His culture provides the raw material of which the individual makes his life. If it is meagre, the individual suffers; if it is rich, the individual has the chance to rise to his opportunity. Every private interest of every man and woman is served by the enrichment of the traditional stores of his civilization. The richest musical sensitivity can operate only within the equipment and standards of its tradition. It will add, perhaps importantly, to that tradition, but its achievement remains in proportion to the instruments and musical theory which the culture has provided. In the same fashion a talent for observation expends itself in some Melanesian tribe upon the negligible borders of the magico-religious field. For a realization of its potentialities it is dependent upon the development of scientific methodology, and it has no fruition unless the culture has elaborated the necessary concepts and tools.

The man in the street still thinks in terms of a necessary antagonism between society and the individual. In large measure this is because in our civilization the regulative activities of society are singled out, and we tend to identify society with the restrictions the law imposes upon us. The law lays down the number of miles per hour that I may drive an automobile. If it takes this restriction away, I am by that much the freer. This basis for a fundamental antagonism between society and the individual is naïve indeed when it is extended as a basic philosophical and political notion. Society is only incidentally and in certain situations regulative, and law is not equivalent to the social order. In the simpler homogeneous cultures collective habit or custom may quite supersede the necessity for any development of formal legal authority. American Indians sometimes say: 'In the old days, there were no fights about hunting grounds or fishing territories. There was no law then, so everybody did what was right.' The phrasing makes it clear that in their old life they did not think of themselves as submitting to a social control imposed upon them from without. Even in our civilization the law is never more than a crude implement of society, and one it is often enough necessary to check in its arrogant career. It is never to be read off as if it were the equivalent of the social order.

Society in its full sense as we have discussed it in this volume is never an entity separable from the individuals who compose it. No individual can arrive even at the threshold of his potentialities without a culture in which he participates. Conversely, no civilization has in it any element which in the last analysis is not the contribution of an individual. Where else could any trait come from except from the behaviour of a man or a woman or a child?

It is largely because of the traditional acceptance of a conflict between society and the individual, that emphasis upon cultural behaviour is so often interpreted as a denial of the autonomy of the individual. The reading of Sumner's *Folkways* usually rouses a protest at the limitations such an interpretation places upon the scope and initiative of the individual. Anthropology is often believed to be a counsel of despair which makes untenable a beneficent human illusion. But no anthropologist with a background of experience of other cultures has ever believed that individuals were automatons, mechanically carrying out the decrees of their civilization. No culture yet observed has been able to eradicate the differences in the temperaments of the persons who compose it. It is always a give-and-take. The problem of the individual is not clarified by stressing the antagonism between culture and the individual, but by stressing their mutual reinforcement. This

253

rapport is so close that it is not possible to discuss patterns
of culture without considering specifically their relation to
individual psychology.

We have seen that any society selects some segment of
the arc of possible human behaviour, and in so far as it
achieves integration its institutions tend to further the
expression of its selected segment and to inhibit opposite
expressions. But these opposite expressions are the congenial responses, nevertheless, of a certain proportion of
the carriers of that culture. We have already discussed
the reasons for believing that this selection is primarily
cultural and not biological. We cannot, therefore, even
on theoretical grounds imagine that all the congenial
responses of all its people will be equally served by the
institutions of any culture. To understand the behaviour
of the individual, it is not merely necessary to relate his
personal life-history to his endowments, and to measure
these against an arbitrarily selected normality. It is necessary also to relate his congenial responses to the behaviour
that is singled out in the institutions of his culture.

The vast proportion of all individuals who are born into
any society always and whatever the idiosyncrasies of its
institutions, assume, as we have seen, the behaviour dictated by that society. This fact is always interpreted by
the carriers of that culture as being due to the fact that
their particular institutions reflect an ultimate and universal sanity. The actual reason is quite different. Most
people are shaped to the form of their culture because of
the enormous malleability of their original endowment.
They are plastic to the moulding force of the society into
which they are born. It does not matter whether, with
the Northwest Coast, it requires delusions of self-reference,
or with our own civilization the amassing of possessions.

254

In any case the great mass of individuals take quite readily the form that is presented to them.

They do not all, however, find it equally congenial, and those are favoured and fortunate whose potentialities most nearly coincide with the type of behaviour selected by their society. Those who, in a situation in which they are frustrated, naturally seek ways of putting the occasion out of sight as expeditiously as possible are well served in Pueblo culture. Southwest institutions, as we have seen, minimize the situations in which serious frustration can arise, and when it cannot be avoided, as in death, they provide means to put it behind them with all speed.

On the other hand, those who react to frustration as to an insult and whose first thought is to get even are amply provided for on the Northwest Coast. They may extend their native reaction to situations in which their paddle breaks or their canoe overturns or to the loss of relatives by death. They rise from their first reaction of sulking to thrust back in return, to 'fight' with property or with weapons. Those who can assuage despair by the act of bringing shame to others can register freely and without conflict in this society, because their proclivities are deeply channelled in their culture. In Dobu those whose first impulse is to select a victim and project their misery upon him in procedures of punishment are equally fortunate.

It happens that none of the three cultures we have described meets frustration in a realistic manner by stressing the resumption of the original and interrupted experience. It might even seem that in the case of death this is impossible. But the institutions of many cultures nevertheless attempt nothing less. Some of the forms the restitution takes are repugnant to us, but that only makes it clearer that in cultures where frustration is handled by giving rein to this potential behaviour, the institutions of that society carry this course to extraordinary lengths. Among the Eskimo, when one man has killed another, the family of the man who has been murdered may take the murderer to replace the loss within its own group. The murderer then becomes the husband of the woman who has been widowed by his act. This is an emphasis upon restitution that ignores all other aspects of the situation — those which seem to us the only important ones; but when tradition selects some such objective it is quite in character that it should disregard all else.

Restitution may be carried out in mourning situations in ways that are less uncongenial to the standards of Western civilization. Among certain of the Central Algonkian Indians south of the Great Lakes the usual procedure was adoption. Upon the death of a child a similar child was put into his place. This similarity was determined in all sorts of ways: often a captive brought in from a raid was taken into the family in the full sense and given all the privileges and the tenderness that had originally been given to the dead child. Or quite as often it was the child's closest playmate, or a child from another related settlement who resembled the dead child in height and features. In such cases the family from which the child was chosen was supposed to be pleased, and indeed in most cases it was by no means the great step that it would be under our institutions. The child had always recognized many 'mothers' and many homes where he was on familiar footing. The new allegiance made him thoroughly at home in still another household. From the point of view of the bereaved parents, the situation had been met by a restitution of the *status quo* that existed before the death of their child.

Persons who primarily mourn the situation rather than

the lost individual are provided for in these cultures to a degree which is unimaginable under our institutions. We recognize the possibility of such solace, but we are careful to minimize its connection with the original loss. We do not use it as a mourning technique, and individuals who would be well satisfied with such a solution are left unsupported until the difficult crisis is past.

There is another possible attitude toward frustration. It is the precise opposite of the Pueblo attitude, and we have described it among the other Dionysian reactions of the Plains Indians. Instead of trying to get past the experience with the least possible discomfiture, it finds relief in the most extravagant expression of grief. The Indians of the plains capitalized the utmost indulgences and exacted violent demonstrations of emotion as a matter of course.

In any group of individuals we can recognize those to whom these different reactions to frustration and grief are congenial: ignoring it, indulging it by uninhibited expression, getting even, punishing a victim, and seeking restitution of the original situation. In the psychiatric records of our own society, some of these impulses are recognized as bad ways of dealing with the situation, some as good. The bad ones are said to lead to maladjustments and insanities, the good ones to adequate social functioning. It is clear, however, that the correlation does not lie between any one 'bad' tendency and abnormality in any absolute sense. The desire to run away from grief, to leave it behind at all costs, does not foster psychotic behaviour where, as among the Pueblos, it is mapped out by institutions and supported by every attitude of the group. The Pueblos are not a neurotic people. Their culture gives the impression of fostering mental health.

Similarly, the paranoid attitudes so violently expressed among the Kwakiutl are known in psychiatric theory derived from our own civilization as thoroughly 'bad'; that is, they lead in various ways to the breakdown of personality. But it is just those individuals among the Kwakiutl who find it congenial to give the freest expression to these attitudes who nevertheless are the leaders of Kwakiutl society and find greatest personal fulfilment in its culture.

Obviously, adequate personal adjustment does not depend upon following certain motivations and eschewing others. The correlation is in a different direction. Just as those are favoured whose congenial responses are closest to that behaviour which characterizes their society, so those are disoriented whose congenial responses fall in that arc of behaviour which is not capitalized by their culture. These abnormals are those who are not supported by the institutions of their civilization. They are the exceptions who have not easily taken the traditional forms of their culture.

For a valid comparative psychiatry, these disoriented persons who have failed to adapt themselves adequately to their cultures are of first importance. The issue in psychiatry has been too often confused by starting from a fixed list of symptoms instead of from the study of those whose characteristic reactions are denied validity in their society.

The tribes we have described have all of them their non-participating 'abnormal' individuals. The individual in Dobu who was thoroughly disoriented was the man who was naturally friendly and found activity an end in itself. He was a pleasant fellow who did not seek to overthrow his fellows or to punish them. He worked for anyone who asked him, and he was tireless in carrying out their commands. He was not filled by a terror of the dark like his fellows, and he did not, as they did, utterly inhibit simple public responses of friendliness toward women closely related, like a wife or sister. He often patted them playfully in public. In any other Dobuan this was scandalous behaviour, but in him it was regarded as merely silly. The village treated him in a kindly enough fashion, not taking advantage of him or making a sport of ridiculing him, but he was definitely regarded as one who was outside the game.

The behaviour congenial to the Dobuan simpleton has been made the ideal in certain periods of our own civilization, and there are still vocations in which his responses are accepted in most Western communities. Especially if a woman is in question, she is well provided for even today in our *mores*, and functions honourably in her family and community. The fact that the Dobuan could not function in his culture was not a consequence of the particular responses that were congenial to him, but of the chasm between them and the cultural pattern.

Most ethnologists have had similar experiences in recognizing that the persons who are put outside the pale of society with contempt are not those who would be placed there by another culture. Lowie found among the Crow Indians of the plains a man of exceptional knowledge of his cultural forms. He was interested in considering these objectively and in correlating different facets. He had an interest in genealogical facts and was invaluable on points of history. Altogether he was an ideal interpreter of Crow life. These traits, however, were not those which were the password to honour among the Crow. He had a definite shrinking from physical danger, and bravado was the tribal virtue. To make matters worse he had attempted to gain recognition by claiming a war honour which was fraudulent. He was proved not to have brought in, as he claimed, a picketed horse from the enemy's camp. To lay false claim to war honours was a paramount sin among the Crow, and by the general opinion, constantly reiterated, he was regarded as irresponsible and incompetent.

Such situations can be paralleled with the attitude in our civilization toward a man who does not succeed in regarding personal possessions as supremely important. Our hobo population is constantly fed by those to whom the accumulation of property is not a sufficient motivation. In case these individuals ally themselves with the hoboes, public opinion regards them as potentially vicious, as indeed because of the asocial situation into which they are thrust they readily become. In case, however, these men compensate by emphasizing their artistic temperament and become members of expatriated groups of petty artists, opinion regards them not as vicious but as silly. In any case they are unsupported by the forms of their society, and the effort to express themselves satisfactorily is ordinarily a greater task than they can achieve.

The dilemma of such an individual is often most successfully solved by doing violence to his strongest natural impulses and accepting the rôle the culture honours. In case he is a person to whom social recognition is necessary, it is ordinarily his only possible course. One of the most striking individuals in Zuñi had accepted this necessity. In a society that thoroughly distrusts authority of any sort, he had a native personal magnetism that singled him out in any group. In a society that exalts moderation and the easiest way, he was turbulent and could act violently upon occasion. In a society that praises a pliant personality that 'talks lots' — that is, that chatters in a friendly fashion — he was scornful and aloof. Zuñi's only reaction to such personalities is to brand them as witches. He was said to have been seen peering through a window from outside, and this is a sure mark of a witch. At any rate, he got drunk one day and boasted that they could not kill him. He was taken before the war priests who hung him by his thumbs from the rafters till he should confess to his witchcraft. This is the usual procedure in a charge of witchcraft. However, he dispatched a messenger to the government troops. When they came, his shoulders were already crippled for life, and the officer of the law was left with no recourse but to imprison the war priests who had been responsible for the enormity. One of these war priests was probably the most respected and important person in recent Zuñi history, and when he returned after imprisonment in the state penitentiary he never resumed his priestly offices. He regarded his power as broken. It was a revenge that is probably unique in Zuñi history. It involved, of course, a challenge to the priesthoods, against whom the witch by his act openly aligned himself.

The course of his life in the forty years that followed this defiance was not, however, what we might easily predict. A witch is not barred from his membership in cult groups because he has been condemned, and the way to recognition lay through such activity. He possessed a remarkable verbal memory and a sweet singing voice. He learned unbelievable stores of mythology, of esoteric ritual, of cult songs. Many hundreds of pages of stories and ritual poetry were taken down from his dictation before he died, and he regarded his songs as much more extensive. He became indispensable in ceremonial life and before he died was the governor of Zuñi. The congenial bent of his personality threw him into irreconcilable conflict with his society, and he solved his dilemma by turning an incidental talent to account. As we might well expect, he was not a happy man. As governor of Zuñi, and high in his cult groups, a marked man in his community, he was obsessed by death. He was a cheated man in the midst of a mildly happy populace.

It is easy to imagine the life he might have lived among the Plains Indians, where every institution favoured the traits that were native to him. The personal authority, the turbulence, the scorn, would all have been honoured in the career he could have made his own. The unhappiness that was inseparable from his temperament as a successful priest and governor of Zuñi would have had no place as a war chief of the Cheyenne; it was not a function of the traits of his native endowment but of the standards of the culture in which he found no outlet for his native responses.

The individuals we have so far discussed are not in any sense psychopathic. They illustrate the dilemma of the individual whose congenial drives are not provided for in the institutions of his culture. This dilemma becomes of psychiatric importance when the behaviour in question is regarded as categorically abnormal in a society. Western civilization tends to regard even a mild homosexual as an abnormal. The clinical picture of homosexuality stresses the neuroses and psychoses to which it gives rise, and emphasizes almost equally the inadequate functioning of the invert and his behaviour. We have only to turn to other cultures, however, to realize that homosexuals have by no means been uniformly inadequate to the social situation. They have not always failed to function. In some societies they have even been especially acclaimed.

Plato's *Republic* is, of course, the most convincing statement of the honourable estate of homosexuality. It is
presented as a major means to the good life, and Plato's
high ethical evaluation of this response was upheld in the
customary behaviour of Greece at that period.

The American Indians do not make Plato's high moral
claims for homosexuality, but homosexuals are often regarded as exceptionally able. In most of North America
there exists the institution of the *berdache*, as the French
called them. These men-women were men who at puberty
or thereafter took the dress and the occupations of women.
Sometimes they married other men and lived with them.
Sometimes they were men with no inversion, persons of
weak sexual endowment who chose this rôle to avoid the
jeers of the women. The berdaches were never regarded
as of first-rate supernatural power, as similar men-women
were in Siberia, but rather as leaders in women's occupations, good healers in certain diseases, or, among certain
tribes, as the genial organizers of social affairs. They
were usually, in spite of the manner in which they were
accepted, regarded with a certain embarrassment. It was
thought slightly ridiculous to address as 'she' a person
who was known to be a man and who, as in Zuñi, would be
buried on the men's side of the cemetery. But they were
socially placed. The emphasis in most tribes was upon the
fact that men who took over women's occupations excelled
by reason of their strength and initiative and were therefore leaders in women's techniques and in the accumulation of those forms of property made by women. One of
the best known of all the Zuñis of a generation ago was the
man-woman We-wha, who was, in the words of his friend,
Mrs. Stevenson, 'certainly the strongest person in Zuñi,
both mentally and physically.' His remarkable memory

for ritual made him a chief personage on ceremonial occasions, and his strength and intelligence made him a leader in all kinds of crafts.

The men-women of Zuñi are not all strong, self-reliant personages. Some of them take this refuge to protect themselves against their inability to take part in men's activities. One is almost a simpleton, and one, hardly more than a little boy, has delicate features like a girl's. There are obviously several reasons why a person becomes a berdache in Zuñi, but whatever the reason, men who have chosen openly to assume women's dress have the same chance as any other persons to establish themselves as functioning members of the society. Their response is socially recognized. If they have native ability, they can give it scope; if they are weak creatures, they fail in terms of their weakness of character, not in terms of their inversion.

The Indian institution of the berdache was most strongly developed on the plains. The Dakota had a saying, 'fine possessions like a berdache's,' and it was the epitome of praise for any woman's household possessions. A berdache had two strings to his bow, he was supreme in women's techniques, and he could also support his *ménage* by the man's activity of hunting. Therefore no one was richer. When especially fine beadwork or dressed skins were desired for ceremonial occasions, the berdache's work was sought in preference to any other's. It was his social adequacy that was stressed above all else. As in Zuñi, the attitude toward him is ambivalent and touched with malaise in the face of a recognized incongruity. Social scorn, however, was visited not upon the berdache but upon the man who lived with him. The latter was regarded as a weak man who had chosen an easy berth instead of the recognized goals of their culture; he did not contribute to the household, which was already a model for all households through the sole efforts of the berdache. His sexual adjustment was not singled out in the judgment that was passed upon him, but in terms of his economic adjustment he was an outcast.

When the homosexual response is regarded as a perversion, however, the invert is immediately exposed to all the conflicts to which aberrants are always exposed. His guilt, his sense of inadequacy, his failures, are consequences of the disrepute which social tradition visits upon him, and few people can achieve a satisfactory life unsupported by the standards of their society. The adjustments that society demands of them would strain any man's vitality, and the consequences of this conflict we identify with their homosexuality.

Trance is a similar abnormality in our society. Even a very mild mystic is aberrant in Western civilization. In order to study trance or catalepsy within our own social groups, we have to go to the case histories of the abnormal. Therefore the correlation between trance experience and the neurotic and psychotic seems perfect. As in the case of the homosexual, however, it is a local correlation characteristic of our century. Even in our own cultural background other eras give different results. In the Middle Ages when Catholicism made the ecstatic experience the mark of sainthood, the trance experience was greatly valued, and those to whom the response was congenial, instead of being overwhelmed by a catastrophe as in our century, were given confidence in the pursuit of their careers. It was a validation of ambitions, not a stigma of insanity. Individuals who were susceptible to trance, therefore, succeeded or failed in terms of their native capacities, but since trance experience was highly valued, a great leader was very likely to be capable of it.

Among primitive peoples, trance and catalepsy have been honoured in the extreme. Some of the Indian tribes of California accorded prestige principally to those who passed through certain trance experiences. Not all of these tribes believed that it was exclusively women who were so blessed, but among the Shasta this was the convention. Their shamans were women, and they were accorded the greatest prestige in the community. They were chosen because of their constitutional liability to trance and allied manifestations. One day the woman who was so destined, while she was about her usual work, fell suddenly to the ground. She had heard a voice speaking to her in tones of the greatest intensity. Turning, she had seen a man with drawn bow and arrow. He commanded her to sing on pain of being shot through the heart by his arrow, but under the stress of the experience she fell senseless. Her family gathered. She was lying rigid, hardly breathing. They knew that for some time she had had dreams of a special character which indicated a shamanistic calling, dreams of escaping grizzly bears, falling off cliffs or trees, or of being surrounded by swarms of yellow-jackets. The community knew therefore what to expect. After a few hours the woman began to moan gently and to roll about upon the ground, trembling violently. She was supposed to be repeating the song which she had been told to sing and which during the trance had been taught her by the spirit. As she revived, her moaning became more and more clearly the spirit's song until at last she called out the name of the spirit itself, and immediately blood oozed from her mouth.

When the woman had come to herself after the first

encounter with her spirit, she danced that night her first initiatory shaman's dance. For three nights she danced, holding herself by a rope that was swung from the ceiling. On the third night she had to receive in her body her power from her spirit. She was dancing, and as she felt the approach of the moment she called out, 'He will shoot me, he will shoot me.' Her friends stood close, for when she reeled in a kind of cataleptic seizure, they had to seize her before she fell or she would die. From this time on she had in her body a visible materialization of her spirit's power, an icicle-like object which in her dances thereafter she would exhibit, producing it from one part of her body and returning it to another part. From this time on she continued to validate her supernatural power by further cataleptic demonstrations, and she was called upon in great emergencies of life and death, for curing and for divination and for counsel. She became, in other words, by this procedure a woman of great power and importance.

It is clear that, far from regarding cataleptic seizures as blots upon the family escutcheon and as evidences of dreaded disease, cultural approval had seized upon them and made of them the pathway to authority over one's fellows. They were the outstanding characteristic of the most respected social type, the type which functioned with most honour and reward in the community. It was precisely the cataleptic individuals who in this culture were singled out for authority and leadership.

The possible usefulness of 'abnormal' types in a social structure, provided they are types that are culturally selected by that group, is illustrated from every part of the world. The shamans of Siberia dominate their communities. According to the ideas of these peoples, they are individuals who by submission to the will of the spirits have been cured of a grievous illness — the onset of the seizures — and have acquired by this means great supernatural power and incomparable vigour and health. Some, during the period of the call, are violently insane for several years; others irresponsible to the point where they have to be constantly watched lest they wander off in the snow and freeze to death; others ill and emaciated to the point of death, sometimes with bloody sweat. It is the shamanistic practice which constitutes their cure, and the extreme exertion of a Siberian séance leaves them, they claim, rested and able to enter immediately upon a similar performance. Cataleptic seizures are regarded as an essential part of any shamanistic performance.

A good description of the neurotic condition of the shaman and the attention given him by his society is an old one by Canon Callaway, recorded in the words of an old Zulu of South Africa:

> The condition of a man who is about to become a diviner is this; at first he is apparently robust, but in the process of time he begins to be delicate, not having any real disease, but being delicate. He habitually avoids certain kinds of food, choosing what he likes, and he does not eat much of that; he is continually complaining of pains in different parts of his body. And he tells them that he has dreamt that he was carried away by a river. He dreams of many things, and his body is muddied [as a river] and he becomes a house of dreams. He dreams constantly of many things, and on awaking tells his friends, 'My body is muddied today; I dreamt many men were killing me, and I escaped I know not how. On waking one part of my body felt different from other parts; it was no longer alike all over.' At last that man is very ill, and they go to the diviners to enquire.
>
> The diviners do not at once see that he is about to have a soft head [that is, the sensitivity associated with shamanism]. It is difficult for them to see the truth; they continually talk

nonsense and make false statements, until all the man's cattle
are devoured at their command, they saying that the spirit
of his people demands cattle, that it may eat food. At length
all the man's property is expended, he still being ill; and
they no longer know what to do, for he has no more cattle,
and his friends help him in such things as he needs.

At length a diviner comes and says that all the others are
wrong. He says, 'He is possessed by the spirits. There is
nothing else. They move in him, being divided into two
parties; some say, "No, we do not wish our child injured. We
do not wish it." It is for that reason he does not get well. If
you bar the way against the spirits, you will be killing him.
For he will not be a diviner; neither will he ever be a man again.'

So the man may be ill two years without getting better;
perhaps even longer than that. He is confined to his house.
This continues till his hair falls off. And his body is dry and
scurfy; he does not like to anoint himself. He shows that he
is about to be a diviner by yawning again and again, and by
sneezing continually. It is apparent also from his being very
fond of snuff; not allowing any long time to pass without
taking some. And people begin to see that he has had what is
good given to him.

After that he is ill; he has convulsions, and when water
has been poured on him they then cease for a time. He
habitually sheds tears, at first slight, then at last he weeps
aloud and when the people are asleep he is heard making a
noise and wakes the people by his singing; he has composed
a song, and the men and women awake and go to sing in concert with him. All the people of the village are troubled by
want of sleep; for a man who is becoming a diviner causes
great trouble, for he does not sleep, but works constantly with
his brain; his sleep is merely by snatches, and he wakes up
singing many songs; and people who are near quit their villages by night when they hear him singing aloud and go to
sing in concert. Perhaps he sings till morning, no one having
slept. And then he leaps about the house like a frog; and the
house becomes too small for him, and he goes out leaping and
singing, and shaking like a reed in the water, and dripping with
perspiration.

In this state of things they daily expect his death; he is now but skin and bones, and they think that tomorrow's sun will not leave him alive. At this time many cattle are eaten, for the people encourage his becoming a diviner. At length [in a dream] an ancient ancestral spirit is pointed out to him. This spirit says to him, 'Go to So-and-so and he will churn for you an emetic [the medicine the drinking of which is a part of shamanistic initiation] that you may be a diviner altogether.' Then he is quiet a few days, having gone to the diviner to have the medicine churned for him; and he comes back quite another man, being now cleansed and a diviner indeed.

Thereafter for life, when he is possessed by his spirits, he foretells events and finds lost articles.

It is clear that culture may value and make socially available even highly unstable human types. If it chooses to treat their peculiarities as the most valued variants of human behaviour, the individuals in question will rise to the occasion and perform their social rôles without reference to our usual ideas of the types who can make social adjustments and those who cannot. Those who function inadequately in any society are not those with certain fixed 'abnormal' traits, but may well be those whose responses have received no support in the institutions of their culture. The weakness of these aberrants is in great measure illusory. It springs, not from the fact that they are lacking in necessary vigour, but that they are individuals whose native responses are not reaffirmed by society. They are, as Sapir phrases it, 'alienated from an impossible world.'

The person unsupported by the standards of his time and place and left naked to the winds of ridicule has been unforgettably drawn in European literature in the figure of Don Quixote. Cervantes turned upon a tradition still honoured in the abstract the limelight of a changed set of practical standards, and his poor old man, the orthodox upholder of the romantic chivalry of another generation, became a simpleton. The windmills with which he tilted were the serious antagonists of a hardly vanished world, but to tilt with them when the world no longer called them serious was to rave. He loved his Dulcinea in the best traditional manner of chivalry, but another version of love was fashionable for the moment, and his fervour was counted to him for madness.

These contrasting worlds which, in the primitive cultures we have considered, are separated from one another in space, in modern Occidental history more often succeed one another in time. The major issue is the same in either case, but the importance of understanding the phenomenon is far greater in the modern world where we cannot escape if we would from the succession of configurations in time. When each culture is a world in itself, relatively stable like the Eskimo culture, for example, and geographically isolated from all others, the issue is academic. But our civilization must deal with cultural standards that go down under our eyes and new ones that arise from a shadow upon the horizon. We must be willing to take account of changing normalities even when the question is of the morality in which we were bred. Just as we are handicapped in dealing with ethical problems so long as we hold to an absolute definition of morality, so we are handicapped in dealing with human society so long as we identify our local normalities with the inevitable necessities of existence.

No society has yet attempted a self-conscious direction of the process by which its new normalities are created in the next generation. Dewey has pointed out how possible and yet how drastic such social engineering would be. For some traditional arrangements it is obvious

271

that very high prices are paid, reckoned in terms of human suffering and frustration. If these arrangements presented themselves to us merely as arrangements and not as categorical imperatives, our reasonable course would be to adapt them by whatever means to rationally selected goals. What we do instead is to ridicule our Don Quixotes, the ludicrous embodiments of an outmoded tradition, and continue to regard our own as final and prescribed in the nature of things.

In the meantime the therapeutic problem of dealing with our psychopaths of this type is often misunderstood. Their alienation from the actual world can often be more intelligently handled than by insisting that they adopt the modes that are alien to them. Two other courses are always possible. In the first place, the misfit individual may cultivate a greater objective interest in his own preferences and learn how to manage with greater equanimity his deviation from the type. If he learns to recognize the extent to which his suffering has been due to his lack of support in a traditional ethos, he may gradually educate himself to accept his degree of difference with less suffering. Both the exaggerated emotional disturbances of the manic depressive and the seclusion of the schizophrenic add certain values to existence which are not open to those differently constituted. The unsupported individual who valiantly accepts his favourite and native virtues may attain a feasible course of behaviour that makes it unnecessary for him to take refuge in a private world he has fashioned for himself. He may gradually achieve a more independent and less tortured attitude toward his deviations and upon this attitude he may be able to build an adequately functioning existence.

In the second place, an increased tolerance in society

toward its less usual types must keep pace with the self-education of the patient. The possibilities in this direction are endless. Tradition is as neurotic as any patient; its overgrown fear of deviation from its fortuitous standards conforms to all the usual definitions of the psychopathic. This fear does not depend upon observation of the limits within which conformity is necessary to the social good. Much more deviation is allowed to the individual in some cultures than in others, and those in which much is allowed cannot be shown to suffer from their peculiarity. It is probable that social orders of the future will carry this tolerance and encouragement of individual difference much further than any cultures of which we have experience.

The American tendency at the present time leans so far to the opposite extreme that it is not easy for us to picture the changes that such an attitude would bring about. Middletown is a typical example of our usual urban fear of seeming in however slight an act different from our neighbours. Eccentricity is more feared than parasitism. Every sacrifice of time and tranquillity is made in order that no one in the family may have any taint of nonconformity attached to him. Children in school make their great tragedies out of not wearing a certain kind of stockings, not joining a certain dancing-class, not driving a certain car. The fear of being different is the dominating motivation recorded in Middletown.

The psychopathic toll that such a motivation exacts is evident in every institution for mental diseases in our country. In a society in which it existed only as a minor motive among many others, the psychiatric picture would be a very different one. At all events, there can be no reasonable doubt that one of the most effective ways in which to deal with the staggering burden of psychopathic

273

tragedies in America at the present time is by means of an educational program which fosters tolerance in society and a kind of self-respect and independence that is foreign to Middletown and our urban traditions.

Not all psychopaths, of course, are individuals whose native responses are at variance with those of their civilization. Another large group are those who are merely inadequate and who are strongly enough motivated so that their failure is more than they can bear. In a society in which the will-to-power is most highly rewarded, those who fail may not be those who are differently constituted, but simply those who are insufficiently endowed. The inferiority complex takes a great toll of suffering in our society. It is not necessary that sufferers of this type have a history of frustration in the sense that strong native bents have been inhibited; their frustration is often enough only the reflection of their inability to reach a certain goal. There is a cultural implication here, too, in that the traditional goal may be accessible to large numbers or to very few, and in proportion as success is obsessive and is limited to the few, a greater and greater number will be liable to the extreme penalties of maladjustment.

To a certain extent, therefore, civilization in setting higher and possibly more worth-while goals may increase the number of its abnormals. But the point may very easily be overemphasized, for very small changes in social attitudes may far outweigh this correlation. On the whole, since the social possibilities of tolerance and recognition of individual difference are so little explored in practice, pessimism seems premature. Certainly other quite different social factors which we have just discussed are more directly responsible for the great proportion of our neurotics and psychotics, and with these other factors civilizations could, if they would, deal without necessary intrinsic loss.

We have been considering individuals from the point of view of their ability to function adequately in their society. This adequate functioning is one of the ways in which normality is clinically defined. It is also defined in terms of fixed symptoms, and the tendency is to identify normality with the statistically average. In practice this average is one arrived at in the laboratory, and deviations from it are defined as abnormal.

From the point of view of a single culture this procedure is very useful. It shows the clinical picture of the civilization and gives considerable information about its socially approved behaviour. To generalize this as an absolute normal, however, is a different matter. As we have seen, the range of normality in different cultures does not coincide. Some, like Zuñi and the Kwakiutl, are so far removed from each other that they overlap only slightly. The statistically determined normal on the Northwest Coast would be far outside the extreme boundaries of abnormality in the Pueblos. The normal Kwakiutl rivalry contest would only be understood as madness in Zuñi, and the traditional Zuñi indifference to dominance and the humiliation of others would be the fatuousness of a simpleton in a man of noble family on the Northwest Coast. Aberrant behaviour in either culture could never be determined in relation to any least common denominator of behaviour. Any society, according to its major preoccupations, may increase and intensify even hysterical, epileptic, or paranoid symptoms, at the same time relying socially in a greater and greater degree upon the very individuals who display them.

This fact is important in psychiatry because it makes

clear another group of abnormals which probably exists in every culture: the abnormals who represent the extreme development of the local cultural type. This group is socially in the opposite situation from the group we have discussed, those whose responses are at variance with their cultural standards. Society, instead of exposing the former group at every point, supports them in their furthest aberrations. They have a licence which they may almost endlessly exploit. For this reason these persons almost never fall within the scope of any contemporary psychiatry. They are unlikely to be described even in the most careful manuals of the generation that fosters them. Yet from the point of view of another generation or culture they are ordinarily the most bizarre of the psychopathic types of the period.

The Puritan divines of New England in the eighteenth century were the last persons whom contemporary opinion in the colonies regarded as psychopathic. Few prestige groups in any culture have been allowed such complete intellectual and emotional dictatorship as they were. They were the voice of God. Yet to a modern observer it is they, not the confused and tormented women they put to death as witches, who were the psychoneurotics of Puritan New England. A sense of guilt as extreme as they portrayed and demanded both in their own conversion experiences and in those of their converts is found in a slightly saner civilization only in institutions for mental diseases. They admitted no salvation without a conviction of sin that prostrated the victim, sometimes for years, with remorse and terrible anguish. It was the duty of the minister to put the fear of hell into the heart of even the youngest child, and to exact of every convert emotional acceptance of his damnation if God saw fit to damn him. It does not matter where we turn among the records of New England Puritan churches of this period, whether to those dealing with witches or with unsaved children not yet in their teens or with such themes as damnation and predestination, we are faced with the fact that the group of people who carried out to the greatest extreme and in the fullest honour the cultural doctrine of the moment are by the slightly altered standards of our generation the victims of intolerable aberrations. From the point of view of a comparative psychiatry they fall in the category of the abnormal.

In our own generation extreme forms of ego-gratification are culturally supported in a similar fashion. Arrogant and unbridled egoists as family men, as officers of the law and in business, have been again and again portrayed by novelists and dramatists, and they are familiar in every community. Like the behaviour of Puritan divines, their courses of action are often more asocial than those of the inmates of penitentiaries. In terms of the suffering and frustration that they spread about them there is probably no comparison. There is very possibly at least as great a degree of mental warping. Yet they are entrusted with positions of great influence and importance and are as a rule fathers of families. Their impress both upon their own children and upon the structure of our society is indelible. They are not described in our manuals of psychiatry because they are supported by every tenet of our civilization. They are sure of themselves in real life in a way that is possible only to those who are oriented to the points of the compass laid down in their own culture. Nevertheless a future psychiatry may well ransack our novels and letters and public records for illumination upon a type of abnormality to which it would not otherwise give credence. In every society it is among this very group of the culturally encouraged and fortified that some of the most extreme types of human behaviour are fostered.

Social thinking at the present time has no more important task before it than that of taking adequate account of cultural relativity. In the fields of both sociology and psychology the implications are fundamental, and modern thought about contacts of peoples and about our changing standards is greatly in need of sane and scientific direction. The sophisticated modern temper has made of social relativity, even in the small area which it has recognized, a doctrine of despair. It has pointed out its incongruity with the orthodox dreams of permanence and ideality and with the individual's illusions of autonomy. It has argued that if human experience must give up these, the nutshell of existence is empty. But to interpret our dilemma in these terms is to be guilty of an anachronism. It is only the inevitable cultural lag that makes us insist that the old must be discovered again in the new, that there is no solution but to find the old certainty and stability in the new plasticity. The recognition of cultural relativity carries with it its own values, which need not be those of the absolutist philosophies. It challenges customary opinions and causes those who have been bred to them acute discomfort. It rouses pessimism because it throws old formulas into confusion, not because it contains anything intrinsically difficult. As soon as the new opinion is embraced as customary belief, it will be another trusted bulwark of the good life. We shall arrive then at a more realistic social faith, accepting as grounds of hope and as new bases for tolerance the coexisting and equally valid patterns of life which mankind has created for itself from the raw materials of existence.

# REFERENCES

## CHAPTER I

PAGE

12 Itard, Jean-Marc-Gaspard. *The Wild Boy of Aveyron*, translated by George and Muriel Humphrey. New York, 1932.
It is probable that some of these children were subnormal and abandoned because of that fact. But it is hardly possible that all of them were, yet they all impressed observers as half-witted.

15 See Boas, Franz. *Anthropology and Modern Life*, 18–100. New York, 1932.

## CHAPTER II

25 For an analysis of puberty rites as crisis ceremonialism, Van Gennep, Arnold. *Les Rites de Passage*. Paris, 1909.

29 Mead, Margaret. *Coming of Age in Samoa*. New York, 1928.

34 Howitt, A. W. *The Native Tribes of South-East Australia*. New York, 1904.

39 Benedict, Ruth. The Concept of the Guardian Spirit in North America. *Memoirs of the American Anthropological Association*, no. 29, 1923.

## CHAPTER III

50 Malinowski, Bronislaw. *The Sexual Life of Savages*, London, 1929; *Argonauts of the Western Pacific*, London, 1922; *Crime and Custom in Savage Society*, London, 1926; *Sex and Repression in Savage Society*, London, 1927; *Myth in Primitive Psychology*, New York, 1926.
Stern, Wilhelm. *Die differentielle Psychologie in ihren Grundlagen*. Leipzig, 1921.

51 Worringer, Wilhelm. *Form in Gothic*. London, 1927.
Koffka, Kurt. *The Growth of the Mind*. New York, 1927.
Köhler, Wilhelm. *Gestalt Psychology*. New York, 1929.
For a summary of the work of the Gestalt school see Murphy, Gardner. *Approaches to Personality*, 3–36. New York, 1932.

52 Dilthey, Wilhelm. *Gesammelte Schriften*, Band 2; 8. Leipzig, 1914–31.
Spengler, Oswald. *The Decline of the West*. New York, 1927-28.

# PATTERNS OF CULTURE

## CHAPTER IV

PAGE

57 The traditional spelling, Zuñi, is misleading. The *n* is pronounced as in any English word.

The following is a selected bibliography on Zuñi. The references in this chapter are numbered as in this list.

Benedict, Ruth.

1. Zuñi Mythology. *Columbia University Contributions to Anthropology*, 2 vol., XXI. New York, 1934.

2. Psychological Types in the Cultures of the Southwest. *Proceedings of the Twenty-Third International Congress of Americanists*, 572–81. New York, 1928.

Bunzel, Ruth L.

1. Introduction to Zuñi Ceremonialism. *Forty-Seventh Annual Report of the Bureau of American Ethnology*, 467–544. Washington, 1932.

2. Zuñi Ritual Poetry. *Ibid.* 611–835.

3. Zuñi Katchinas. *Ibid.* 837–1086.

4. Zuñi Texts. *Publications of the American Ethnological Society*, XV. New York, 1933.

Cushing, Frank Hamilton.

1. Outlines of Zuñi Creation Myths. *Thirteenth Annual Report of the Bureau of American Ethnology*. Washington, 1926.

2. Zuñi Folk Tales. New York, 1901.

3. My Experiences in Zuñi. *The Century Magazine*, n.s. 3, 4, 1888.

4. Zuñi Breadstuffs. *Publications of the Museum of the American Indian, Heye Foundation*, VIII. New York, 1920.

5. Zuñi Fetishes. *Second Annual Report of the Bureau of American Ethnology*. Washington, 1883.

Kroeber, A. L. Zuñi Kin and Clan. *Anthropological Papers of the American Museum of Natural History*, vol. XVIII, part 2. New York, 1917.

Parsons, Elsie Clews. Notes on Zuñi, I and II. *Memoirs of the American Anthropological Association*, vol. 4, no. 3, 1927.

Stevenson, Matilda Cox.

1. The Zuñi Indians. *Twenty-Third Annual Report of the Bureau of American Ethnology*. Washington, 1904.

2. The Religious Life of the Zuñi Child. *Ibid.*, V. Washington, 1887.

58 Kidder, A. V. *Southwest Archæology*. Yale University Press. New Haven, 1934.

# REFERENCES

PAGE

61 Zuñi ritual prayers are recorded in Bunzel 2.

62 Bunzel 2:626.

63 Bunzel 2:689.

64 Bunzel 2:645; 2:716.

65 Bunzel 2:666–67.
   See Bunzel, 1 and 3.

69 Stevenson 1:94–107.

72 *Ibid.* 407–576.

74 For the mildness of Zuñi behavior upon separation of spouses see, however, below, p. 108, for the fist fight in which two women may engage.

78 Nietzshe, Friedrich. *The Birth of Tragedy.* New York, 1924.

79 'Measure in the Hellenic sense,' *ibid.* 40.
   'And retains his civic name,' *ibid.* 68.

81 Benedict, Ruth. The Vision in Plains Culture. *American Anthropologist,* n.s. 24:1–23. 1922.

85 Reo F. Fortune. Secret Societies of the Omaha. *Columbia University Contributions to Anthropology,* XII. New York, 1932.
   Benedict 1.

86 Lewin, Louis. Weber Anhalonium Lewinii und andere Cacteen. Zweite Mitteilung. *Separatdruck aus dem Archiv für experimentelle Pathologie und Pharmakologie,* Bd. XXXIV. Leipzig, 1894.
   Wagner, Günther. Entwicklung und Verbreitung des Peyote-Kultes. *Baessler Archiv,* 15:59–144. Hamburg, 1931.

87 Benedict 2.
   Quotation, Bunzel 1:482.

88 Stevenson, *Thirtieth Report of the Bureau of American Ethnology,* 89.

91 For the Cactus initiation, Cushing 3 (vol. 4): 31–32.
   For the Fire initiation, *ibid.* 30–31; Stevenson 1:526.

93 D. H. Lawrence. *Mornings in Mexico,* 109–10. New York, 1928.

94 For the Cora dance upon the altar, Preuss, K. T. *Die Nayarit Expedition,* 55. Leipzig, 1912.
   For the Hopi dance, Voth, H. R. Oraibi Summer Snake Ceremony. *Field Columbian Museum Publication,* no. 83, 299. Chicago, 1903.

99 Quotations, Bunzel 1:480.

101 Malinowski, B. *Sex and Repression in Primitive Society,* 74–82. New York, 1927.

102 Junod, Henri A. *Story of a South African Tribe,* I: 73–92. Neuchâtel, 1912. The description is of the Bathonga.

104 This folk tale, Benedict 1, vol. II (in press), is based on an event that happened about 1850, and is described by the daughter of the household, Bunzel 4:35–38.

281

# PATTERNS OF CULTURE

107 For a cultural discussion of jealousy, see Mead, Margaret, Jealousy, Primitive and Modern. In *Woman's Coming of Age*, edited by S. D. Schmalhausen and V. F. Calverton. New York, 1931.

109-110 Parsons, Elsie Clews. Isleta, New Mexico. *Forty-Seventh Annual Report of the Bureau of American Ethnology*, 248-50; and Goldfrank, Esther Schiff, MS.

111 Prayer to dead wife, Bunzel 2:632.
For mourning on the Plains, see Grinnell, George Bird. *The Cheyenne Indians*, II:162. Yale University Press, 1923.

112 For the mourner's reluctance to leave the grave, *ibid*. II: 162.
For continued visiting of the grave, Donaldson, Thomas. The George Catlin Indian Gallery in the U. S. National Museum, 277. (*Smithsonian Institution*), *Report of the Board of Regents of the Smithsonian Institution to July*, 1885, Part V. Washington, 1886.
For Dakota mourning, Deloria, Ella, MS.
The quotation is from Denig, Edwin T. The Assiniboine, 573. *Forty-Sixth Annual Report of the Bureau of American Ethnology*. Washington, 1930.

113 For discussion of the aberrant, see below, Chapter VII.

114 Bunzel 2:679-83.

116 Grinnell, George Bird. *The Cheyenne Indians*, II:8-22. New Haven, 1923.
For clowning at the scalp dance, *ibid*. 39-44.

118 Benedict 1.

121 Bourke, John J. Notes on the Cosmology and Theogony of the Mojave Indians of the Rio Grande, Arizona, 175. *Journal of American Folklore*, II (1889), 169-89.

123 For instances of Hopi fecundity symbolism, see Haeberlin, H. K., The Idea of Fertilization in the Culture of the Pueblo Indians, 37-46. *Memoirs of the American Anthropological Association*, III, no. 1, 1916.

124 For the race between men and women in Peru, Arriaga, P. J., *Extirpacion de la Idolatria del Peru*, 36, Lima, 1621.

125 For an extreme instance of Zuñi misinterpretation see Parsons, Elsie Clews, Winter and Summer Dance Series in Zuñi in 1918, 199. *University of California Publications in American Archæology and Ethnology*, 17, no. 3, 1922.
Cushing, 1:379-81.

126 'Amiable disciplinary means,' is Dr. Bunzel's phrase, Bunzel 3:846.

127 The quotations are from Bunzel 1:486; 497.

# REFERENCES

128 The quotation concerning Zuñi lack of resignation is from Bunzel
1:486.
The extracts from the ritual are found in Bunzel 2:784; 646; 807–08.


## CHAPTER V

130 This chapter is based on the field study, *The Sorcerers of Dobu*,
by Reo F. Fortune, New York, 1932. The present chapter can
be only an abridgment of Dr. Fortune's full account and to
facilitate consultation page references are given on special points.
137 For Dobuan totems, Fortune 30–36.
139 For the Manus marriage, see Mead, Margaret. *Growing up in
New Guinea*. New York, 1930.
145 The quotation is from Fortune 16.
146 For the ritual of the garden, Fortune 106–31.
149 The version given here is condensed. See Fortune 139–40.
152 For accounts of vada, see Fortune 158–64, and for comparative
data, 284–87.
154 Malinowski, Bronislaw. *Argonauts of the Western Pacific*. London,
1922.
For the economic background of the Kula, Fortune 200–10.
159 Fortune 216–17.
160 For mourning observances at the death of a spouse, Fortune 11;
57; 194.
163 Fortune 11, for quotation.
164–165 Fortune 197–200.
166 Fortune 23, for statement of sullen suspicion in mourning exchange.
Fortune 170.
167 For this behavior toward yams, Fortune 222.
169 Fortune 78.
170 Fortune 85.
171 Fortune 109.


## CHAPTER VI

173 The following is a selected bibliography on the Kwakiutl by
Franz Boas:
1. The Social Organization and Secret Societies of the Kwakiutl
Indians, *Report of the U.S. National Museum for 1895*, 311–
738. Washington, 1897.
2. Kwakiutl Texts, by Franz Boas and George Hunt. *The
Jesup North Pacific Expedition*, III, *Memoir of the American
Museum of Natural History*. New York, 1905.

3. Ethnology of the Kwakiutl, 2 vols. *Thirty-Fifth Annual Report of the Bureau of American Ethnology.* Washington, 1921.
4. Contributions to the Ethnology of the Kwakiutl. *Columbia University Contributions to Anthropology*, III. New York, 1925.
5. The Religion of the Kwakiutl Indians, vol. II. *Columbia University Contributions to Anthropology*, X. New York, 1930.

175 The performances of the secret societies are described in Boas 1.
176 Quotation, Boas 1:466.
   *Ibid.* 513; 467.
177 *Ibid.* 459.
178 For the cannibal dance, *ibid.* 437–62; 500–44.
181 Exorcism, Boas 3: 1173.
188 For the endogamy of the Bella Coola, Boas, Franz. The Mythology of the Bella Coola Indians, 125. *Publications of the Jesup North Pacific Expedition* I, 25–127, *Memoirs of the American Museum of Natural History.* New York, 1898.
189 'We fight with property.' Boas 1:571.
190–191 Boas 3:1291; 1290; 848; 857; 1281.
192 *Ibid.* 1288; 1290; 1283; 1291.
194 Boas 1:622.
195–197 *Ibid.* 346–53.
197–199 Hunt, George, The Rival Chiefs. *Boas Anniversary Volume*, 108–36. New York, 1906.
200 Boas 3:744.
   Boas 1:581.
201 Boas 4:165–229.
203 Boas 1:359 ff.; 421 ff.
205 *Ibid.* 422.
206 Quotation, *ibid.* 424. For the marriage contest, *ibid.* 473.
207 Boas 3:1030.
208 Boas 1:366.
209 Boas 3:1075.
   Boas 3:1110–17.
210 Boas 2:441 etc.
211 'Of the order of spirits,' Boas 3:740.
   Demonstrating the privileges of a shaman, Boas 5:18, 30.
212 Killing a shamanistic competitor, Boas 5:31–33.
213 Shamanistic spies, Boas 5:15; 270.
   *Ibid.* 277–288.
214 *Ibid.* 271.

# REFERENCES

PAGE

215 The capsized canoe, Boas 4:133.
The broken cannibal mask, Boas 1:600.
The bankrupt gambler, Boas 2:104.
216 'Craziness strikes,' Boas 3:709.
For this head-hunting, Boas 3:1385.
*Ibid.* 1363.
217 Boas MS.
219 Boas 3:1093–1104.
221 Quoted from Mayne. Boas, F., Tsimshian Mythology, 545.
*Thirty-Fifth Annual Report of the Bureau of American Ethnology.*
Washington, 1916.
Boas 1:394.

## CHAPTER VII

231 Durkheim, Émile. *Les Règles de la méthode sociologique.* 6th
edition. Paris, 1912.
Kroeber, A. L. The Superorganic. *American Anthropologist,*
n.s., XIX (1917), 163–213.
For discussion, see Folsom, J. R. *Social Psychology,* 296 ff. New
York, 1931.
For condemnation of the group fallacy, Allport, F. H. *Social
Psychology.* Boston, 1924.
232 Rivers, W. H. R. Sociology and Psychology, in *Psychology and
Ethnology.* London, 1926.
236 Murphy, Gardner. *Experimental Psychology,* 375.
239–240 Boas 5:202; Boas 3:1309. See complete titles under preceding chapter.
242 Westermarck, E. A. *History of Human Marriage.* 3 vols. 5th
edition. London, 1921.

## CHAPTER VIII

253 Sumner, William Graham. *Folkways.* Boston, 1907.
256 Jones, William. Mortuary Observances and the Adoption Rites
of the Algonkin Foxes of Iowa, 271–77. *Quinzième Congrès International des Américanistes,* 273–77. Quebec, 1907.
257 For mourning practices of the Plains, see above, p. 282.
258 Fortune, R. F. *Sorcerers of Dobu,* 54. New York, 1932.
261 For a native account of this witchcraft incident in Zuñi, see
Bunzel, Ruth L. *Publications of the American Ethnological Society,* XV:44–52. New York, 1933.
263 For description of various Zuñi men-women, see Parsons, Elsie

# PATTERNS OF CULTURE

PAGE

Clews. The Zuñi Łámana. *American Anthropologist*, n.s. 18 (1916), 521–28.

For Mrs. Stevenson's description of We-wha, Stevenson, Mathilda C. The Zuñi Indians. *Twenty-Third Annual Report of the Bureau of American Ethnology*, 37; 310–331; 374.

264 Deloria, Ella, MS.

265–270 From Benedict, Ruth. Culture and the Abnormal. *Journal of General Psychology*, 1934, I, 60–64.

266 Dixon, Roland B. The Shasta. *Bulletin of the American Museum of Natural History*, XVII:381–498. New York, 1907.

267 For a convenient summary, Czaplicka, M. A. *Aboriginal Siberia.* Oxford, 1914.

268 Callaway, Canon H. Religious System of the Amazulu. *Publications of the Folklore Society*, XV:259 ff. London, 1884.

270 Sapir, E., in *Journal of Abnormal and Social Psychology*, XXVII (1932), 241.

271 Dewey, John. *Human Nature and Conduct.* New York, 1922.

273 Lynd, Robert and Helen. *Middletown.* New York, 1929.

277 Such individuals are favourite subjects in the novels and short stories of May Sinclair and Tchekhov.

# INDEX

Aberrants, 258–74; Dobu, 258; Plains Indians, 259; Zuñi, 260–62

Abnormal, categories of: extreme development of cultural type, 276–78; inferiors, 274; unsupported by their culture, 258–74

Abnormality, inadequacy of characterization by fixed symptoms, 258–78; by inadequate functioning, 275

Adolescence, 24–30; Apache, 28, 102; Australia, 26, 102; Carrier, 28; Central Africa, 27; Kwakiutl, 202; Nandi (East Africa), 27; Plains Indians, 25; Plateau of British Columbia, 26; Samoa, 29; Western civilization, 24; Zuñi, 69, 91, 102

Africa, Central Africa, adolescence, 27; Nandi, adolescence, 27; South Africa, adolescence, 102; South Africa, shamanism, 268–70

Allport, F. H., 231

Analytical studies in anthropology, 48

Anthropology, analytical studies in, 48; comparative studies in, 242; configuration studies in, 229; definition of, 1; functional studies in, 50; individual vs. culture, 251–54; preliminary propositions of, 3–9; typological studies in, 238; value in social sciences, 16–18

Apache, adolescence, 28, 102; alcohol, 90; punishment of wife's infidelity, 107.

Apollonian, 79

Art and religion, 38

Australia, adolescence, 26, 102; behaviour at death, 119; marriage in, 33

Authority, right to exercise, Zuñi, 99–104

Aztecs, 85; self-torture, 90; use of datura, 86, 88; war, 30

Bella Coola, 188

Biological inheritance in behaviour, 233–36; ants, 12; man, 12–15

Blake, William, 79

British Columbia, plateau of, adolescence, 26; lack of cultural integration, 224, 225; religion, 39

Bunzel, Ruth, 66, 69, 99, 107, 126

California, shamanism, 42, 92, 266, 267. *See also* Mission Indians

Cannibalism, 131, 164, 178

Capitalism, Western civilization, 250

Carrier Indians, adolescence, 28

Cervantes, 270

Clan, Dobu, 132, 133, 136; Northwest Coast, 185, 186; Zuñi, 75, 76, 78, 101, 105

Closed group and the alien, 7

Comparative school in anthropology, 242, 244

Crow Indians, 259

Cultural change, control of, 271; fears of, 36; inevitability of, 10; technique of control, 248–50

Culture, as an organism, 230–32; biological interpretation of, 233–36; historical factors in, 232, 233, 236; importance of, 2; integration of, 23, 46, 48, 223; psychological interpretation of, 35, 232; selection in, 24, 46; variety in, 3; and the individual, 251–78

Custom. *See* Culture

Dakota, homosexuality, 264; mourning, 112

Dance, Hopi, 94; Kwakiutl, 92, 175–81; Maidu, California, 92; Northern Mexico, 92, 94; Northwest Coast, 92; Zuñi, 92; absence of, Dobu, 133; Ghost Dance of American Indians, 92

287

# INDEX

Darwin, 4, 56

Datura, 86, 88

Death, behaviour at, 243, 244; Australia, 119; Central Algonkian, 256; Dobu, 160–65; Kwakiutl, 215–18, 239; Navajo, 119; Plains Indians, 111–13; Pueblo, 109, 120; Zuñi, 110, 120, 243

Dewey, John, 271

Diffusion, 241

Dilthey, Wilhelm, 52

Dionysian, 79, 175, 181

Divination, Dobu, 132, 171; Zuñi, 87

Divorce, Dobu, 138, 139; Kwakiutl, 208–09; Zuñi, 74, 108

Dobu, 130–72; aberrant individual, 258; cannibalism, 131, 164; clan, 132, 133, 136; consistency in cultural behaviour, 239; death, behaviour at, 160–65, 244; divination, 132, 171; dourness, 166; economic life, 130, 139–41, 146, 147, 153–60, 162–64; frustration, behaviour at, 255; government, 131, 169; homicide, 152, 166; ideal character, 142, 168, 172, 250; Kula ring, 154–59, 171; legality, 169, 170; magic, 132, 142–53, 156–61, 171; marriage, 133–41, 160, 168; medicine charms, 148–53, 160; mother's brother, 138, 142, 144, 145; personal names, use of, 137; religion, 142–53, 156–58; sex, 138, 139, 147, 167, 168; sorcery, 131, 132, 133, 152; suicide, 139, 173; supernaturals, 142; totems, 137; villages, 132, 133, 141; war, 131; wabuwabu, 158–60

Drugs and religion, 85–89

Dualisms in social theory, 251

Durkheim, 231

Economic laws, 248

Economic life, 243; Dobu, 130, 139–41, 146, 153–60, 162–64; Kwakiutl, 173–75, 182–86, 188, 193–211; Zuñi, 63, 64, 76, 105

Evolution, 4; in anthropological theory, 18–19

Fasting and religion, 88

Fertility cult, Hopi, 123; Peru, 124; Zuñi, 122

Fortune, R. F., 139, 144, 152, 165, 171

Frazer, *The Golden Bough*, 49

Frustration, behaviour at, 255–57

Gestalt school in psychology, 51

Government, Dobu, 131, 169; Kwakiutl, 183, 185; Zuñi, 100

Greece, 79, 238, 263

Group fallacy, 231

Headhunting, Kwakiutl, 216–18

Homicide, 45; Dobu, 152, 166; Eskimo, 256; Kwakiutl, 207, 210, 212; Zuñi, 117

Homosexuality, American Indians, 263; Dakota, 264–65; Greece, 263; Western civilization, 262, 265; Zuñi, 263–64

Hopi, fertility magic, 123; snake dance, 94

Ideal character, Dobu, 142, 168–72, 250; Kwakiutl, 200, 214, 220, 222, 250; Plains, 98; Zuñi, 98

Incest groups, 33

Inconsistencies in cultural behaviour, Dobu, 239; Kwakiutl, 239–41; Western civilization, 239, 241; Zuñi, 241

Individual, malleability of, 113, 254; and society, 251–78

Integration, emphasis upon in psychology, 50; in social studies, 52

Integration, cultural, 23, 46, 48, 223; lack of, 223–26; Western civilization, 229, 230

Intoxication, religious, 85

Isleta, 109, 119

Jealousy, marital, Dobu, 138; Zuñi, 107

Kroeber, A. L., 231

Kula ring, Dobu, 154–59, 171

Kwakiutl, 173–222; adolescence, girls', 202; bear dance, 176; cannibal dance,

288

# INDEX

177–81; cannibalism, 178; cultural integration, historical, 226–28; dances, 175–81; death, behaviour at, 215–18, 239, 243; economic life, 173–75, 182–86, 188, 193–211; evaluation of culture, 246–48; frustration, behaviour at, 255; headhunting, 216–18; homicide, 207, 210, 212; ideal character, 200, 214, 220, 222, 250; inconsistencies in cultural behaviour, 239–41; marriage, 174, 186, 203–10, 219, 220; potlatch, 174, 184–86, 190, 191, 195–211; psychiatric view of, 258; religion, 175–81, 210–14, 221; rivalry, 189–202, 212–14; shamanism, 211–14, 219; shame, 215, 216, 218–21; social organization, 182–87; suicide, 215, 218, 219, 220; supernaturals, 221; titular names, 183–87, 189

Lawrence, D. H., 93
Lowie, R. H., 259

Magic, Dobu, 132, 142–53, 156–61, 171; Zuñi, 61
Maidu, California, 92
Malinowski, B., 50, 101, 130, 154
Manus, 139
Marriage, 243; and economic transfer, 43; and religion, Western civilization, 43; asocial developments of, Australia, 34; Dobu, 133–41, 160–68; Dutch New Guinea, 136; Kwakiutl, 174, 186, 187, 203–10, 219, 220; Zuñi, 73, 101, 105, 107, 110
Mead, Margaret, 29
Medicine, charms, Dobu, 148–53, 160; societies, Zuñi, 71, 72
Menstruation, Zuñi, 120
Mental hygiene, Western civilization, 245, 272–74
Mexico, Northern, religious use of alcohol, 85; whirling dance, 94. *See also* Aztecs
*Middletown*, 247, 273
Mission Indians, California, adoles-

cence, 103; proverb of, 21; use of datura, 86; war, 31
Mojave, shamanism and sorcery, 121; use of datura, 86

Navajo, mourning, 119
Nietzsche, 78
Northwest Coast, dance, 92; prerogatives, 227. *See also* Kwakiutl

Œdipus complex, Zuñi, 101
Orgy, traces in Zuñi, 124
Osage, totemism among, 40

Penitentes, 90
Personality differences within a culture, 253
Peyote, 85, 89
Pima, purification of slayer, 115; religious intoxication, 85
Plains Indians, aberrant individual, 259; adolescence, 25; behaviour at death, 111–13, 257; homosexuality, 264; ideal of character, 98; Omaha, 85; purification of slayer, 116; self-torture, 90; shamanism, 97; suicide, 118; the vision, 81; totemism, Osage, 40
Plato, 263
Potlatch, Kwakiutl, 174, 184–86, 190, 191, 195–211
Primitive, romantic return to the, 19–20
Primitive societies, value of as social laboratory, 16–20, 55
Psychiatry, 257; and psychotic types, 49
Psychological origins of culture, 232
Psychology, experimental, 236; integration studies in, 50; and culture, 35
Pueblos, behaviour at death, 109, 120; prehistory of, 57. *See also* Zuñi
Purification of slayer, Pima, 115; Plains Indians, 116; Zuñi, 113
Puritanism, 276; Dobu, 168; Western civilization, 126; Zuñi, 126

# INDEX

Race and culture, 233–36
Race prejudice, 9, 11, 15, 44
Racial inheritance, 15
Rasmussen, K., 31
Religion, the closed group and the alien in, 8; and adolescence, 39; and art, 38; and dance, 92–95; and drugs, 85; and economic exchange, 43; and feasting, 88; and intoxication, 85; and marriage, 43; and self-torture, 90; and social organization 40; and shamanism, 96; and trance, 42; Dobu, 142–53, 156–58; Kwakiutl, 175–81, 211–14, 221; Pima, 85; Plains Indians, 81; Zuñi, 59–73, 221; shamanism and sorcery, 121
Rivalry, 247; Kwakiutl, 189–202, 212–14
Rivers, W. H. R., 232

Salish, 226, 227
Samoa, adolescence, 29
Sapir, E., 270
Selection, in art forms, 47; in cultural configurations, 237, 254; in cultural forms, 24, 47; in linguistic forms, 23
Self-torture, Aztec, 90; Penitentes, 90; Plains Indians, 90; Zuñi, 91
Sense of sin, Western civilization, 126; Zuñi, 126
Sex, Dobu, 138, 139, 147, 167, 168; Kwakiutl, 240, 241; Zuñi, 73–75, 101, 107, 108, 111, 124–26, 168
Sexual symbolism, Zuñi, 125
Shamanism, 96–98; and sorcery, Mojave, 121; California, 42; Kwakiutl, 211–14, 219; Shasta Indians, 42, 266, 267; Siberia, 267, 268; Zulu, 268–70
Shasta, 42, 266, 267
Siberia, religious art, 38; shamanism, 267, 268
Snake dance, Hopi, 94
Social organization, 32–35; Dobu, 131–33, 136; Kurnai, Australia, 34; Kwakiutl, 182–87; Osage, 40; Zuñi, 73, 75, 76, 78, 101, 105

Sorcery, Dobu, 131, 132, 133; North America, 120
South America, adolescence, 102; religious art, 38
Spengler, Oswald, 52
Stern, Wilhelm, 50
Struktur school in psychology, 51
Suicide, 46; Dobu, 139, 173; Kwakiutl, 215, 218, 219, 220; Plains Indians, 118; Zuñi, 117
Supernaturals, Dobu, 142; Kwakiutl, 221; Zuñi, 67, 71, 126, 128

Taos, peyote in, 89
Totemism, Dobu, 137; Osage, 40
Trance, 265–70; Shasta Indians, 42
Trobriand Islands, 130, 154, 161
Typology in cultural studies, 238

Utopias, 248

Value, problem of, 246–50
Vision, the, in North America, 39–43, 81–92, 96, 97; Kwakiutl, 177, 212
War, Aztecs, 30; Dobu, 131; Eskimo, 30; Mission Indians of California, 31; Plains Indians, 98; Western civilization, 32, 45, 250
Westermarck, 242
Western civilization, aberrant individuals, 260, 270; adolescence, 24; art and religion, 38; artists, 260; attitudes toward children, 245; behaviour at death, 257; capitalism, 250; cultural integration, 229; economics, 36; ego extensions, 245; ego-gratification, 277; forms of, not biologically conditioned, 36; hobos, 260; homosexuality, 262, 265; inconsistencies in behaviour, 239; inferiority complex, 274; integration in, 53; intolerance, 273, 274; marriage and religion, 43; mental hygiene, 245, 272–74; position of women and Christianity, 44; possibility of cultural control, 248–50, 271, 272;

# INDEX

paranoia, 222; Puritan divines, 276; puritanism, 126; race and prejudice, 44; religion, 249; rivalry, 248; sanity in, 237; spread over world, 5; trance, 265; war, 31, 250

Wild children of the Middle Ages, 12

Witchcraft, Pueblo, 122, 127

Women, position of, and Christianity, 34

Worringer, W., 51

Zuñi, 57–129; aberrant individual, 260–62; adolescence, 69, 91, 102; Apollonian type, 79; authority, 99–104; authority in the family, 101; clan, 75, 76, 78, 101, 105; crime, 100; dance, 92; datura, 88; death, behaviour at, 110, 120, 243; death of spouse, 110; divination, 87; divorce, 74, 108; economic life, 73, 74, 76, 105; evaluation of culture, 246; fasting, 88; fertility cult, 122, 124; frustration, behaviour at, 255; good and evil, 127; government, 100; group sanction, 103–06; homicide, 117; homosexuality, 263, 264; ideal of character, 98; initiation, 69, 91, 102; intoxication, 89; kachina cult, 67–71; magical technique, 60; marriage, 73, 101, 105, 107, 110; medicine societies, 71–73; menstruation, 120; moderation in emotional life, 106, 120, 243; Œdipus complex, 101; orgy, traces of, 124; prayer, 61; priests, 65, 121; priest, character of the, 96; psychiatric view of, 257; purification of the slayer, 113; puritanism, 126; religion, 59–73, 221; religion, object of, 63; religious art, 38; resignation, 128; ritual, importance of, 59; sense of sin, 126; sex, 73–75, 101, 107, 108, 111, 124–26, 168; sexual symbolism, 125; self-torture, 91; shamanism, absence of, 96; social organization, 73, 75, 76, 78, 101, 105; suicide, 117; supernaturals, 67, 71, 126, 128; wealth, 76; witchcraft, 122, 127

# Sentry Editions